Clarke County Virginia

Personal Property Tax Lists, 1836–1870

Volume 1
1836–1853

Marty Hiatt, CG

HERITAGE BOOKS
2015

HERITAGE BOOKS
AN IMPRINT OF HERITAGE BOOKS, INC.

Books, CDs, and more—Worldwide

For our listing of thousands of titles see our website
at
www.HeritageBooks.com

Published 2015 by
HERITAGE BOOKS, INC.
Publishing Division
5810 Ruatan Street
Berwyn Heights, Md. 20740

Copyright © 2015 Marty Hiatt, CG

All rights reserved. No part of this book may be reproduced or transmitted in any form or by any means, electronic or mechanical, including photocopying, recording or by any information storage and retrieval system without written permission from the author, except for the inclusion of brief quotations in a review.

International Standard Book Numbers
Paperbound: 978-0-7884-5670-1
Clothbound: 978-0-7884-6237-5

Clarke County, Virginia Personal Property Tax Lists 1836-1853

Contents

Introduction	vii
1836	1
1837	10
1838	19
1839	29
1840	39
1841	49
1842	58
1843	67
1844	77
1845	87
1846	97
1847	107
1848	118
1849	129
1850	140
1851	151
1852	164
1853	177
Recapitulations from 1836-1850 tax lists.	189
Index	193

Clarke County, Virginia Personal Property Tax Lists 1836-1853

Heritage Books by Marty Hiatt:

Clarke County, Virginia Register of Births, 1853–1896
Clarke County, Virginia Personal Property Tax Lists, 1836–1870: Volume 1, 1836–1853
Clarke County, Virginia, Personal Property Tax Lists, 1836-1870: Volume 2, 1854-1870
Early Church Records of Loudoun County, Virginia, 1745–1800

Loudoun County, Virginia Death Register, 1853–1896
Elizabeth R. Frain and Marty Hiatt

New Jerusalem Lutheran Church Cemetery
Marty Hiatt and Craig R. Scott

Northern Virginia Genealogy: Volume 1, Numbers 1, 1996
Northern Virginia Genealogy: Volume 1, Number 2, April 1996
Northern Virginia Genealogy: Volume 1, Number 3, July 1996
Northern Virginia Genealogy: Volume 1, Number 4, October 1996
Northern Virginia Genealogy: Volume 2, Number 1, January 1997
Northern Virginia Genealogy: Volume 2, Number 2, April 1997
Northern Virginia Genealogy: Volume 2, Number 3, July 1997
Northern Virginia Genealogy: Volume 2, Number 4, October 1997
Northern Virginia Genealogy: Volume 3, Number 1, January 1998
Northern Virginia Genealogy: Volume 3, Number 2, April 1998
Northern Virginia Genealogy: Volume 3, Number 3, July 1998
Northern Virginia Genealogy: Volume 3, Number 4, October 1998
Northern Virginia Genealogy: Volume 4, Number 1, Winter 1999
Northern Virginia Genealogy: Volume 4, Number 2, Spring 1999
Northern Virginia Genealogy: Volume 4, Number 3, Summer 1999
Northern Virginia Genealogy: Volume 4, Number 4, Fall 1999

Northern Virginia Genealogy: Volume 5, 2000
Northern Virginia Genealogy: Volume 6, 2001
Northern Virginia Genealogy: Volume 7, 2002
Northern Virginia Genealogy: Volume 8, 2003
Northern Virginia Genealogy: Volume 9, 2004

*Those at Rest: Lovettsville Union Cemetery,
Loudoun County, Virginia, 1879–1999*

Clarke County, Virginia Personal Property Tax Lists 1836-1853

Dedication

To Virginia S. Dunn, *Archives Research Services Manager* at the Library of Virginia. Ginny graciously provided photocopies of pages that were missing from the microfilms of these tax lists. Her dedication and response is extraordinary.

Appreciation

Many thanks to Betty Frain, my friend who offered to format information in this book. Without her skills and generosity this information would still be a manuscript.

Clarke County, Virginia Personal Property Tax Lists 1836-1853

Clarke County, Virginia Personal Property Tax Lists 1836-1870

Introduction

Personal property taxes have been assessed and collected in Virginia almost annually since 1782. Names of all free adult men, and women who owned taxable items, were collected by a commissioner of revenue or his deputies. The poll tax (on heads of adult men) was used to support county needs. Taxes on slaves, horses, carriages, clocks and other items were sent to the state. The taxable age for white males varied from 16 to 21 years, depending on the time frame.

An explanation of the columns on the first page for each year tells the age at which men were *supposed* to be taxed. This isn't to say that every 16-20 year-old young man was named or even indicated by a number in the lists. People didn't enjoy paying taxes any more in the 19th century than they do today. When a man's name does appear on a Clarke County tax list, you can be fairly certain that he was head of a household.

This book presents abstracts of information found on the original lists. Basically the heads of households, slaves, and horses are indicated. Some years have names of men who were merchants and free Negroes who owned property. The dates that the individual lists of men and taxable property were received by the commissioner are found on the original lists for most years. Space did not allow for their inclusion in this book.

Clarke County, Virginia Personal Property Tax Lists 1836-1870

More information about using tax records for research purposes can be found in Research Notes No. 3, *Using Personal Property Tax Records in the Archives at the Library of Virginia*. This helpful pamphlet is available on the web-site of the Library of Virginia.

Additional information about the taxable protery families owned can be determined by reading the complete tax lists that are available at the Library of Virginia. Microfilm of the lists can be ordered through inter-library loan.

>Auditor of Public Accounts, Clarke County
>microfilm reel No. 88 (1836-1850)
>microfilm reel No. 469 (1851-1860).

When reading the tax lists in this book:
- Always check the first page of each year to determine the column headings.
- Brackets were used to enclose comments by the compiler. [sic] means "as written." In other words the name was misspelled. If the name is not clear, and could be interpreted more than one way a question mark [?] was added after the name.
- A few abbreviations are found, mainly Est. for estate; Rev. or Revd. for reverend; Dr. or Doct. for doctor, and various military ranks.
- Periods were not used after abbreviated given names in the original or this book.
- When there are no numbers after a woman's name, it means she was not married (a widow or a spinster) and paying taxes on property that was not extracted for this book.
- Occasionally you will see "back of book." That refers to the original tax booklet, not this book. Look at the end of that year's list for additional information.

Clarke County, Virginia Personal Property Tax Lists 1836-1870

1836

Columns: 1) Tithes over 16 year of age, 2) Slaves over 12 years of age, 3) Horses, mules, etc.

Name	Values	Name	Values
Jane Anderson	0-0-2	George Bolen	1-0-0
David Anderson	1-0-0	Francis O. Byrds	1-13-8
Philip Ayreheart	1-0-1	Philip Burlin	1-3-3
John Ashly	2-0-4	John M. Blakemore	1-1-2
David H. Allen	3-21-65	John Burchill	1-4-8
Robert Ashby	3-0-5	Squire Bell	1-1-6
Joseph Anderson	2-3-10	Thomas Blakemore	1-7-9
Thomas Anderson	1-0-1	James Beck	1-0-0
Samuel Armour	1-1-1	Samuel Bonham	1-11-21
Mary Alexander	0-2-2	Humphrey Brooke	1-4-1
Buckner Ashby	1-13-25	Daniel S. Bonham	1-5-10
Philip Ayreheart	1-1-0	Andrew Bellmyre	2-0-1
John Alexander	3-15-17	Hiram Brisin	1-9-18
Mason Anderson	1-1-0	William Brawner	1-0-0
William Allen	1-3-5	George N. Barnett	1-0-0
Charles W. Andrew	1-0-4	John Bourine	1-1-2
John Ambrous	2-0-6	Mildred Bourine	0-0-1
William Ambrous	1-0-3	John Bragg	3-0-2
Algernon S. Allen	1-9-11	William Baker	1-7-6
John Ambrous Jr.	2-0-0	Isaac Burlin	2-0-1
William Allen	1-0-2	Samuel Burlin	1-2-1
Thompson F. Anderson	1-0-0	Juliett Barton	0-2-1
Hathaway Alexander	1-0-1	Rudolph F. C. Bouel	1-0-0
		Thomas H. Burwell	1-18-20
		Mariah M. Burwell	1-10-3
Thomas Briggs	6-3-7	George H. Burwell	1-39-38
William Berry	1-11-12	Philip Burwell	1-33-16
Carv [?] W. Bayless	1-1-0	Nathaniel Burwell	1-51-36
Charles Butler	1-7-14	Edward Bruer	1-0-0
Benjamin Barr	1-1-0	Thomas T. Byrd	1-5-7
John Brownley	1-15-18	Amos A. Bonham	1-7-10
William Brownley	1-1-2	John M. Byrd	0-0-5
Robert Burchill	1-5-10	Samuel Byrarly	1-7-10
Thomas Byrds Estate	0-1-0	Hector Bell	1-16-15

Clarke County, Virginia Personal Property Tax Lists 1836-1853
1836

Pheneas Brown	2-4-10	Thomas & David	
Lewis Brumley	1-0-5	Clevenger	2-0-4
James Bulger	1-0-0	Elizabeth N. Castro	0-3-1
Joseph Bulgar	1-0-0	William Carrington	1-1-0
William Beesley	1-1-2	Thomas T. Castleman	1-0-0
Samuel Beck	1-0-2	Alexander Coal	1-1-0
Aron Beck	1-0-1	Henry Catlett	1-8-16
James Bell Jr.	1-0-0	Peter Carper	1-0-0
Westley Brabham	1-0-0	John Copenhaven	2-2-9
John C. Bazzle	1-0-2	George F. Calmes	1-2-5
Abram Beevers	1-0-3	Jane Calmes	0-0-0
Ezekiel Barton	1-0-0	Elizabeth Carter	1-2-4
Isabella Burson	1-4-3	William Carper Jr.	1-0-4
John Blake	1-0-0	Alfred Clevenger	1-1-2
Nancy Blake	1-0-1	Samuel Casio	1-0-0
James Bell	1-0-10	Peter Crum	2-0-1
Hiram P. Bell	1-0-3	Charles Cain	1-0-0
Strother Bell	1-3-6	John Cooper	1-0-0
Henry Brown	1-0-1	John Carpenter	1-5-5
		Patrid Carroll	1-0-3
James Cross	2-4-9	John Carroll	1-0-1
Jesse Calvert	1-0-5	Thomas Cornwell	1-0-0
James Castleman	2-15-12	Fielding Cornwell	1-0-0
John Castleman	1-4-10	Dabney Cothen	1-0-2
Martha P. Castleman	0-9-3	George Cornwell	2-0-2
Alfred Castleman	1-6-7	William Castleman	1-16-24
William H. Colston	1-1-1	Elizabeth	
William A. Castleman	1-0-1	Carnagey [sic]	0-23-23
Thomas H. Crow	3-2-1	William Clark	1-1-6
Elijah Cleaveland	1-0-0		
Nelson Colier	2-0-2	John Drish	1-0-0
Daniel P. Conrad	2-3-1	William Dowty	1-0-2
Craven & John Craig	2-3-6	Gersham Drake	1-0-0
Parkeson &		Seth Davo	1-0-2
Ebbin Craig	2-1-6	William Deahl	1-0-0
John P. Chamberlain	2-1-9	Henry Dick Sr.	1-0-0
Baalis Casteleman	1-0-1	Henry Dick Jr.	1-0-2
George Castleman	2-0-3	Baalis Davis	1-1-1
Carter B. Chandler	2-12-10	Walter Downs	1-0-0

Clarke County, Virginia Personal Property Tax Lists 1836-1853
1836

Name	Value	Name	Value
David Denny	2-0-5	Archibald Fleming	1-0-1
Turner Dawson	1-0-1	Joseph Fleming	1-0-1
James Downing	1-0-2	John D. Ferguson	2-12-10
Benjamin Downing	2-0-2	McFarland Fuller	1-0-0
Gary Davis	1-0-1		
Robert Dewk	1-0-0	James Green	3-9-13
Peter Dearmont	2-5-5	George Green	1-1-6
Michael Dearmont	1-3-5	Richard Green	1-2-4
		Darias Grubb	1-0-0
John B. Earle	2-12-24	Stephen J. Gantt	1-2-3
Jacob Enders	1-4-6	William Graves	1-0-0
Sarah Earle	2-2-2	Lewis Glover	1-1-1
William G. Everheart	2-1-2	William Goodin	1-0-0
Benjamin Franks	1-0-1	Thomas Gold	2-5-10
John Ferguson	1-1-1-	Alice Gold	1-0-3
George Fyst	3-2-14	Monroe C. Garton	1-0-1
Martha Foster	0-3-10	William Green	1-0-0
William Fridley	1-0-1	John Gantt	2-5-13
John Foster	1-2-6	John Greenley	1-2-7
Jane H. Foster	0-2-0	Jemima Green	0-1-2
Edward Franks	1-1-1	1 free negro over 16 years	
Martin Feltner	1-0-0	William Gourley	1-1-6
John F. Fauntleroy	1-2-4	Thomas Grubb	1-0-1
Margaret Funston	0-5-2	John C. Grigg	1-2-1
Samuel P. Ferrer [?]	1-0-0	Henry N. Grigsby	1-4-8
Marcus Feehrer	1-0-1	James V. Glass	1-8-8
Noah Frasher	2-11-16	Hiram Gibbons	1-0-0
Robert Florence	1-0-2	John Grantt	3-3-5
Strother Franks	1-0-1	Joseph George	1-1-3
Ann Farnsworth	2-0-3	Catherine W. Groves	0-1-1
Moses Furr	1-0-1	George Gordon	1-0-0
William Fowler	1-0-2	John Gordon	1-0-1
John Furlow	1-0-0	Francis & Harrison	
Henry Franks Sr.	1-0-2	Gordon	2-0-4
Henry Franks Junr.	1-0-0	James T. Grantham	1-0-9
John Furr	1-0-0	Abrahm Grim	1-0-0
Jesse Furr	1-0-0	Washington Garrison	1-0-1
Daniel Furr	1-0-3	Dandridge Garrison	1-0-1
James Jurr	1-0-0	James Gibbs	1-0-0

Clarke County, Virginia Personal Property Tax Lists 1836-1853
1836

Name	Values	Name	Values
Nimrod Glasscock	1-1-2	William Holtzclaw	2-0-0
Nelson Garrison	1-0-3	Alexander Holtzclaw	1-0-1
Thornberry Grubb	1-0-0		
		William Johnston	1-0-0
Henry D. Hooe	1-2-2	William Jackson	1-0-1
George Hefflebour	2-3-15	Thomas Jordan	1-0-0-1
Edwin Hart	1-2-1	Solomon R. Jackson	1-1-2
Samuel L. Hesser	1-0-0		
John Hay	1-3-3	Joseph Hicks	2-0-0
Abraham Huiett	2-0-5		
John Huiett	1-0-4	Thomas Jackson	1-13-9
Richard Homes	0-3-0	Jane Jackson	0-4-3
Samuel Heflebour	1-1-2	Jacob Isler	3-10-16
Robert Haynie [?]	1-0-2	John J. Johnston	1-9-11
Presley N. Helm	1-3-6	Elizabeth Jackson	1-1-5
James M. Hite	1-20-30	John Johnston Senr.	1-0-0
James Hay	1-18-16	John Johnston Jr.	1-0-1
William T. Helm	1-6-7	Horace H. Jordan	1-0-0
Philip Hart [?]	1-0-0	Reubin R. Jordan	1-2-5
Mary Howard	0-1-1	George Johnston	1-0-2
Richard Hardesty	3-2-11	Herod Jenkins	1-0-1
Ann &			
John B. Helm	1-3-6	Jacob Kimmerly	1-0-0
James Howard	1-0-0	James Kean	1-2-7
George Heida	1-1-1	Thomas Keenan	1-0-0
Thomas Hiatt	1-0-3	George Kitchen	1-6-8
Levi &		George Knight	1-7-12
Joseph Hiatt	2-0-6	Thomas Knight	1-0-3
James P. Hughes	2-2-6	Joseph Kline	1-0-1
Abram Haines	1-0-5	John Kerfoot	2-18-20
William Hurst	0-2-4	William C. Kerfoot	1-8-11
Moses Hicks	2-1-1	Franklin J. Kerfoot	1-7-14
Rodero [?] Hoffman	1-0-1	William G. Kerfoot	1-5-12
William Hummer	1-0-2	Jacob Kline	1-0-0
Bushrod Hoff	1-0-0	Joseph Kirby	1-0-0
Joseph Hoff	1-0-0	John Koble	1-1-0
Harrison Hoff	1-0-0	Benjamin Kent	1-0-0
Whiting Hamilton	1-0-0	Jon Keene	1-0-1
Cornelius Hoff	1-0-0	Thomas Kennerley	1-0-0

Clarke County, Virginia Personal Property Tax Lists 1836-1853
1836

Sarah Lundrey	0-2-0	Bushrod McCormick	1-1-1
James Lyons Senr.	1-0-3	John Morgan	1-6-8
Richard Lanham	1-0-0	Cyrus McCormick	1-0-1
Samuel Lloyd	1-0-1	John Mayers	1-0-3
John B. Larue	1-15-18	Samuel & Thos	
John Lloyd	1-0-0	McCormick	2-16-17
Hamilton Lay	1-0-0	Benjamin Morgan	1-19-28
Francis Larue	1-7-8	Province McCormick	1-1-0
Jacob Luke	1-3-6	Francis McCormick	1-11-19
Samuel Larue	2-10-15	James McCormick	1-6-10
Richard K. Littleton	2-1-6	Stephen R. Mount	1-16-21
Lorenzo Lewis	1-34-19	James Murphey	2-0-1
George S. Lane	1-7-11	Isaac McCormick	1-5-12
John Louthard	2-2-1	Sylvanus Morse	1-0-1
Robert H. Little	3-11-8	Peer McMurray	1-2-9
Mary Lefever	0-1-1	Otway McCormick	2-6-2
William H. Luckett	1-0-0		
James Larue	1-3-6	[Tape over next 8 names, makes	
John Lock	2-0-7	them difficult to read.]	
William Lock	3-0-6	Shelton [?] McDaniel	1-0-0
John Lancaster	1-0-0	Susan Marshall	0-4-6
Timothy Lessinger	1-0-0	John Mitchell	1-1-2
James Lyons Jr.	1-0-0	Matilda [?] Mitchell	1-1-2
Josiah Lee	1-0-0	____ Myers [?]	
Louisa Littleton	0-1-1	____ Meade [?]	
John Longerbone	1-0-1	____ Milton	
Washington Lee	1-0-1	[illegible]	
George Longerbone	1-0-0		
William Longerbone	1-0-0	Philip N. Meade	2-8-9
John Loyd	1-0-0	John Myers	0-2-5
Henry Loyd	1-0-0	Robert McCandless	0-3-7
Elizabeth Lanham	0-0-2	Alexander McLoy	1-0-0
Edgar Lanham	1-0-0	Henry Mack	2-1-6
		John Mack	1-0-2
Warner Muse	2-2-5	Richard Morgan	2-0-4
John Marshall	1-0-1	McCormick &	
John J. Monroe	1-1-5	Ballenger	1-3-6
William Morgan	2-4-5	Jacob May	1-0-0
George McCormick	2-9-18	Lott McDaniel	2-1-1

Clarke County, Virginia Personal Property Tax Lists 1836-1853
1836

Name	Values	Name	Values
William D. McGuire	2-11-12	Matthew Page	1-8-15
James Mason	2-0-0	George Pults	2-0-1
Charles McCormick	2-20-30	Mann R. Page	1-9-17
Elijah Milton	1-0-0	Thomas Preston	1-0-0
Tenley Murphey	1-0-1	Daniel Powers	1-3-2
William Mason	1-0-0	Mary Pine	0-1-0
Lucy Mustin	0-2-1	Washington Pagett	1-1-1
John Martz	2-0-1	Ann R. Page	0-7-0
Jesse Messer	1-0-0	John Page Jr.	1-7-12
George Moulder	2-0-3	Robert Page	1-21-22
Levi Marcus	1-0-3	Judith Page	0-3-0
Alfred Moore	1-0-2	John Pierce	2-4-8
Edward Moore	1-0-0	John Page Senr.	1-50-18
Jesse McConehay	1-0-1	John E. Page	1-8-12
John & James Mitchem	2-0-3	Elizabeth Page	0-2-1
James Mitchell	1-5-6	William B. Pages Est.	0-8-10
Josiah Murphey	1-0-1	Paul Pierce	1-7-6
		Isaac E. Pigeon	2-0-1
George H. Norriss	2-17-19	Isaac Pigeon	3-0-6
John Noell	1-0-0	John W. Packett	1-0-0
Joseph Noble	1-0-0	William Pagett	2-0-0
Lewis Neill	1-5-11	Evan Peyton	1-0-0
William H. Nicklin	1-0-2	Philip Puller	1-0-3
Joseph M. Nicklin	1-4-1	Richard E. Parker	2-14-16
James H. Newell	1-1-0		
James Newman	1-0-0	Matthew Royston	1-0-6
Thomas J. Needler	1-0-0	Peter Royston	1-0-0
Philip Nelson	1-24-15	William Reiley	1-0-0
Thomas F. Nelson	2-16-20	Isaac Ramey	2-1-3
William Nicewander	1-0-2	Benjamin Richards	2-4-1
		John Russell Senr.	1-2-0
Dennis OConner	2-5-11	Joshua Roseberry	1-0-0
Enoch ORear	1-5-10	John Reed	1-0-0
Elizabeth ORear	0-8-7	Robert C. Randolph	1-10-13
Aquilla Osburne	2-0-4	John Richardson	2-25-30
James Osburne	1-2-2	Daniel B. Richards	1-0-0
		John Roush	1-0-0
John W. Page	2-1-14	Jacob Rhodes	1-1-1
Robert P. Page	1-17-19	Bennett Russell	1-1-6

Clarke County, Virginia Personal Property Tax Lists 1836-1853
1836

Daniel Richards	1-0-1		Horace P. Smith	1-1-0
John Ross	1-0-0		Philip Shaver	1-0-0
John Reiley	1-0-0		Robert Smith	1-0-1
Jane Richardson	1-1-1		Daniel Shotts	1-0-0
James Rice	1-1-0		George Smedley	2-0-1
Levi Rogers	1-0-1		Enoch Strother	1-2-3
George Ritter	1-0-0		Fielding L. Sowers	2-8-14
John Ratliffe	1-0-0		1 free negro over 16 years	
Addison Romine	1-0-2		James Sowers	1-15-18
Uriah Royston	1-1-0		William Steel	1-0-1
Joseph Ross	1-0-0		George K. Sowers	1-6-10
Matthew Rust	1-2-3		John W. Sowers	1-4-9
Richard Ridgway	4-0-6		John Shipe	2-1-1
William Reed	2-0-6		Daniel Stoner	1-0-0
Jonas Ridgway	1-1-4		Horace Stringfellow	1-2-1
Joseph Ridings	1-0-3		Daniel W. Sowers	1-9-13
Jacob Rookingbaugh	1-2-1		John Scroggins	1-8-12
James Ryan	1-1-0		John Stewart	1-0-1
William Ross	1-0-0		Edward Sheckles	1-0-1
George Renno	1-0-0		James H. Sowers	1-8-20
			Catherine Sowers	0-4-6
Lewis A. Smith	2-11-17		Moses Scott	2-0-3
Parkeson D. Shepherd	1-2-2		James Stevens	2-2-5
Jacob Shoup	1-0-0		William Steward	3-2-10
Treadwell Smith	2-8-4		Edward Stonestreet	1-0-0
John Ship	1-13-22		Samuel Stonestreet	1-0-0
Emanuel Shores	5-2-1		Isaac Starkey	1-0-0
Edward J. Smith	2-2-42		Moses Stickle	1-0-1
Jacob Shively	2-10-13		Joseph Stonestreet	1-0-0
Joseph F. Stephenson	3-0-2		John Shaun [?]	1-0-0
Henry W. Snyder	1-2-2		Barnett Smallwood	1-0-0
Philip Smith	2-22-30		Sarah Smallwood	1-0-01
Henry Stipe	2-2-10		John Smallwood	1-0-0
Joseph Shepherd	2-6-14		Thomas Stillions	1-0-2
John Strother	1-7-5		John Stillions	1-0-1
Erasmus G. Ship	1-4-4		James Shoemate	1-1-7
William Sowers	1-8-14		Mary T. Ship	0-1-0
1 free negro over 16 years			James Strother	1-0-2
Samuel Stipe	1-4-3		Elizabeth Strother	0-5-5

Clarke County, Virginia Personal Property Tax Lists 1836-1853
1836

Samuel Taylor	3-15-14	John Vancleave	1-1-3
William Taylor	1-18-21	Jacob Vanmeter	0-4-4
Joshua H. Thomas	1-1-2		
John B. Taylor	1-15-36	Harrison S. Wiatt	1-0-3
Nancy Taylor	1-8-11	Josiah W. Ware	2-13-11
Jesse Taylor	2-1-3	Allen Williams	1-9-11
John Thompson	1-3-2	Leroy P. Williams	2-4-9
John Trussell	2-2-6	James Williams	1-7-8
Moses Trussell	3-0-4	Henry Weaver	1-0-0
Warner W. Throckmorton	0-3-4	William P. Wigginton	2-3-12
		James Wigginton	1-0-1
Richard M. S. Timberlake	2-8-12	Alexander H. Washington	1-4-1
Samuel Trinary	1-0-1	Elizabeth W. Washington	0-1-0
Stephen Timberlake	1-0-0		
Alfred Tobin	1-0-1	Stephen Whittelsey [?]	1-0-1
Emanuel Trinary	1-0-1	Osburne Willing [?]	1-0-0
Adam Towner	1-0-0	John K. Wood	2-1-6
Minor M. Towner	1-0-0	Bennett Wood	1-0-0
Joseph Tuley	2-20-31	Obed Willingham	1-0-0
David Timberlake	2-12-14	John Willingham	1-0-3
David Trisler	1-2-4	William Willingham	1-0-0
Edward Tegner	1-0-0	Francis B. Whiting	1-23-17
Abigail Tanquary	0-0-2	Richard Wagner	1-1-2
John C. Taylor	1-9-10	James Whittington	1-0-1
Mary Thomas	1-2-4	William Welch	1-0-0
Henry H. Taylor	1-0-1	Grantham Way	1-0-0
William Tintsman	1-0-0	Hezekiah Wiley	1-0-2
William Turner	1-0-0	James Wiley	1-0-1
Enoch Triplett	1-0-0	Samuel Wiley	1-0-1
Joseph Vincent	1-1-1	Samuel Yakle	2-0-0
James M. Voldineer	2-0-5	George Young	2-0-0
Gary Vaughn	1-0-0	Samuel Young	1-0-2
James Violett	1-0-1	Simeon Yowell	1-0-0

Clarke County, Virginia Personal Property Tax Lists 1836-1853
1836

Names of Free Negroes

Columns: 1) Free negroes over 16 years, 2) Slaves over 12 years, 3) Horses

John Fletcher	1-0-0		Ben Fairfax	1-0-0
Buster Smith	1-0-1		Alfred Dickson	1-0-0
Thomas Whiting	2-4-0		George Brister	1-0-0
John Clifton	1-0-0		Mowin Harris	1-0-0
Robert Cook	1-0-1		George Ransome	1-0-0
Burwell Cook	1-0-1		John Jackson	1-0-2
Daniel Wilkins	1-0-1		Sampson Robeson	1-0-1
Isaac _____	1-0-0		Joseph Grayson	1-0-1
Horace McDaniel	1-0-0			

Clarke County, Virginia Personal Property Tax Lists 1836-1870

1837

Columns: 1) White males above 16, 2) Slaves 12-16 years, 3) Slaves over 16 years, 4) Horses mares, mules, etc.

Name	Values	Name	Values
William Armstrong	1-0-0-0	Samuel Bonham	1-1-12-18
William Allen	1-0-3-5	Lewis Bromley	1-0-0-5
John Ambrous	3-0-0-6	Juliet Boyston	0-0-0-1
Robert Ashby	3-0-0-6	Rudolph T. C. Boude	1-0-0-0
Thomas Anderson	1-0-0-0	Thomas H. Burwell	1-1-8-17
David H. Allen	3-5-18-53	Samuel Briarly	2-0-7-6
Algernon S. Allen	1-1-7-18	Philip Berlin	2-1-2-3
Buckner Ashby	1-2-10-26	Phineas Bowen	2-1-3-9
Charles W. Andrews	1-0-0-4	Jacob Beaty	1-0-0-0
Evan Anderson	1-0-0-0	John Burchell	1-0-4-8
John B. Andrews	1-0-0-0	George Boling	1-0-0-1
Philip Ayreheart Senr.	1-0-0-2	Francis O. Byrd	1-4-10-13
Mary Alexander	0-0-2-2	Thomas T. Byrd	1-1-4-6
Mason Anderson	1-0-1-0	Isaac Berlin	2-0-0-1
Peyton Ashby	1-0-0-0	Humphrey Brooke	1-0-3-1
John Alexander	3-2-10-16	Thomas Blackmore	1-1-5-10
Samuel Armar	1-1-1-2	Robert Burchell	1-1-5-8
1 free negro		John M. Blackmore	3-1-1-1
William Ambrous	1-0-0-0	Strother Bell	1-0-2-4
Jane Anderson	0-0-0-2	Philip Burwell	2-5-28-14
David Anderson	1-0-0-0	James Bell	1-5-48-31
William Allen	1-0-0-0	Thomas Briggs	6-0-3-11
Hathaway Allexander	2-0-0-1	William Baker	1-1-4-5
Joseph Anderson	2-0-3-9	Maria M. Burwell	0-0-5-3
John Ashby	1-0-0-3	John Brounley	1-1-12-17
Martin Ashby	1-0-0-3	Thomas T. Byrd's	
Augustine Athey	2-0-0-3	Estate	0-0-1-0
		George H. Burwell	1-7-32-36
Lewis Burwell	1-2-5-12	Lucy Burwell	0-2-7-0
Robert Binns	1-0-0-1	George N. Barnett	1-0-0-0
John Bourne	1-0-2-2	Hiram O. Bell	1-0-0-3
Daniel S. Bonham	2-1-5-9	James A. Bonham	1-2-5-16

Clarke County, Virginia Personal Property Tax Lists 1836-1870
1837

William Brounley	1-0-1-3		Elizabeth Carter	1-0-3-4
William Berlin	1-0-1-1		Elizabeth N. Carter	0-0-3-1
James Boggs	1-0-0-0		Daniel D. Conner	2-0-0-1
Henry Bell	1-0-1-0		Alfred Clevnger	1-0-2-4
James Bulger	1-0-0-0		John Copenhaver	1-0-3-9
William Benjamin	1-0-0-0		Carter B. Chandler	1-1-9-9
Joseph Bulger	1-0-0-0		Peter Crum	1-0-0-1
John Boling	1-0-0-0		Thomas & David	
Napoleon B. Balthrop	1-0-0-1		Clevenger	2-0-0-4
Henry Brown	1-0-1-1		Parkerson &	
Isabella Benson	1-1-3-8		Eben Craig	2-1-2-7
George C. Blackmore	1-0-0-0		William H. Colts	1-1-0-1
Hiram Bruen	2-1-6-21		Craven Craig	1-0-2-6
William Brawner	1-0-0-0		James Castleman	2-4-10-22
John Berresyer [?]	1-0-0-0		William D. Castleman	1-1-2-4
Nancy Blake	1-0-0-1		William Castleman	1-0-8-18
John Blake	1-0-0-0		John Castleman	2-0-3-9
William Berry	1-4-6-13		Martha R. Castelman	2-1-8-4
Charles Butler's Estate	0-0-7-15		Thomas H. Crow	1-1-2-0
Benjamin Barr	1-0-0-0		Jane Calmes	0-1-0-1
Squire Bell	1-0-2-6		Elijah Cleveland	1-0-0-0
Andrew Billmyer	3-0-0-1		Benjamin Crampton	1-1-0-1
Carr Baylinolls	1-0-0-0		George F. Calmes	1-1-3-6
John C. Bazzle	1-0-0-2		William Clark	1-0-0-3
Abraham Beavers	1-0-0-4		Henry Catlett	1-2-7-15
Daniel Barr	1-0-0-0		Osman Chamberlane	1-0-1-0
Henry W. Brabham	1-0-0-0		Baalis Castleman	1-0-0-3
Thomas W. Burns	1-0-0-0		Frederick Clopton	1-1-3-7
James Beck	1-0-0-1		John G. Chapman	1-0-0-1
Hector Bell	1-1-21-18		Jacob Crim	1-0-0-0
James Bell Junr.	1-0-0-1		James Cain	1-0-0-0
			Robert A. Colston	1-0-3-5
George Castleman	1-0-1-4		Alfred Castleman	1-0-5-7
John Carroll	1-0-0-1		Joseph Carter	1-0-0-0
Patrick Carroll	1-0-0-3		James Cannon	1-0-0-0
George Cornwell	2-0-0-2		John P. Chamberlane	1-0-2-7
Hiram Craig	1-0-0-0		William Carper	1-0-0-4
Nelson Colier	1-0-0-0		Frederick Carper	1-0-0-0
James Cross	3-1-3-5		Martha Chapman	1-0-0-0

Clarke County, Virginia Personal Property Tax Lists 1836-1870
1837

Elizabeth Carnagey [sic]	0-1-18-19	Sarah Earle	0-1-2-2	
		John B. Earle	1-0-11-22	
William Cornwell	1-0-0-0	Christopher Ellett	1-0-0-1	
Fielding Cornwell	1-0-0-0	Jacob Enders	1-0-2-4	
Thomas Cornwell	1-0-0-0	William G. Everheart	3-0-1-2	
John Carpenter	1-1-3-2	John Elyett	1-0-0-0	
John Cooper	1-0-0-1			
Dabney Cother	2-0-0-0	Margaret Funston	0-0-5-2	
Parkenson Corder	1-0-0-0	George Fyste	2-0-2-19	
Alexander Cole	1-1-0-0-	James C. Ford & Co.	3-0-2-11	
		John J. Fauntleroy	1-0-3-4	
William Davidson	1-0-0-0	John D. Furguson Junr.	1-0-0-1	
Sidney Dean	0-0-1-0	Martha Foster	0-1-2-8	
Thomas Davis	1-0-0-3	William Fridley	1-0-0-1	
Moses Dillon	1-0-0-0	Robert Florence	1-0-1-2	
William Deahl	1-0-0-0	John M. Fillan	1-0-0-0	
James Davis	2-0-0-0	Edward Franks	1-0-1-1	
Gersham Drake	1-0-0-0	Ann Farnsworth	2-0-0-2	
Henry Dick Senr.	1-0-0-0	Moses Furr	1-0-0-2	
Henry Dick Junr.	1-0-0-2	John Furlow	1-0-0-0	
Baalis Davis	1-2-1-1	Benjamin Franks	1-0-0-2	
Seth Dero [?]	1-0-0-3	William Fowler	1-0-0-2	
Benjamin Downing	2-0-0-2	John Foster	1-0-2-6	
William Doughty	1-0-3-5	Jane H. Foster	0-0-2-0	
Peter Dearmont	2-1-3-6	McFarland Fuller	1-0-0-0	
John Dow	1-0-0-1	Joseph Flemming	1-0-0-1	
Henson Dorsey	1-0-0-1	Archibald Flemming	1-0-0-4	
David Denney	2-0-0-4	Marcus Feehrer	1-0-0-1	
John Doran	1-0-0-0	Strother Franks	1-0-0-1	
Gurey Davis	1-0-0-0	Henry Franks	1-0-0-2	
John Drish	1-0-0-0	John Furr	1-0-0-0	
Michael Dearmont	1-0-3-4	Jesse Furr	1-0-0-1	
		Daniel Furr	1-0-0-3	
James Downing	1-0-0-2	Thomas & Washington Furguson	2-0-0-3	
Robert Duke	1-0-0-0			
Thomas Duke	1-0-0-0	John D. Furguson Senr.	1-0-12-11	
		James Furr	1-0-0-0	
Levi Elliott	1-0-0-0			
Hiram P. Evans	2-1-1-2	Richard Green	1-0-2-6	

Clarke County, Virginia Personal Property Tax Lists 1836-1870
1837

John Gantt	2-0-5-12		
John Gregg	2-0-1-1	Richard Hardesty	3-1-1-10
Henry N. Grigsby	1-1-3-5	George Heida	1-0-0-0
James V. Glass	1-6-0-9	Henry Hooe	1-0-1-2
John Greenley	2-1-0-5	John Hay	1-0-4-1
Stephen J. Gantt	1-1-2-3	Thomas Hiatt	1-0-0-3
Lewis Glover	1-0-2-9	James R. Hughes	1-1-0-4
Thomas Gould	2-2-2-10	James M. Hite	1-3-15-30
Alice Gould	0-0-0-3	James Hay	1-2-13-16
Dandridge Garrison	1-0-0-1	William T. Helm	1-2-5-7
Hiram Gibbons	1-0-0-0	George Hefflebower	2-1-3-16
James Green	3-1-9-16	Robert Haney	1-0-0-2
John Grantt	1-0-3-5	John Huyett	1-0-0-4
William Graves	1-0-0-1	Abraham Huyett	2-0-0-5
Thomas Grub	1-0-0-0	Abraham Hayns	1-0-0-6
William Garner	1-0-0-0	Samuel Hill	3-0-0-0
William Gourley	1-1-0-6	Edwin Hart	1-0-1-1
Jemima Green	0-0-0-1	Decatur Heaton	1-0-0-1
Joseph George	1-0-1-3	Samuel Hefflebower	1-0-1-1
Edward Gorman	1-0-0-0	Mary Howard	0-2-0-0
William Green	1-0-0-0	George D. Harrison	0-1-1-7
Catharine Grove	0-0-0-1	William H. Harvey	1-0-0-0
John Gordon	1-0-0-3	Whiting Hamiton [sic]	1-0-0-0
James Grantham	0-0-1-0	William Hummer	1-0-0-2
Harrison Gordon	3-0-0-4	Bushrod Hoff	1-25-25-6
Abraham Grim	1-0-0-0	William Hollslaw [sic]	2-0-0-0
Robert Gill	1-0-0-0	Joseph Hoff	1-0-0-0
Monroe C. Garton	1-0-0-1	Cornelius Hoff	1-0-0-0
George Green	1-0-2-6	Levi & Joseph Hiatt	2-0-0-2
Samuel Grub	1-0-0-0		
James Galway	1-7-30-6	Thomas Knight	1-0-0-3
William Goodwin	1-0-0-0		
Davis Grub	1-0-0-1	Elizabeth Jackson	0-0-2-4
Thornbury Grub	2-0-0-1	Solomon N. Jackson	1-0-1-2
Stephen Glascock	1-0-0-0	John Joliff	2-1-5-9
Nelson Garrison	2-0-0-4	George Johnston	1-0-0-2
Nimrod Glascock	1-0-0-2	Thomas Jackson	1-2-12-11
James Gibbs	1-0-0-0	John J. Johnston	1-2-7-10
Washington Garrison	1-0-0-1	Jacob Isler	2-1-8-10

Clarke County, Virginia Personal Property Tax Lists 1836-1870
1837

Jane Jackson	0-1-0-2	George S. Lane	2-0-7-12
John Johnston Senr.	1-0-0-0	Samuel Larue	1-2-9-12
John Johnston Junr.	1-0-0-1	Mary Lefever	0-0-1-1
Reuben N. Jordan	1-0-2-5	William H. Luckett	1-0-0-1
Reuben Jordan	1-0-1-2	William Lee	1-0-0-0
Thomas Jordan	1-0-0-1	George F. Ludwig	2-0-1-1
William Johnston	1-0-0-0	Hamilton Lay	1-0-0-0
Jeremiah Jordan	1-0-0-0	Samuel Lancaster	1-0-0-0
Herod Jenkins	1-0-0-1	John B. Larue	1-3-9-18
Ebenezer Jackson	1-0-0-0	Edgar Lanham	1-0-0-0
Elias Johns	1-0-0-0	Elizabeth Lanham	0-0-0-2
		George Longerbeam	1-0-0-0
John Kerfoot	2-0-16-17	Sarah Longerbeam	1-0-0-0
George L. Kerfoot	1-3-8-15	William Longerbeam	1-0-0-0
William C. Kerfoot	1-1-3-11	John W. Luke	1-0-0-0
Franklin C. Kerfoot	1-1-7-13	James Lamb	1-0-0-0
Thomas Kennerly	1-0-0-0	Sarah Lindsey	1-0-2-0
John Kable	1-0-1-0	James Lyons	1-0-0-3
George Kitchen	1-3-3-8	Henry Loyd	1-0-0-0
George Knight	1-2-5-11	Richard Lanham	1-0-0-0
James Kean	1-0-2-6	William Lock	2-0-0-4
Joseph Kirby	1-0-0-0	James Loyd	1-0-0-0
Middleton Kealor	1-0-0-0	James Lanham	1-0-0-0
Thomas Kneedler	1-1-0-1	Samuel Loyd	2-0-0-2
Joseph Kline	1-0-0-2	John Loyd	1-0-0-0
Benjamin Kent	1-0-0-0	Louisa K. Littleton	0-0-1-0
John Keene	1-0-0-1		
Jacob Kemmerly	1-0-0-0	Otway McCormick	0-0-2-0
		Willougby McCormick	1-0-0-0
Bushrod Longerbeam	1-0-0-0	Stephen R. Mount	1-4-16-19
Washington Lee	1-0-0-1	Peter McMurry	1-0-0-8
Jacob Luke	1-0-2-5	Cyrus McCormick	1-0-0-1
John Lock	1-0-0-6	Sam & Thomas	
Frances Larue	0-0-5-9	McCormick	2-2-11-15
Richard S. E. Littleton	1-0-1-4	William Morgan	4-2-4-9
James Larue	2-0-3-10	Province McCormick	1-0-0-1
Robert H. Little	3-0-10-8	James McCormick	1-1-5-10
Lorenzo Lewis	1-6-32-28	Isaac McCormick	1-0-4-13
John Louthen	1-0-1-1	Bushrod McCormick	1-0-2-0

Clarke County, Virginia Personal Property Tax Lists 1836-1870
1837

Benjamin Morgan	1-1-16-26	John & James Mitchell	2-0-0-3
David Meade	1-2-7-9	Susan Marshall	1-1-3-6
Rebecca S. Meade	0-1-3-2	John Myers	1-0-0-0
Philip N. Meade	2-1-4-7	Lucy Mustin	0-0-0-1
Robert McCandless	0-0-4-7	John Martz Senr.	2-0-0-1
McCormick &		Jesse Messer	1-0-0-0
Ballinger	1-0-3-8	George Moulder	2-0-0-3
William D. McGuire	1-1-9-10	Edward Moore	1-0-0-0
David H. McGuire	1-0-9-7	Jesse McConnehay	1-0-0-1
William Mason	1-0-0-1	John Martz Junr.	1-0-0-1
James Mitchell	1-2-6-3	Stephen Marlow	1-0-0-1
William McDaniell	1-0-0-0	James Murphey	1-0-0-1
Alexander Marshall	1-0-0-1		
Francis McCormick	1-2-7-20	George H. Norris	2-2-9-18
Elizabeth Morgan	0-2-2-0	Joseph Noble	1-1-1-1
James Murphey	1-0-0-1	William H. Nicklin	1-0-0-0
Henry Mark	2-0-0-6	Joseph M. Nicklin	1-0-4-3
Mary Morgan	1-0-0-1	Philip Nelson	1-5-21-17
John Mayers	1-0-0-4	Thomas F. Nelson	2-4-13-15
John Mark	1-0-0-2	James Newman	1-0-0-0
Alexander McCloy	2-0-0-0	James H. Neville	1-1-0-1
John Mahue	2-0-0-0	William Nicewander	1-0-0-2
Moses McCarty	1-0-0-0	Ann Neel	0-1-2-5
John Miller	1-0-0-0	John Noel	1-0-0-0
Lott McDaniell	1-0-0-1	Philip N. Nicholas	0-1-1-0
Samuel McCormick	1-0-0-0		
Richard Morgan	1-0-0-0	Dennis OConnor	2-0-3-10
Isaac Manuel	1-0-0-0	John W. Owen	1-0-0-1
Levi Marcus	1-0-0-3	Mason Oram	1-0-0-0
George McCormick	2-1-9-17	Enoch Orear	1-0-5-9
Charles McCormick	3-0-19-31	Aquilla Osbourne	2-0-0-4
Elijah Milton	1-0-0-0	Elizabeth Orear	1-0-6-8
James Mason	1-0-1-0	James Osbourn	0-0-0-1
Alfred Moore	1-0-0-2		
John Marshall	1-0-1-2	John Pierce	2-2-2-5
Sylvanus Moore	1-0-0-0	Mathew Page's Estate	0-2-8-15
Shelton McDaniell	1-0-0-0	Paul Pierce	1-2-4-5
Henry Murphey	1-0-0-0	John Page Senr.	1-6-4-18
John Morgan	1-2-6-10	John E. Page	1-0-8-12

Clarke County, Virginia Personal Property Tax Lists 1836-1870
1837

Name	Values	Name	Values
Robert P. Page	1-1-14-19	Samuel Redman	1-0-0-1
Eliza M. Page	0-0-2-1	Eliza Romine	1-0-0-1
William B. Page's Estate	1-1-7-9	Lydia Romine	0-0-1-0
		Levi Rodgers	1-0-0-1
John Page Junr.	2-1-6-12	Jacob Roehenbauch	1-0-0-1
Robert Page	1-2-17-21	James Ryan	1-0-1-0
Ann N. Page	0-1-2-0	John Reed	1-0-0-0
Judith Page	0-1-3-1	John Russell	1-0-0-2
John H. Page	3-2-10-15	John Richardson	1-3-17-35
Mary Pine	0-0-1-0	John Roush	1-0-1-0
William Parker	1-0-0-0	Daniel B. Richards	1-0-0-1
Richard E. Parker	1-0-16-20	William Ross	1-0-0-1
Mann R. Page	1-1-7-12	Jane Richardson	1-0-1-1
Daniel Powers	1-1-3-2	John Riley	0-0-0-0
James Pine	1-0-0-0	George Renno	1-0-0-0
William B. Peake	1-0-0-1	Daniel Richards	1-0-0-1
Isaac Pidgeon	2-0-0-5		
Isaac E. Pidgeon	2-0-0-1	James Seevers	1-0-0-0
John Padget	1-0-0-0	Robert Smith	1-0-0-4
George Pultz	2-1-0-1	Thomas Simpson	1-0-1-2
Washington Padget	1-0-1-1	Thomas Sprint	2-0-0-0
Joseph E. Peyton	1-0-0-1	Daniel Stoner	1-0-0-0
Thomas Preston	1-0-0-0	James H. Sowers	1-4-6-16
		Joseph Shepherd	2-0-5-12
William Rieley	1-0-0-0	Emanuel Showers	4-0-0-1
Isaac Ramey	2-0-1-4	Treadwell Smith	2-2-9-5
George Rutter	1-0-0-0	William Seevers	1-0-0-2
Mathew Rust	1-0-2-4	Joseph F. Stephenson	1-0-0-1
Uriah Royston	1-0-0-1	Joseph Smith	3-0-0-2
Addison Romine	1-0-0-1	Benjamin F. Seevers	1-0-0-8
Bennett Russell	2-1-5-7	Edward J. Smith	2-2-21-37
Elizabeth Roots	0-0-2-0	Parkinson D. Shepherd	1-0-2-2
Jonas Ridgway	1-0-1-4	John Ship	1-2-10-28
William Reed	2-0-0-6	Erasmus Ship	1-1-4-6
Solomon Redman	1-0-0-0	Horace P. Smith	2-0-4-1
Richard Ridgway	2-0-0-6	Fielding S. Sowers	1-0-5-13
Mathew Royston	1-0-1-3	James Sowers	1-0-12-15
Peter Royston	1-0-0-4	John M. Sowers	1-1-4-9
Robert C. Randolph	1-2-11-12	Horace Stringfellow	1-0-2-1

Clarke County, Virginia Personal Property Tax Lists 1836-1870
1837

Philip Smith	1-2-22-29	George Smedley	1-0-0-0
John H. Sweaney	1-0-0-1	Benjamin Starkey	1-0-0-0
George K. Sowers	1-2-5-11	Edward Sheckles	1-1-0-1
Jacob Shireley	1-2-7-14		
Henry Stipe	3-0-2-7	Adam Towner	1-0-0-0
Samuel Stipe	1-0-4-6	Jesse Taylor	2-0-2-3
Thomas Shumate	1-1-2-6	Isaac Tanquary	1-0-0-1
Daniel W. Sowers	1-1-8-12	Abigail Tanquary	0-0-0-2
Daniel Shotts	1-0-0-0	Mary Thomas	1-0-0-4
John Stewart	1-0-0-0	John Thompson	1-1-3-4
Catharine Sowers	0-0-4-8	Warner W.	
Franklin Sheppard	1-0-0-2	Throcmorton [sic]	0-0-3-7
James Smith	1-0-0-2	Samuel Taylor	2-3-12-13
John Scroggins	1-1-8-16	John C. R. Taylor	2-5-8-7
Joseph Sherman	2-1-0-7	Nancy Taylor	1-1-7-11
Enoch Strother	1-0-2-3	Richard M. S.	
Elizabeth Strother	0-0-5-5	Timberlake	1-0-8-15
Henry Shepherd	1-0-0-1	Joseph Tuley	2-5-28-24
Champ Shepherd	1-0-0-1	William Taylor	2-0-0-0
Henry W. Snyder	1-0-2-3	William Turner	1-0-0-0
John Strother	1-1-2-6	Harrison Thompson	1-0-0-1
Philip Shanck [?]	1-0-0-0	Enoch Triplett	1-0-0-0
Jacob Shoup	1-0-0-0	Greenbury Thompson	1-0-0-2
William Sowers	1-3-4-16	Thomas Stillions	1-0-0-2
Edward Stonestreet	1-0-0-0	William Timberlake	0-0-2-0
William Steward	3-0-2-9	Mathew Talbot	1-0-0-0
Moses Stickles	1-0-0-0	Alfred Tobin	2-3-1-3
Barnet Smallwood	1-0-0-0	1 free negro	
Van Smallwood	1-0-0-0	Stephen Timberlake	1-0-0-0
Alfred Smallwood	1-0-0-0	David Timberlake	2-1-11-14
Joseph Stonestreet	1-0-0-0	William Trinary	1-0-0-1
Sarah Smallwood	1-0-0-1	Samuel Trinary	1-0-0-1
Joseph Stewart	1-0-0-1	John B. Taylor	1-0-15-36
John N. Sowers	1-0-0-0	William Taylor	1-3-15-20
John Shaver	2-0-0-1	Joshua H. Thomas	1-0-2-2
Isaac Starkey	1-0-0-1	David Trisler	1-0-0-4
James Strother	1-0-0-1	William Tumbil	1-0-0-0
John Shipe	1-0-1-1	Nimrod Trussell	2-1-0-5
John Stillions	1-0-0-2	John Trussell	1-2-0-5

Clarke County, Virginia Personal Property Tax Lists 1836-1870
1837

Henry H. Taylor	1-0-0-1	Elizabeth W.	
Benjamin Thompson	1-0-0-2	Washington	0-1-1-0
William Tintsman	1-0-0-1	Bennett Wood	1-0-0-0
Samuel Tintsman	1-0-0-0	Allen Williams	1-1-9-11
Felix Triplett	1-0-0-0	John Wallingham	1-0-0-0
Moses Trussell	2-1-0-5	Obed Wallingham	1-0-0-0
		William Wallingham	1-0-0-0
Joseph Vincent	1-0-2-1	Josiah W. Ware	2-3-6-12
James Valdenar	1-0-3-7	John Wood	2-0-0-5
John Vanmeter	0-0-3-12	Hezekiah Wiley	2-0-0-1
James Violett	1-0-0-1	Samuel Wiley	1-0-0-1
John Vancleave	1-0-1-3	James Wiley	1-0-0-0
		Richard Waggoner	1-0-1-1
Francis B. Whiting	2-4-17-16	Herbert Washington	0-0-1-1
Henry Weaver	1-0-0-0	Lucinda Washington	0-0-3-2
Grantham Way	1-0-0-0		
Leroy P. Williams	1-1-3-7	Samuel Young	1-0-1-4
James Williams	1-1-6-7	George Young	2-0-0-2
James Wigginton	3-0-4-4	Samuel S. Yakle	1-0-0-1
Francis H. Whiting	1-0-4-6	Isaac Young	1-0-0-0
Hamilton Washington	1-0-3-1	Simeon Yowell	1-0-0-0

Free Negroes & Mulattoes

Columns: 1) Free males above 16, 2) Slaves 12-16 years, 3) Slaves over 16 years, 4) Horses mares, mules, etc.

Jack Adams	1-0-0-1	William Murry	1-0-0-0
Henry Brady	1-0-0-0	Sampson Robinson	1-0-0-3
Robert Cook	1-0-0-2	John Robinson	1-0-0-0
Burwell Cook	1-0-0-0	George Ransom	1-0-0-2
John Clifton	1-0-0-0	Thomas Whiting	1-0-4-1
John Diggs	1-0-0-0	Daniel Wilkinson	1-0-0-0
Wiley Finch	1-0-0-0	Isaac Busey	1-0-0-0
Thomas Gray	1-0-0-0	William Jones	1-0-0-0
Joseph Grayson	1-0-0-2	William Butler	1-0-0-0
Lydia Ball	1-0-0-0	Daniel Lewis	1-0-0-0
Mowen Harris	1-0-0-1	Philip Martin	1-0-0-0
Anthony Lucas	1-0-0-4	George Brutus	1-0-0-0
Aaron Lee	1-0-0-0	Brister Smith	1-0-0-0

Clarke County, Virginia Personal Property Tax Lists 1836-1853

1838

Columns: 1) White males above 16, 2) Slaves 12-16 years, 3) Slaves over 16 years, 4) Horses mares, mules, etc.

William C. Alexander	0-0-0-5	Robert Boyston	0-0-2-1
Mary Alexander	0-0-1-1	Philip Berlin	2-2-1-5
Mason Anderson	0-0-0-1	Samuel Berlin	1-0-3-2
William Allen	1-0-2-5	Mary Berlin	1-0-0-0
Thomas Anderson	1-0-0-3	John Brown	1-0-0-0
Algernon S. Allen	1-2-7-18	Humphrey Brooke	1-0-3-1
David H. Allen	3-8-19-18	John Brounley	1-1-11-19
Charles W. Andrews	1-0-0-6	William Brounley	1-0-1-2
Buckner Ashby	1-4-9-24	James Boggs	1-0-0-0
John Alexander	1-2-6-10	Isaac Bushmel	2-0-0-4
Joseph Anderson	2-0-2-7	William Baker	1-2-5-5
Peyton Ashby	1-0-0-0	Hector Bell	1-1-17-19
Samuel Armar	1-0-1-3	Samuel Briarly	2-0-7-6
1 free negro		Philip Burwell	1-6-29-13
John B. Ambrows	1-0-0-0	Thomas H. Burwell	1-1-10-14
Evan Anderson	1-0-0-0	Thomas Blackmore	1-1-7-10
John Ashby	1-0-0-0	Robert Burchell	1-0-3-8
Martin Ashby	1-0-0-3	John W. Blackmore	2-1-1-1
Robert Ashby	2-0-0-3	George H. Burwell	1-4-32-38
Nimrod Ashby	1-0-0-1	Nathaniel Burwell	1-10-45-38
John Arnell	1-0-0-0	Lucy Burwell	0-0-6-0-
John Ambrous	3-0-0-6	Maria M. Burwell	0-0-5-3
Robert Ashby Jr.	1-0-0-1	Thomas Briggs	1-0-3-13
Jane Anderson	0-0-0-2	Hiram O. Bell	1-0-1-3
William Allen	1-0-0-1	James Bell	1-2-6-8
Hathaway Alexander	2-0-0-2	Strother Bell	1-0-3-6
Augustine Athey	2-0-0-5	Isaac Berlin	2-1-0-1
		William Berlin	2-0-0-1
Lewis Burwell	1-2-4-12	Squire Bell	1-0-1-5
Daniel S. Bonham	2-1-5-8	John Burchell	1-0-4-8
John Borne	1-0-0-2	Francis O. Byrd	1-3-10-13
Samuel Bonham	1-3-10-18	Thomas T. Byrd	1-0-5-5
Lewis Bromley	2-0-0-6	Nathaniel Burwell	
Phineas Bowen	2-1-3-unk	(of Wm N. B)	1-0-0-1

Clarke County, Virginia Personal Property Tax Lists 1836-1853
1838

Amos Bonham	1-1-6-12	George T. Calmes	1-1-5-7
William Berry	1-4-7-10	Henry Catlett	1-1-7-16
James Bulger	1-0-0-0	Frederick Clopton	1-1-4-8
Joseph Bulge	1-0-0-0	Frederick Carper	1-0-0-0
John Bouling	1-0-0-0	Elizabeth	
Hiram Bruen	2-0-0-16	Carnagey [sic]	0-3-18-20
John Ballinger	1-0-2-6	William Carter	1-0-0-1
Henry Bell	1-0-0-0	Peter Crum	1-0-0-1
John Berringer	1-0-0-0	John Copenhaver	2-1-2-11
Henry Brown	2-0-1-6	Carter B. Chandler	2-1-12-11
Andrew Billmyer	0-0-0-1	James Castleman	2-2-14-20
Izabella Benson	1-1-4-3	William Castleman	1-2-8-17
John & Aaron Blake	2-0-0-1	John Castleman	2-0-3-9
Carr Baylinolls	1-0-0-0	William A. Castleman	1-1-3-7
John C. Bazzle	1-0-0-0	Baalis Castleman	1-0-0-3
Abraham Beavers	1-0-0-2	George Castleman	1-0-0-4
Henry W. Brabham	1-0-0-0	Thomas H. Crow	1-0-2-0
James Bell Jr.	1-0-0-1	Benjamin Crampton	1-1-0-1
James Beck	1-0-0-1	William Clark	1-0-1-6
Jesse Bouling	1-0-0-1	Hiram Craig	1-0-0-1
Napoleon B.		Nelson Colier	1-0-0-0
Balthrope	1-0-0-1	Alfred Castleman	1-0-4-9
Wesley Brown	1-0-0-1	Joseph Carter	1-0-0-0
John W. Bird	1-1-12-1	James Cannon	1-0-0-0
Robert Binns [?]	1-0-0-0	John P. Chamberlane	1-1-2-6
Thomas T. Byrds Est.	0-0-1-0	Osmon Chamberlane	1-0-1-0
George Bouling	1-0-0-1	William Carper	1-0-0-4
		Elijah Cleveland	1-0-0-1
John G. Chapman	1-0-0-0	Martha Castleman	2-1-8-4
George Cornwell	2-0-0-2	William Carrington	1-0-0-1
William Cornwell	1-0-0-1	Craven Craig	1-0--4
Fielding Cornwell	1-0-0-0	William H. Colston	1-0-0-1
Thomas Cornwell	1-0-0-1	Robert A. Colston	1-0-2-7
Thomas Cross	1-1-2-2	Edward Cornwell	1-0-0-0
Elizabeth Carter	2-1-2-6	Madison Chapman	1-0-0-0
Elizabeth N. Carter	0-0-3-1	James H. Clark	2-1-1-0
Alfred Clevinger	1-1-1-6	Samuel Cain	1-0-0-0
David Clevinger	1-0-0-3	John Carpenter	1-1-2-2
Thomas Clevinger	1-1-0-3	John Cooper	1-0-0-1

Clarke County, Virginia Personal Property Tax Lists 1836-1853
1838

Dabney Cother	1-0-0-1		Margaret Funston	0-0-3-2
Parkinson Corder	1-0-0-0		Oliver Funston	1-0-0-1
Alexander Cole	1-1-0-0		George Fyste	4-0-0-17
Patrick Carroll	0-0-0-3		James C. Ford & Co.	1-1-3-7
Parkinson &			John J. Fauntleroy	1-2-2-3
Ebin Craig	2-0-3-9		John D. Furguson Jr.	1-0-3-4
Andrew Cage	1-0-0-0		Martha Foster	0-2-2-7
			William Fridley	1-0-1-1
Andrew K. Davis	1-0-0-2		Robert Florence	1-0-0-2
George Dunn	1-0-0-0		Edward Franks	1-0-1-1
Thomas Davis	1-0-0-3		Ann Farnsworth	2-0-0-3
Samuel Davis	1-0-0-1		Moses Furr	1-0-0-3
William Deahl	2-0-0-0		Benjamin Franks	1-0-0-4
James Davis	2-0-0-0		William Fowler	1-0-0-2
Henry Dick Senr.	1-0-0-0		John Furlow	1-0-0-0
Henry Dick Junr.	1-0-0-2		John Foster	1-0-2-6
Baalis Davis	2-2-1-0		Jane H. Foster	0-0-2-0
Benjamin			McFarland Fuller	1-0-0-0
Downing [?]	2-0-0-2		Joseph Flemming	1-0-0-1
William Doughty	1-0-1-2		Archibald Flemming	1-0-0-3
John Dow	1-0-0-1		Marcus Feehrer	1-0-0-1
Hanson Dorsey	1-0-0-1		Strother Franks	1-0-0-9
James Doran	1-0-0-0		Henry Franks	1-0-0-0
Garey Davis	1-0-0-0		John Furr	1-0-0-0
Peter Dearmont	2-1-4-6		Jesse Furr	1-0-0-0
Michael Dearmont	1-7-2-5		Daniel Furr	1-0-0-3
John Drish	1-0-0-0		James Furr	1-0-0-0
James Downing	1-0-0-3		Thomas Furguson	1-0-0-1
Thomas Duke	1-0-0-0		Washington Furguson	1-0-0-1
			John D. Furguson	1-0-12-11
Hiram P. Evans	2-1-1-1			
Sarah Earle	0-0-2-2		Richard Green	1-0-0-2
John B. Earle	1-0-11-21		John Gantt	2-0-5-12
Jacob Enders	1-0-0-1		John Gregg	3-0-1-6
Levi Ellett	1-0-0-0		Henry N. Grigsby	1-1-3-9
William G. Everheart	2-0-1-2		James V. Glass	1-1-6-7
Jacob Everheart	1-0-0-0		Lewis Glover	1-0-2-1
Henry Edwards	1-0-0-0		John Greenley	1-1-1-5
John Ellyett	1-0-0-0		Stephen J. Gantt	1-1-1-5

Clarke County, Virginia Personal Property Tax Lists 1836-1853
1838

Thomas Gould	2-1-4-10		John Hay	1-0-3-1
Dandridge Garrison	1-0-0-1		William T. Helm	1-1-6-7
Hiram Gibbons	1-0-0-1			
James Green	5-2-9-24		Churchill C. Gibson	1-0-0-0
William Graves	2-0-0-1			
Thomas Grub	1-0-0-0		George Hefflebower	2-1-4-12
William Garner	1-0-0-0		Thomas Hiatt	1-0-0-4
Alice Gould	1-0-0-2		James P. Hughs	1-0-0-5
William Gourley	1-1-0-6		James M. Hite	2-5-15-29
Jemima Green	0-0-1-1		1 free negro	
Joseph George	1-0-1-3		James Hay	1-2-15-17
Catharine Grove	0-0-0-1		Levi Hiatt	0-0-0-3
William Green	1-0-0-0		Robert Haney	1-0-0-1
John Gordon	1-0-0-2		John Huyett	2-0-0-4
James Grantham	0-0-1-0		Abraham Hayns	1-0-0-7
George Gordon	3-0-0-5		Edwin Hart	1-0-0-1
Robert Gill	1-0-0-0		Samuel H.	
Monroe C. Garton	1-0-0-2		Hefflebower	1-0-1-2
William S.			Mary Howard	0-1-1-0
Greenlease	1-0-0-6		George D. Harrison	0-0-1-4
Samuel Grub	1-0-0-0		Whiting Hamilton	1-0-0-1
James Galway	1-0-0-0		William H. Harvey [?]	1-0-0-0
William Goodwin	1-0-0-0		William Hummer	1-0-0-2
Jacob Gates	1-0-0-1		Bushrod Hoff	1-0-0-0
Thornbury Grub	1-0-0-1		Joseph Hoff	1-0-0-0
Stephen Glasscock	1-0-0-0		Cornelius Hoff	1-0-0-0
Nimrod Glasscock	1-0-0-0		William Hollslaw	1-0-0-0
James Gibbs	1-0-0-0		John Hugley	0-0-1-0
Washington Garrison	1-0-0-1		John Hopkins	1-0-1-1
Nelson Garrison	2-0-0-5			
Edward Gorman	1-0-0-0		Thomas Knight	1-0-0-3
John H. Hefflin	1-0-0-0		Mathew Jones	3-0-0-7
Richard Hardesty	4-2-1-11		Elizabeth Jackson	1-1-1-6
James Harris	1-0-3-6		Larkin D. Jennings	1-0-0-0
George Heida	1-0-0-0		Solomon R. Jackson	1-0-1-2
Rudolph Houtt	1-0-0-4		John Joliff	
William Houtt	1-0-0-0		[may be erased ?]	0-0-0-0
Henry Hooe	1-0-0-2		George Johnston	1-0-0-2

Clarke County, Virginia Personal Property Tax Lists 1836-1853
1838

Thomas Jackson	1-3-11-10	Frances Larue	0-0-8-8
John J. Johnston	1-0-7-12	Samuel Larue	2-3-9-11
Jane Jackson	0-0-0-2	Richard K. Littleton	1-0-1-3
		Lorenzo Lewis	1-7-31-23
Jacob Isler	3-0-8-11	John Louther	1-1-2-1
		George S. Lane	1-0-7-10
John Johnston Sen.	1-0-0-0	George F. Ludwig	1-0-1-2
John Johnston Junr.	1-0-0-1	Samuel Lancaster	1-0-0-0
Reubin R. Jordan	1-0-2-4	Edgar Lanham	1-0-0-0
Reubin Jordan	1-0-2-2	George Longerbeam	1-0-0-0
Richard Johnston	1-0-0-0	John B. Larue	1-3-9-20
Jeremiah Jordan	1-0-0-0	Sarah Longerbeam	2-0-0-0
Herod Jenkins	1-0-0-1	William Longerbeam	1-0-0-0
William M. Jackson	1-0-1-1	Sarah Lindsey	1-1-2-1
Ebenezer Jackson	2-0-0-1	James Lindsey	1-0-0-2
Elias Johns	1-0-0-0	James Lyons	2-0-0-5
		Henry Loyd	1-0-0-2
John Kerfoot	2-2-13-17	William Lanham	1-0-0-0
George L. Kerfoot	1-2-8-15	William Lock	3-0-0-4
William C. Kerfoot	1-1-7-12	James Loyd	1-0-0-0
Franklin C. Kerfoot	1-1-6-12	Charles Leech	2-0-0-1
George Kitchen	1-3-2-10	Hugh Lindsey	1-0-0-0
Thomas Kennerly	1-0-1-0	James Lanham	1-0-0-0
John Kable	1-0-0-0	Richard Lanham	1-0-0-0
James Kean	1-0-2-5	John Lock	1-0-0-6
Joseph Kirby	1-0-0-0	William Lock Junr.	1-0-1-1
Midleton Kealor	1-0-0-0	Robert H. Little	3-0-9-8
Thomas Kneedler	1-0-0-1	Samuel Loyd	2-0-0-2
Benjamin Kent	1-0-0-0	John Loyd	1-0-0-0
John Keene	1-0-0-2	William Littleton	2-0-1-3
Jacob Kemmerly	1-0-0-0	Louisa Littleton	0-0-1-0
George Knight	3-2-7-9		
		James Morris	1-0-0-1
Franklin Lock	1-0-0-1	Otway McCormick	1-2-6-7
Uriah Lock	1-0-2-7	Peter Morgan	1-0-0-0
Bushrod Longerbeam	1-0-0-0	Stephen R. Mount	1-4-16-18
James Lee	1-0-0-0	Peter McMurry	1-0-1-8
Washington Lee	1-0-0-1	Cyrus McCormick	1-0-0-1
Jacob Luke	1-0-3-4		

23

Clarke County, Virginia Personal Property Tax Lists 1836-1853
1838

Saml & Thos		Thomas Murphey	1-0-0-0
McCormick	2-2-11-15	John Mayers	1-0-0-2
William Morgan	1-1-3-9	John Mark	1-0-0-2
James McCormick	1-1-4-8	John McCloy	1-0-0-1
Isaac McCormick	2-1-4-10	Alexander McCloy	1-0-0-0
Benjamin Morgan	1-2-16-24	Franklin Mahue	1-0-0-0
David Meade's Estate	1-2-6-9	John Mahue	1-0-0-0
Rebecca S. Meade	0-0-3-2	John Miller	1-0-0-0
Philip N. Meade	1-0-5-8	Lott McDaniel	1-0-1-1
Francis Meade	1-0-4-6	Samuel McCormick	1-0-0-0
John Mattox	2-0-0-1	Richard Morgan	1-0-0-0
William D. McGuire	1-0-10-13	Levi Marcus	1-0-0-4
David H. McGuire	1-0-7-15	George McCormick	2-0-9-16
William Mason	1-0-0-1	Charles McCormick	3-1-12-27
James Mitchell	2-1-3-1	Elijah Milton	1-0-0-0
William McDaniel	1-0-0-0	Susan Marshall	0-0-2-5
John McFillan	1-0-0-0	Alfred Moore	1-0-0-1
Francis MCormick	1-1-7-15	John Marshall	1-0-1-2
Elizabeth Morgan	0-0-3-0	Sylvanus Moore	1-0-0-0
James Murphey	1-0-0-1	Asa Mathews	1-0-0-0
Mary Morgan	1-0-0-1	Jacob May	1-0-0-0
Warner Muse	2-0-1-4	Isaac Manuel	1-0-0-0
Alexander Marshall	1-0-0-1		
Lewis Metcalf	1-0-0-1	George H. Norris	3-1-8-18
Henry Murphey	1-0-0-0	Joseph Noble	1-0-0-0
John Morgan	1-1-7-10	Pierce Nolen	1-0-0-0
John & James		Joseph M. Nicklin	1-0-3-1
Mitchell	2-0-0-3	Philip Nelson	1-3-15-17
Lucy Mustin	0-0-1-1	Thomas F. Nelson	1-3-14-16
John Myers	1-0-0-0	James Newman	1-0-0-0
John Martz Senr.	1-0-0-2	James H. Neville	1-1-1-1
William Marts	1-0-0-0	William Nicewander	1-0-0-2
Jesse Messer	1-0-0-0	Ann Neil	0-1-2-3
George Moulder	2-0-0-3	Philip N. Nicholas	0-1-1-0
Edward Moore	1-0-0-0		
Jesse McConnehay	1-0-0-1	John W. Owen	1-0-0-1
John Murphey	1-0-0-0	Mason Oram	1-0-0-0
Stephen Marlow	1-0-0-1	Enoch Orear	1-0-0-0
James Murphey	1-0-0-0	Joab Osbourn	1-0-1-0

Clarke County, Virginia Personal Property Tax Lists 1836-1853
1838

Name	Values	Name	Values
Aquilla Osbourn	2-0-0-4	Elizabeth Roots	0-0-1-0
Elizabeth Orear	0-2-7-7	Jonas Ridgway	2-0-1-6
		Mathew Royston	1-0-0-8
John Page		Peter Royston	1-0-0-0
(of Wm B. Page)	0-0-1-0	Robert C. Randolph	1-2-10-11
John Pierce	2-1-3-4	Samuel Redman	1-0-0-1
Walter & Francis K.		Jacob Roehenbauch	1-0-1-1
Page	1-0-2-5	James Ryan	1-0-0-0
Mathew Page's Estate	0-2-6-11	John Reed	0-0-0-0
Paul Pierce	1-2-3-5	John Russell Sen.	0-0-1-0
John Page Senr.	1-9-45-29	John Richardson	1-1-19-26
John P. Page	1-0-6-10	John Roush	1-0-0-0
Robert P. Page	1-3-14-17	Daniel B. Richards	1-0-0-0
Eliza M. Page	0-0-1-0	Lidia Romine	0-0-0-1
William B. Page	0-0-2-3	William Reed	2-0-0-6
John Page Junr.	3-1-7-9	Solomon Redman	1-0-0-1
Robert Page	0-0-15-21	Richard Ridgway	2-0-0-6
Ann R. Page	0-1-4-0	William Ross	1-0-0-0
John W. Page	2-2-10-15	Jane Richardson	2-0-2-1
Judith Page	0-0-3-2	John Rieley	1-0-0-0
Mary Pine	0-1-0-0	George Renno	1-0-0-0
Richard E. Parker	1-1-12-19	Joseph Ross	1-0-0-0
Mann R. Page	1-2-8-17	Levi Rogers	1-0-0-0
Daniel Powers	1-2-2-3		
James Pine	1-1-0-1	James Seevers	1-0-0-4
Isaac Pidgeon	2-0-0-5	James Smith	1-0-0-1
Isaac E. Pidgeon	2-0-0-1	Thomas Sprint	1-0-0-0
John Padget	1-0-0-0	James H. Sowers	1-2-6-15
Washington Padget	1-0-0-1	Joseph Shepherd	3-0-5-14
Joseph E. Peyton	1-0-0-1	Emanuel Showers	5-2-0-1
Thomas Preston	1-0-0-0	Treadwell Smith	2-2-9-6
George Pultz	1-0-0-1	William Seevers	1-0-0-2
		Joseph Smith	3-0-0-2
Isaac Ramey	2-1-0-4	Benjamin F. Seevers	1-0-3-5
George Rutter	0-0-0-1	Edward J. Smith	2-2-18-30
Mathew Rust	1-0-2-4	Parkinson D.	
Uriah Royston	1-0-0-1	Shepherd	1-1-1-2
Addison Romine	1-0-0-1	John Ship	1-2-10-15
Bennett Russell	1-1-4-10	Erasmus Ship	1-1-4-5

Clarke County, Virginia Personal Property Tax Lists 1836-1853
1838

Horace P. Smith	1-0-4-1	Burr Smallwood	1-0-0-1
Fielding S. Sowers	1-1-8-11	Van Smallwood	1-0-0-0
Daniel Sowers	1-1-3-7	Alfred Smallwood	1-0-0-0
James Sowers	1-2-10-14	Joseph Stonestreet	1-0-0-0
John M. Sowers	1-2-3-10	John R. Sowers	2-0-1-1
Horace Stringfellow	1-0-3-1	John Shaver Senr.	1-0-0-1
Henry Seevers Junr.	1-0-0-5	John Shaver Jur	1-0-0-0
Philip Smith	1-3-18-22	Adam Stipe	1-0-0-1
Moses & Abraham Shipe	2-0-0-0	Isaac Starkey	2-0-0-2
		Benjamin Starkey	1-0-0-0
John H. Sweaney	1-0-1-1	Edward Sheckles	1-1-0-1
George K. Sowers	1-2-4-10	John Stillions	1-0-0-1
Jacob Shireley	1-2-7-10	George Smedley	1-0-0-0
Henry Stipe	3-0-2-8		
Daniel W. Sowers	1-0-8-13	Adam Towner	1-0-0-0
Daniel Shotts	1-0-0-0	Jesse Taylor	1-0-0-2
Thomas Shumate	1-0-2-7	Abigail Tanquary	0-0-0-1
John Stewart	2-0-0-1	John Thomas	1-0-2-4
Catharine Sowers	0-0-4-6	John Thompson	1-1-3-2
Franklin Shepherd	1-0-0-2	Warner W. Throckmorton	0-0-3-4
James Strother	1-0-0-1		
John Scroggins	1-2-9-14	Samuel Taylor	1-3-11-11
Joseph Sherman	1-1-1-7	Susan B. Taylor	0-0-6-7
Enoch Strother	1-0-2-4	Nancy Taylor	1-1-7-9
Elizabeth Strother	0-0-5-5	Richard M. S. Timberlake	2-0-8-14
Philip Shanck	1-0-0-0		
Jacob Shoup	1-1-0-0	Joseph Tuley	1-3-20-22
William Sowers	3-3-6-13	William Turner	1-0-0-0
Benjamin Stonestreet	1-0-0-0	Harrison Thompson	1-0-0-1
Edward Stonestreet	1-0-0-0	Enoch Triplet	1-0-0-0
Henry Shepherd	1-0-0-1	Greenbury Thompson	1-0-1-2
Champ Shepherd	1-0-0-1	William Timberlake	0-0-2-0
Henry W. Snyder	1-0-2-3	Stephen Timberlake	1-0-0-1
John Strother	1-1-2-8	David Timberlake	2-2-12-17
Samuel Stipe	1-0-4-7	William Trinary	1-0-0-1
William Steward	3-0-2-9	Jonas Trinary	1-0-0-1
Moses Stickles	1-0-0-1	John B. Taylor	1-1-10-18
Simon Stickles	1-0-0-1	William Taylor	1-2-15-15
Barnet Smallwood	1-0-0-1	Joshua H. Thomas	1-1-1-2

Clarke County, Virginia Personal Property Tax Lists 1836-1853
1838

David Trisler	1-0-0-3		James Wigginton	3-0-3-4
William Tumbil	1-0-0-1		Francis H. Whiting	1-0-9-8
Nimrod Trussell	1-0-0-1		Hamilton Washington	1-0-2-0
John Trussell	1-0-2-3		Elizabeth Washington	0-0-2-0
Henry H. Taylor	0-0-0-1		Bennett Wood	1-0-0-0
Benjamin Thompson	1-0-0-4		Allen Williams	1-2-8-10
William Tintsman	1-0-0-0		John Wallingham	1-0-0-0
Felix Triplet	1-0-0-0		William Wallingham	1-0-0-0
Moses Trussell	1-0-0-1		Obed Wallingham	1-0-0-0
			Josiah W. Ware	1-3-17-22
Joseph Vincent	1-0-1-1		John Wood	2-0-1-5
James Valdenar	1-0-3-5		Hezekiah Wiley	1-0-0-1
John Vancleave	1-0-0-4		Samuel Wiley	1-0-0-1
Jacob Vanmeter	0-0-1-14		James Wiley	1-0-0-0
James Violet	1-0-0-1		Richard Waggoner	1-0-1-2
Samuel Vancleave	1-0-0-1		Herbert Washington	0-0-1-1
Jacob Vorous	1-0-0-0		Lucinda Washington	0-0-3-2
			James H. Weaver	1-0-0-0
Grantham Way	1-0-0-0			
Francis B. Whiting	2-4-18-16		Samuel Young	1-0-1-4
Henry Weaver	1-0-0-0		George Young	1-0-0-2
Ephraim Watson	1-0-0-2		Samuel S. Yakle	1-0-0-1
William Wilson	1-0-0-0		Isaak Young	1-0-0-0
Leroy P. Williams	1-2-4-6		Simeon Youell	1-0-0-0
James Williams	1-1-6-7		Washington Young	1-0-0-0

Clarke County, Virginia Personal Property Tax Lists 1836-1853
1838

[Free negroes, but not labeled as such]

Columns: 1) Free male negroes over 16 years, 2) Slaves over 12 & under 16 years, 3) Slaves over 16 years, 4) Horses, etc.

John Adams	1-0-0-2	Philip Martin	1-0-0-0
William Butler	1-0-2-0	John Robinson	1-0-0-0
Robert Cook	1-0-0-2	Hannah Robinson	0-0-0-1
John bleffron [sic]	1-0-0-0	George Ranson	1-0-0-1
Burwell Cook	1-0-0-0	Brister Smith	1-0-0-0
John Diggs	1-0-0-0	Griffin Taylor	1-0-0-1
Wiley Finch	1-0-0-0	Thomas Whiting	2-0-4-1
Lydia Hall	1-0-0-1	George Wells	1-0-0-0
Mowen Harriss	1-0-0-0	Daniel Wilkinson	1-0-0-1
Aaron Lee	1-0-0-0	Isaac Busey	1-0-0-0
William Murry	1-0-0-0		

Clarke County, Virginia Personal Property Tax Lists 1836-1853

1839

Columns: 1) White males above 16, 2) Slaves 12-16 years, 3) Slaves over 16 years, 4) Horses mares, mules, etc.

William Allen	1-0-0-1		Daniel S. Bonham	1-1-4-6
John Ambrous	3-0-0-5		Samuel Bonham	1-3-11-18
Robert Ashby Senr.	2-0-0-4		Lewis Bromley	2-0-0-6
Nimrod Ashby	1-0-0-0		Juliet Boyston	0-0-2-1
Robert Ashby Junr.	1-0-0-1		Thomas H. Burwell	1-1-10-18
Thomas H. Anderson	1-0-0-3		Nathaniel	
David H. Allen	1-7-21-50		Burwell Junr.	1-0-7-1
Algernon S. Allen	1-2-7-5		Samuel Briarly	2-1-7-11
Buckner Ashby	1-1-8-19		Philip Berlin	2-1-2-4
John B. Ambrous	1-0-0-1		Phineas Bowen	2-1-2-7
Mary Alexander	0-0-1-1		Francis O. Byrd	1-3-10-12
Mason Anderson	1-0-0-1		Thomas T. Byrd	1-0-4-5
Peyton Ashby	1-0-0-1		Isaac Berlin	2-1-0-1
John Alexander	1-2-6-11		Samuel Berlin	1-0-0-1
Samuel Aumar	1-0-0-3		Humphrey Brooke	0-0-2-0
1 free black			Thomas Blackmore's	
William Ambrous	1-0-0-4		Est.	0-0-1-0
Jane Anderson	0-0-0-2		Robert Burchell	1-0-3-3
David Anderson	1-0-0-0		John M. Blackmore	3-1-1-1
John Arnold	1-0-0-0		Strother Bell	1-0-3-6
Hathaway Alexander	2-0-0-1		Philip Burwell	2-8-23-13
Joseph Anderson	2-1-2-8		Nathaniel Burwell	1-11-42-40
John Ashby	1-0-0-1		James Bell	1-3-6-8
Martin Ashby	1-0-0-2		Thomas Briggs	8-1-4-15
Augustine Athey	2-0-0-5		William Baker	1-2-4-3
William C. Alexander	1-3-6-10		Maria M. Burwell	0-2-10-11
Thomas Alexander	1-0-0-1		John Brounley	1-1-11-17
			Thomas T. Byrd's Est.	0-0-1-0
John W. Bird	1-0-13-7		George H. Burwell	1-7-36-43
Preston Brown	1-0-0-0		Lucy Burwell	0-1-5-0
Napoleon B. Balthrop	1-0-0-1		John Burchell	1-1-3-8
Blackmore &			Mary Berlin	1-0-0-0
Richardson	2-0-0-0		John Brown	1-0-0-0
Samuel Bowser	1-0-0-0		George Bartlett	1-0-0-1
John Bourne	1-1-1-3		Neil Barnett	1-0-0-1

Clarke County, Virginia Personal Property Tax Lists 1836-1853
1839

Name	Values	Name	Values
Hiram O. Bell	1-0-0-3	Edward Cornwell	1-0-0-0
Amos A. Bonham	1-1-6-12	Henry Chew	1-0-0-0
William Brounley	1-0-1-2	Jacob Crim	1-0-0-0
William Berlin	2-0-2-1	Nelson Colier	1-0-0-0
James Boggs	1-0-0-0	James Cross	1-3-1-8
James Bulger	1-0-0-0	Elizabeth Carter	1-1-2-6
Joseph Bulger	1-0-0-0	Elizabeth N. Carter	0-0-2-1
John Bouling	1-0-0-0	John Copenhaver	2-1-2-11
John Blue	1-1-0-5	Michael Copenhaver	1-0-0-0
Henry Brown	1-0-1-4	Carter B. Chandler	2-1-13-12
Isabella Benson	1-1-4-4	Peter Crum	1-0-0-1
John Berringer	1-0-0-0	Alfred Clevinger	1-0-0-5
William Berry	1-4-6-10	David Clevinger	1-0-0-4
Squire Bell	1-0-2-3	Parkinson Craig	1-2-1-6
William Billmyer	1-0-0-0	Ebin Craig	1-0-0-2
Andrew Billmyer	1-0-0-0	William H. Colston	1-0-1-2
Abraham Beavers	1-0-0-2	James Castleman	3-0-13-20
Henry W. Brabham	1-0-0-0	William A. Castleman	1-1-3-6
Oliver Binns	1-0-0-0	John Castleman	1-1-3-9
John Ballinger	1-0-1-9	William Castleman	1-2-8-18
James Beck	1-0-0-1	Martha P. Castleman	2-1-8-4
Hector Bell	1-3-16-15	John G. Chapman	1-0-0-0
Marcus Blackmore's Est.	0-0-1-0	Stephen Cother	1-0-0-0
Wesley Brown	1-0-0-1	Thomas H. Crow	2-0-2-1
Robert Binns	1-0-0-1	Elijah Cleveland	1-0-0-1
James Bell Junr.	1-0-0-1	Joshua Chapman	1-0-0-0
George Brent	1-0-0-0	Benjamin Crampton	1-0-0-1
		George F. Calmes	1-2-4-7
		William Clark	1-0-0-6
George Castleman	1-0-1-4	Henry Catlett	1-1-6-10
James H. Clarke	2-1-1-0	Osman Chamberlane	1-0-1-0
John B. Castleman	1-0-0-0	Frederick Clopton	1-1-4-8
Alfred Castleman	1-1-4-8	Philip Corbin	1-0-0-0
Baalis Castleman	1-0-0-3	Samuel Cain	1-0-0-0
John Carroll	1-0-0-1	Robert A. Colston	1-0-2-4
Patrick Carroll	1-0-0-2	James Carter	1-0-0-0
Thomas Carter	1-1-13-19	James Cannon	1-0-0-0
William Carrington	2-1-0-1	John R. Chamberlane	1-1-1-6
George Cornwell	2-0-0-2	William Carper	1-0-0-4

Clarke County, Virginia Personal Property Tax Lists 1836-1853
1839

Elizabeth		John Ellyett	1-0-0-1
Carnagey [sic]	0-3-18-22	Byrd A. Evans	1-0-0-0
James Grogan	1-0-3-6	Job D. Eichelberger	1-0-3-7
William Cornwell	1-0-0-0		
Fielding Cornwell	1-0-0-0	Margaret Funston	1-0-7-2
Thomas Cornwell	1-0-0-0	Oliver Funston	1-0-0-1
John Carpenter	1-0-1-0	George Fyste	6-0-1-14
Aaron Chamblan	0-0-0-1	John F. Fauntleroy	1-2-2-3
John Cooper	2-0-0-1	John D.	
Parkinson Corder	1-0-0-0	Furguson Junr.	1-0-3-5
William Carter	1-0-0-1	Hiram P. Evans	1-0-0-1
Andrew Cage	1-0-0-0	James C. Ford & Co.	3-0-2-7
Henry Corbin	1-0-0-0	John Foster	1-0-1-6
David Caldwell	1-0-0-0	Jane H. Foster	0-0-2-0
Dabney Cother	1-0-0-2	Martha Foster	0-1-4-7
Andrew Collins	1-0-0-0	Robert Florence	1-0-0-[?]
		James Furr	1-0-0-1
Andrew H. Davis	1-0-2-2	Edward Franks	1-0-0-1
Samuel Davis	1-0-0-1	Ann Farnsworth	1-0-0-3
William Deahl	2-0-1-0	Moses Furr	1-0-0-2
Baalis Davis	2-3-1-1	John Fuston	1-0-0-0
Benjamin Downing	2-0-0-3	Benjamin Franks	1-0-0-2
Peter Dearmont	2-1-2-6	William Fowler	1-0-0-2
Hanson Dorsey	1-0-0-1	Stephen Few	1-0-0-0
James Doran	1-0-0-0	Joseph Flemming	1-0-0-1
Garey Davis	1-0-0-0	Archibald Flemming	1-0-0-2
John Drish	1-0-0-0	Marcus Feehrer	1-0-0-1
Michael Dearmont	1-0-2-5	Strother Franks	1-0-0-1
James Downing	2-0-0-2	John Furr	1-0-0-0
Thomas Duke	1-0-0-1	Jesse Furr	1-0-0-0
_____ Dyser	1-0-0-0	Daniel Furr	1-0-0-0
		Thomas Washington	
Sarah Earle	0-0-2-2	Furguson	1-0-0-2
John B. Earle	1-2-11-21	John D.	
Levi Ellett	1-0-0-0	Furguson Senr.	1-0-11-11
Christopher Elliott	1-0-0-0	McFarland Fuller	1-0-0-0
Jacob Enders	1-0-0-1	James Fitzimmons	1-0-0-0
William G. Everheart	3-0-1-3	John Fletcher	1-0-0-0
Henry Edwards	1-0-0-0	_____ Fulton	1-0-0-0

31

Clarke County, Virginia Personal Property Tax Lists 1836-1853
1839

Enos Farnsworth	1-0-0-0	Alice Gould	0-0-0-2
John Gantt	2-0-5-11	Isaac I. Hite	1-0-0-1
John Grigg	2-0-3-6	Cornelius Hoff	1-0-0-0
Henry N. Grigsby	1-2-1-5	John Hopkins	1-0-2-1
Henry Franks	1-0-0-0	James Gibbs	1-0-0-0
		John Groves	1-0-0-0
Marshall Green	1-0-0-1		
Richard Green	1-0-2-3	William Hobbs	1-0-0-0
John Greenley	1-2-1-6	John Hefflin	1-0-0-0
James V. Glass	1-1-6-7	Richard Hardesty	4-1-2-10
Stephen Gantt	1-1-1-5	James Harris	2-0-3-8
John Grantt	2-0-0-4	Rudolph Hout	1-0-0-2
Lewis Glover	1-0-2-1	Henry D. Hooe	1-0-0-3
Thomas Gould	2-1-5-10	John Hay	1-0-3-1
Dandridge Garrison	1-0-0-1	Levi Hiatt	1-0-1-4
Hiram Gibbons	1-1-0-1	Thomas Hiatt	2-0-0-4
John Gordon	1-0-0-1	James M. Hite	1-4-18-28
James Green	4-2-9-16	1 free black	
William Graves	1-0-0-4	James Hay	1-2-12-20
Thomas Grub	1-0-0-0	William Helm	1-1-6-9
William Garner	1-0-0-0	George Hefflebower	2-1-5-13
George Garner	0-0-0-0	Robert Haney	1-0-0-1
William Gourley	1-0-1-6	Johy Huyett	2-0-0-5
Joseph George	1-0-0-3	Abraham Huyett	2-0-0-5
Edward Gorman	1-0-0-0	Abraham Haynes	1-0-0-8
Catharine Grove	0-0-0-1	Edwin Hart	0-1-0-1
John Gordon	1-0-0-2	Samuel Hefflebower	1-0-1-1
James Grantham	0-0-1-0	Mary Howard	0-0-1-1
George Gordon	2-0-0-6	George D. Harrison	0-0-1-8
Monroe C. Garton	1-0-0-1	Whiting Hamilton	1-0-0-1
Samuel Grub	1-0-0-0	William Hummer	1-0-0-2
William Goodwin	1-0-0-1	Bushrod Hoff	1-0-0-0
Jacob Gates	1-0-0-0	Jonathan Hunsucker	1-0-0-1
Thornbury Grub	1-0-0-1	Joseph Hoff	1-0-0-0
Thomas P. Glasscock	1-2-0-1	Blackwell Hollslaw	1-0-0-0
Nimrod Glasscock	1-0-0-1	William Hollslaw	2-0-0-1
Charles Gillett	1-0-0-0	Richard R. Harrison	1-0-1-1

Clarke County, Virginia Personal Property Tax Lists 1836-1853
1839

William M. Jackson	1-0-1-1		Thomas Kneedler	1-1-0-1
Mathew Jones	4-0-0-8			
Elizabeth Jackson	1-1-1-6		Uriah Lock	1-1-2-7
Solomon K. Jackson	1-0-1-1		James Lee	1-0-0-1
John Jolliff	1-0-6-10		Jacob Luke	1-0-4-5
1 free black			John Lock	1-0-0-6
Thomas Jackson	1-1-13-10		Frances Larue	0-1-7-10
George Johnston	1-0-0-2		Richard K. Littleton	1-1-2-2
John J. Johnston	1-0-7-16		Clarissa Larue	0-0-2-2
Jane Jackson	0-0-1-2		John & James Larue	2-0-5-7
Jacob Isler	3-0-7-11		J. Phil [?] Larue	1-0-0-1
John Johnston Senr.	1-0-0-0		Robert H. Little	3-0-8-8
John Johnston Junr.	1-0-0-1		Lorenzo Lewis	1-7-31-23
Reubin R. Jordan	1-0-1-3		John Louther	1-0-1-1
Reubin Jordan	1-0-2-2		George L. Lane	2-0-6-12
John Jones	1-0-0-0		Samuel Larue	2-3-10-13
Thomas Jordan	1-0-0-1		George F. Ludwig	1-0-1-2
Jeremiah Jordan	1-0-0-0		Samuel Lancaster	1-0-0-0
Herod Jenkins	1-0-0-1		John Lindsey	1-0-0-1
Ebenezer Jackson	1-0-0-0		John B. Larue	1-3-9-20
Elias Johns	1-0-0-0		Thomas Lewis	1-0-0-0
Richard Johnston	1-0-0-0		Edgar Lanham	1-0-0-[?]
			Henry Lanham	1-0-0-0
John Kerfoot	2-3-9-16		William Longerbeam	1-0-0-[?]
William C. Kerfoot	1-0-8-16		George Longerbeam	1-0-0-0
George L. Kerfoot	1-2-6-15		Bushrod Longerbeam	1-0-0-0
George Kitchen	1-1-4-9		Sarah Lindsey	0-0-2-1
George Knight	3-2-6-11		James Lindsey	1-0-1-2
Franklin J. Kerfoot	1-1-8-12		Henry Loyd	1-0-0-2
Thomas Knight	1-0-0-2		Richard Lanham	1-0-0-0
Thomas Kennely [sic]	1-0-0-0		James Loyd	1-0-0-0
Jacob Kemmerly [sic]	1-0-0-0		Washington Lee	1-0-0-1
Robert Kable	2-0-1-0		Charles Luck	2-0-0-1
James Kean	1-0-2-5		Samuel Loyd	2-0-0-1
Joseph Kerby	1-0-0-0		John Loyd	1-0-0-0
John Knight	1-0-0-0		William Littleton	1-0-1-3
Benjamin Kent	1-0-0-0		Louisa K. Littleton	0-0-1-1
Middleton Kealor	1-0-0-0		Sarah Longerbeam	2-0-0-1
John Keene	1-0-0-1			

33

Clarke County, Virginia Personal Property Tax Lists 1836-1853
1839

Name	Values	Name	Values
Otway McCormick	1-1-6-10	Marcus McCloy	1-0-0-0
Peter Morgan	1-0-0-0	Alexander McCloy	1-0-0-0
Stephen K. Mount	1-4-16-18	John Mahue	1-0-0-0
Peter McMurry	1-0-2-7	John Miller	1-0-0-0
Cyrus McCormick	1-0-0-1	Samuel McCormick	1-0-0-0
Samuel & Thomas McCormick	2-1-12-17	Levi Marcus	1-0-0-4
		George McCormick	2-1-9-16
William Morgan	1-0-4-8	Charles McCormick	2-1-13-29
Province McCormick	1-0-1-2	Elijah Milton	1-0-0-0
John Mayers	1-0-0-2	William Martz	1-0-0-0
James McCormick	1-1-4-8	John Marshall	1-0-1-2
Isaac McCormick	1-1-4-10	Sylvanus Moore	1-0-0-0
Benjamin Morgan	1-1-14-28	Jacob May	1-0-0-0
David Meade's Estate	1-0-6-9	Daniel May	1-0-0-0
Philip N. Meade	1-0-5-8	James Murdock	1-0-0-0
Francis Meade	1-0-4-7	Lewis Metcalf	1-1-0-1
Warner Muse	1-0-0-4	Thomas Murphey	1-0-0-0
Isaac Manuel	1-0-0-0	John Morgan	1-1-6-15
		John & James Mitchem	2-0-0-2
James Lanham	1-0-0-0		
William Lock	3-0-0-4	Susan Marshall	0-1-2-5
Samuel Lanham	1-0-0-0	Lucy Musten	0-1-1-1
		John Martz Senr.	1-0-0-3
AlbertMcCormick	1-0-0-1	John Martz Junr.	1-0-0-0
John Mattox	2-0-0-1	Jesse Mercer	1-0-0-1
Richard Morgan	1-0-0-0	George Moulden	1-0-0-2
Jonathan Montgomery	1-0-0-0	Edward Moore	1-0-0-1
		Stephen Marlow	1-0-0-1
William D. McGuire	1-1-8-9	Alfred Moore	1-0-0-1
David H. McGuire	1-0-6-9	Henry Murphy	1-0-0-0
William Mason	1-0-0-1	John McFillan	1-0-0-0
James Mitchell	2-0-2-1	S. Medcalf	1-0-0-0
William McDaniel	1-0-0-0		
Alexander Marshall	1-0-0-1	George H. Norris	2-0-13-14
Francis McCormick	1-1-9-14	Joseph Noble	1-1-0-0
James McDaniel	1-0-0-0	Joseph M. Nicklin	1-1-2-1
John J. Monroe	1-0-2-2	Philip Nelson	1-3-14-17
Elizabeth Morgan	0-1-3-0	Thomas F. Nelson	1-4-13-15
James Murphy	1-0-0-0	William Nelson	1-0-0-0

Clarke County, Virginia Personal Property Tax Lists 1836-1853
1839

Name	Values	Name	Values
James Newman	1-1-0-0	Thornton Pendleton	1-0-0-1
Hugh Nelson	1-0-0-3	John Page	
James W. Neville	1-1-0-1	(of W. B. Page)	0-0-1-0
William Nieswander	1-0-0-2	Walker G. Page	1-0-0-3
Ann Niel	0-1-2-2	James Pine	1-0-0-0
Philip N. Nicholas	0-0-2-0		
Abby Nelson & Mary		Isaac Ramey	2-0-1-3
Pickens	0-0-2-0	George W. Rutter	1-1-0-0
		Mathew Rust	1-0-2-4
John W. Owen	1-0-0-1	Uriah Royston	1-0-0-2
Mason Oram	1-0-0-0	Bennett Russell	1-1-3-7
Enoch Orear	1-1-4-7	James Russell	1-0-0-0
Aquilla Osbourne	2-0-0-3	Jane Richardson	1-0-2-4
Elizabeth Orear	0-1-6-7	Elizabeth Roots	0-0-1-0
John ODonnell	1-0-0-0	Jonas Ridgway	1-0-0-6
		Richard Ridgway	3-0-0-4
Robert P. Page	1-2-15-17	Mathew Royston	1-0-0-6
John Pierce	2-1-3-8	Peter Royston	1-0-0-0
Mathew Page's		William Reed	2-0-0-6
Estate	0-2-6-9	Solomon Redman	1-0-0-3
Paul Pierce	1-1-6-7	Nancy Redman	0-0-0-1
John Page Senr.		Samuel Redman	1-0-0-1
Estate	0-11-42-23	Robert C. Randolph	1-2-11-13
John E. Page	1-0-6-10	James Ryan	1-0-0-0
Eliza M. Page	0-0-1-0	John Ried	1-0-0-1
William B. Page	0-0-2-3	Joseph Ried	1-0-0-0
John Page Senr.	2-1-8-12	John Russell Senr.	0-0-1-0
John W. Page	2-1-10-12	John Richardson	1-4-14-26
Robert Page	1-1-14-21	John Roush	1-0-1-0
Judith Page	0-0-3-2	Daniel B. Richards	1-0-0-0
Richard E. Parker	1-0-12-16	Thomas W. Reynolds	2-0-2-3
Mann R. Page	1-2-8-18	Joseph Ross	1-0-0-0
Daniel Powers	1-2-2-3	George Renno	1-0-0-1
Isaac Pidgeon	2-0-0-6		
Isaac E. Pidgeon	1-0-0-1	Bur Smallwood	1-0-0-1
John Pidgeon	1-0-0-0	James Seevers	2-0-0-5
George Pultz	1-0-0-1	James Smith	1-0-0-3
Joseph E. Peyton	1-0-0-1	Thomas Sprint	1-1-0-0
Thomas Preston	1-0-0-0	William G. Steele	1-0-1-1

Clarke County, Virginia Personal Property Tax Lists 1836-1853
1839

James H. Sowers	1-2-6-12		Richard M. Sydner	1-0-0-0
William K. Seevers	1-0-0-2		Sarah Smallwood	0-0-0-1
Joseph Smith	2-0-1-3		John Shaver Senr.	1-0-0-1
Benjamin F. Seevers	1-1-4-6		John Shaver Junr.	1-0-0-0
Edward J. Smith	2-4-14-28		John W. Sowers	2-0-1-1
Parkinson T. Shepherd	1-1-1-1		James Strother	1-0-0-1
			Adam Shipe	1-0-0-1
Barnett Smallwood	1-0-0-1		Treadwell Smith	2-0-12-12
John Ship	1-3-10-13		George Smedley	1-1-0-1
Erasmus Ship	1-0-4-5		Richard Swift	1-0-0-0
Horace P. Smith	2-0-4-1		Benjamin Starkey	1-0-0-0
Fielding L. Sowers	1-0-7-13		Edward Sheckles	1-0-0-1
Daniel Sowers	1-0-4-8			
John W. Sowers	1-2-3-10		Adam Towner	1-0-0-0
James Sowers	1-1-12-17		Jesse Taylor	2-0-0-4
Horace Stringfellow	1-0-3-1		Abigail Tanquary	0-0-0-1
Amos Shepherd	1-0-0-0		John Thompson	1-1-2-2
Henry Seevers Junr.	1-0-0-7		Warner Throckmorton	0-0-3-6
Philip Smith	1-4-16-22		Samuel Taylor	1-2-12-11
George K. Sowers	1-2-6-10		Susan B. Taylor	0-0-9-7
Jacob Shively	1-1-8-7		William Talley	1-0-0-0
Franklin Sheppard	1-0-0-2		Nancy Taylor	1-1-7-9
John Scroggins	1-0-3-14		Richard M. S. Timberlake	
Enoch Strother	1-0-2-4		1 free black	1-0-7-14
Elizabeth Strother	0-0-5-4		Joseph Tuley	1-3-25-22
Champ Shepherd	1-0-0-1		William Turner	1-0-0-0
Henry W. Snyder	1-0-2-2		Harrison Thompson	1-0-0-1
John Strother	1-1-2-9		Greenbury Thompson	1-0-0-2
Philip Shanch	1-0-0-0		William Timberlake	0-0-2-0
Jacob Shoup	1-1-0-0		Felix Triplet	1-0-0-0
William Sowers	2-4-5-12			
Samuel Stipe	1-0-4-7		Simon Stickles	1-0-0-1
Thomas Shumate	1-0-2-7			
Daniel W. Sowers	1-0-7-12			
Daniel Shotts	1-0-0-0		John Tutt	1-0-0-0
Benjamin Stonestreet	1-0-1-0		Stephen Timberlake	1-0-0-1
Edward Stonestreet	1-0-0-0		William Trenary	1-0-0-1
John Stewart	3-0-0-3		John B. Taylor	1-1-11-18
Alfred Smallwood	1-0-0-0			

Clarke County, Virginia Personal Property Tax Lists 1836-1853
1839

Joshua H. Thomas	1-2-1-1	William Whitescarver [?]	1-0-0-0
David Trisler	1-0-0-5	Elizabeth Washington	0-0-2-0
William Tumbil	2-0-0-1	Bennet Wood	1-0-0-0
Nimrod Trussell	1-0-0-0	Allen Williams	1-2-8-11
John Trussell	1-1-2-2	William Wallingham	1-0-0-1
Timothy A. Todd	1-0-0-0	Josiah W. Ware	1-3-18-20
Henry H. Taylor	1-0-0-1	John Wood	2-0-2-6
Benjamin Thompson	1-0-0-4	Hezekiah Wiley	1-0-0-2
William Tintsman	1-0-0-0	James Wiley	1-0-0-1
John Thomas	0-0-2-0	Samuel Wiley	1-0-0-0
Moses Trussell	1-0-0-3	Herbert Washington	0-0-1-0
William Taylor	1-1-14-18	William Wise	1-0-0-0
		Lucinda Washington	0-0-4-2
		James H. Weaver	1-0-0-0
Joseph Vincent	1-0-1-1	Henry Weaver	1-0-0-0
James Valdemar	1-0-3-8	John Wallingham	1-0-0-1
John Vancleave	1-0-1-5	Jonas Whitacre	1-0-0-1
Jacob Vanmeter	0-0-1-7	Burwell Whiting	11-0-3-6
James Violett	1-0-0-1	Alexander Wood	1-1-0-0
Samuel Vancleave	1-0-0-0		
		George Young	1-0-0-1
James Wigginton	1-1-0-2	Washington Young	1-0-0-0
Francis B. Whiting	1-4-16-18	Samuel S. Yeakle	
H. F. Wheat	2-0-2-2	Simeon Youell	1-0-0-0
Grantham Way	1-0-0-0		
Ephraim Watson	1-0-0-4	Mary Pine	0-1-0-0
Leroy P. Williams	1-3-4-8	Omitted in its proper place & Now added to the whole amount	
James Williams	1-1-6-7		
Francis Whittington	1-0-0-0	Joseph Shepherd	3-0-5-14
Charles Wheeler	1-0-0-1	Emanuel Showers	5-2-0-1
David Timberlake	1-2-12-17	Francis H. Whiting	1-1-2-7

Clarke County, Virginia Personal Property Tax Lists 1836-1853
1839

Free blacks

Jack Adams	1-0-0-1		Jackson Newman	1-0-0-0
_____ Brady	1-0-0-0		James Murry	1-0-0-0
Robert Cook	1-0-1-2		_____ Newton	1-0-0-0
John Cliffton	1-0-0-0		Hannah Robinson	0-1-0-1
John Diggs	1-0-0-0		George Ransom	1-0-0-0
Wiley French	1-0-0-0		Philip Martin	1-0-0-0
William Gray	1-0-0-0		Brister Smith	1-0-0-0
Lydia Hall	1-0-0-1		George Wells	1-0-0-0
William Butler	1-0-0-0		Henry Wheeler	1-0-0-0
Mowen Harris	1-0-0-0		Roderick Tribee [?]	1-0-0-0
Frederick Cooper	1-0-0-0		John Robinson	1-0-0-0
James Irvine	1-0-0-0		David Whiting	1-0-0-0
Lewis Nickens	1-0-0-0			

Clarke County, Virginia Personal Property Tax Lists 1836-1853

1840

Columns: 1) White males above 16, 2) Slaves 12-16 years, 3) Slaves over 16 years, 4) Horses mares, mules, etc.

Name	Values	Name	Values
Robert Ashby	4-0-0-5	Joseph Bulger	1-0-0-0
Thomas H. Anderson	1-0-0-4	Nathaniel Burwell Jr.	1-0-7-10
Mason Anderson	1-0-1-2	William Benson	1-0-3-5
John Alexander	1-2-7-9	John Burchell	1-1-3-8
William C. Alexander	1-2-7-13	Archibald Bowen	1-0-2-5
Augustine Athey	2-0-0-5	Philip Sherrick	1-0-0-0
David H. Allen	7-8-21-38	Hiram O. Bell	1-0-3-6
Samuel Armor	2-1-1-4	Phineas Bowen	3-0-3-11
Wm Ambrouse	1-0-0-4	Francis Otway Byrd	1-3-8-10
Benjn P. Ashby	1-0-0-1	John Bourne	1-0-1-3
John Ambrouse	3-0-0-8	Philip Berlin	2-1-2-7
John B. Ambrouse	1-0-0-2	William Berlin	2-0-1-1
Buckner Ashby	1-2-7-15	Geo Carter	
Evan P. Anderson	1-1-0-1	Blakemore	1-0-1-1
Thos H. Alexander	2-0-0-1	John Bowlin	1-0-0-0
Miss Ann Alexander	0-0-1-1	Neile Barnett	1-0-0-1
Geo Anderson	1-0-0-0	John Ballinger	1-0-1-8
Joseph Anderson	3-0-2-8	Wm O. Bond	1-0-0-1
William Allen	1-0-3-4	Thomas W. Briggs	1-0-0-2
Algernon S. Allen	1-0-8-16	Amos A. Bonham	1-1-6-13
1 free black		Danl S. Bonham	1-1-4-9
Joseph Alexander	1-0-0-1	James Boggs	1-0-0-0
Hathaway Alexander	2-0-0-1	John Brownley	1-4-8-19
Mrs. Jane Anderson	1-0-0-2	William Brownly	1-0-1-2
John Ashby	2-0-0-1	William Baker	1-2-5-4
Nicholas Anderson	1-0-0-1	Isaac Berlin	3-0-1-2
Samuel Alexander	1-0-0-1	Strother Bell	1-0-4-8
Westley Ashby	1-0-0-0	Robert Burchell	1-1-3-9
Robert Ashby Jr.	1-0-0-1	William Brawner	1-0-0-0
Martha Ashby	1-0-0-3	H. W. Brabham	1-0-0-0
		Squire Bell	1-0-2-4
T. T. Byrd Sr. Est.	0-0-2-0	Samuel Berlin	1-0-0-1

Clarke County, Virginia Personal Property Tax Lists 1836-1853
1840

William Billmyer	1-0-0-0	Thomas F. Blakemore	1-0-0-1
Juliet Boston	0-0-2-1	Thomas H. Burwell	1-1-10-20
Philip Burwell	1-8-22-13	Mrs. Lucy Burwell	0-1-5-0
Thomas W. Byrne	1-0-0-0	Napolean Balthrop	1-0-0-0
John D. Barr	1-0-0-0	Alfred Castleman	1-1-7-6
John H. Berringer	1-0-0-0	John Campbell	1-0-0-0
John W. Byrd	1-0-12-8	Parkerson Craig	1-0-1-8
Thomas Briggs	8-2-3-14	Osmin Chamberlain	1-0-1-0
Lewis Bromley	2-0-0-7	John P. Chamberlain	1-1-1-4
John C. Bonham	1-0-1-0	Joshua Chapman	1-0-0-0
James W. Beck	1-0-0-4	Jacob Crim	1-0-0-0
Andrew Billmyer	1-0-0-1	Frederick Clopton	2-0-6-8
[Margin: P. D. Shepherds]		George F. Calmese	1-1-4-9
Nathaniel Burwell Sr.	1-11-41-25	William Carrington	4-2-1-2
Blackemore & Richardson	2-0-0-2	William Carper	1-0-0-3
Samuel Bonham	1-2-10-17	C. B. Chandler	1-1-10-11
John Blue	1-2-1-5	Elizabeth Carnegy	0-3-18-24
T. T. Byrds Est.	0-0-4-5	Robert A. Colston	1-0-2-6
Mrs. Mariah Burwell	0-1-4-3	John B. Castleman	1-0-0-1
Col. James Bell	1-3-5-9	Wm M. Clark	1-1-0-7
Wesley Brown	1-0-0-1	Wm H. Colston	1-0-3-4
Robert Ben	1-0-0-3	Peter Crum	1-0-0-1
William Berry	1-2-9-9	Elizabeth K. Carter	2-0-3-6
Jesse C. Bolen	1-0-0-1	John Copenhaver	1-0-4-12
Hector Bell	1-2-17-18	Mariam & Sarah Catlett [&] Henry Catlett	1-2-6-13
A. H. Beevers	1-0-0-2	Michael Copenhaver	1-0-0-0
George H. Burwell	1-5-38-43	Wm Cornwell	1-0-0-2
James Bulger	1-0-0-0	Thomas Cornwell	1-0-0-1
George Bartlett	1-0-0-2	John Cullerton	1-0-0-0
James Boyles	3-0-0-1	John Castleman	1-2-3-7
Saml Briarly	2-1-7-8	James H. Clarke	1-0-2-0
Christian Bowser	2-0-1-1	Wm Castleman	1-2-12-17
Jacob Bowser	1-0-0-0	Thomas H. Crow	2-0-3-1
James Bell Jr.	1-0-0-1	John G. Chapman	1-0-0-0
Thomas Blakemores Est.	0-0-1-0	Wm A. Castleman	1-1-3-11
		Alfred Clevinger	1-0-0-6

Clarke County, Virginia Personal Property Tax Lists 1836-1853
1840

John Cooper	2-0-0-4	James Downing	1-0-0-1
Baalis D. Castleman	1-0-0-4	Joseph Deaver	1-0-0-0
Elizabeth Crampton	0-0-1-1	Thomas Duke	2-0-0-1
James Castleman	3-1-14-26	James Doren	1-0-0-0
S. B. T. Caldwell	2-1-1-1		
Martha P.		A. H. Evans	1-0-0-0
Castleman	2-0-9-6	Job D. Eichelberger	1-0-3-8
Thomas Carter	1-1-14-17	Charles Eckardt	1-0-0-1
Pressley Cooper	1-0-0-0	Henry Edwards	1-0-0-1
Parkerson Carder	1-0-0-0	Wm G. Everhart	4-0-1-5
Edward Cornwell	1-0-0-0	John Eleyett	1-0-1-1
Benjamin Criglar	1-0-0-1	Sarah Earle	0-0-3-2
Fielding Cornwell	1-0-0-0	John B. Earle	2-1-11-21
John Carrol	2-0-0-2	Hiram P. Evans	3-0-1-1
Patrick Carrol	1-0-0-2	Jacob Enders	1-0-2-2
John Carpenter	1-0-1-0	Christopher Elliott	1-0-0-1
Dabney Cauthorn	2-0-0-2		
Stepehn Cauthorn	1-0-0-1	Edward Franks	1-0-1-1
Elijah Cleveland	1-0-0-2	John Furr	1-0-0-0
Nelson Collier	1-0-0-0	Ephraim Furr	1-0-0-0
James Carter	1-0-0-0	Jesse Furr	2-0-0-3
Geo Castleman	3-0-1-8	George Fyst	4-0-0-10
Elizabeth N. Carter	0-0-2-1	1 free black	
		Daniel Feagans	1-0-2-1
Peter Dearmont	2-2-4-5	Feagans & Mount	2-0-1-5
Andrew R. Davis	1-0-1-2	John F. Fauntleroy	1-1-2-3
Dr. H. Dorsey	1-0-0-1	M. R. Feehrer	2-0-1-1-
George Dunn	1-0-0-0	Margaret Funstan	0-1-5-2
Joseph Drake	1-0-1-0	David Funston	1-0-0-1
Thomas G. Dowdle	1-0-1-0	John Forster	1-2-0-7
Wm Deahl	2-0-1-0	Jane H. Forster	0-0-2-0
Samuel Davis	1-0-0-1	James Flore	1-1-2-1
Dolphin Drew	1-0-0-0	Flore & Keyes	3-0-0-0
James Davis	2-0-0-0	John Furlow	1-0-0-0
John Drish	1-0-0-0	Moses Furr	1-0-0-4
Michael Dearmont	1-2-2-7	Martha Forster	0-1-4-7
Baalis Davis	1-2-1-2	Geo Farnsworth	1-0-0-2
Thomas Dwyer	1-0-0-0	Thomas Ferguson	1-0-0-1
Benjamin Downing	1-0-0-2	Archibald Flemming	2-0-0-4

Clarke County, Virginia Personal Property Tax Lists 1836-1853
1840

John D. Ferguson Sr.	1-0-14-10		
James Furr	1-0-0-2	John H. Greer	1-0-0-0
John D. Ferguson Jr.	2-1-3-6	James D. Gibson	1-0-0-1
Wm P. Flood	1-0-0-1	John Grant	1-0-1-6
Thoms Forres [?]	1-0-0-0	William Gourly	1-0-1-9
Wm Fowler	1-0-0-3	Francis Griffin	1-0-0-1
Benj Franks	1-0-0-2	Emanuel Garmong	1-0-0-1
[Margin: N. B.]		Thornberry Grubbs	1-0-0-1
Henry Franks	1-0-0-0	Samuel Grubbs	1-0-0-0
[Margin: W. D. Mc G]		Derias Grubbs	1-0-0-0
		Nimrod Glasscock	1-0-0-0
Richard Green	2-0-2-4	Carey Gover	1-0-0-0
Monro C. Garton	1-0-0-1	[Margin: S.B.T.C.]	
Thomas E. Gold	2-1-4-10	David E. Graham	1-0-0-0
John Greenly	1-0-2-5	Alice Gold	1-0-0-1
Wm Graves	2-0-0-5	Charles Gillet	1-0-0-0
Harrison &			
Geo Gordon	2-0-0-5	Whiting Hamilton	1-0-0-1
James Green	1-0-4-6	Henry D. Hooe	2-0-1-4
Geo Wm &		George D. Harrison	1-0-1-9
Richd Green	3-2-7-10	Rudolph Hout	1-0-0-2
John Gant	2-1-5-10	Henry Horuer	1-0-0-1
Stephen J. Gant	1-1-1-4	Edwin Hart	1-0-1-3
John C. Gregg	2-0-2-7	Abram Hewit	2-0-0-5
James J Grogan	1-0-5-7	James Harris	2-0-4-9
Edward Gorman	1-0-0-1	James Hay	1-4-13-20
Thomas Grubb	1-0-0-0	Thomas Hiett	1-0-1-6
Joseph George	1-0-1-2	John Hopkins	1-0-2-1
Catharine Groves	0-1-0-1	[Margin: J.E.P.]	
John S. Gordon	2-0-0-3	Levi Hiett	2-1-2-9
[Margin: A.S.A.]		Isaac Irvine Hite	2-2-8-4
John Gordon	1-0-0-2	1 free black	
James V. Glass	2-2-7-8	James M. Hite	2-5-15-30
Henry N. Griggsby	1-0-3-6	Jefferson Hackley	1-1-0-0
Wm Gardner	1-0-0-0	William T. Helm	2-1-6-9
Dandridge Garrison	1-0-0-1	John Hewitt	2-0-0-5
Jacob Gater	1-0-1-2	William Hummer	1-0-0-3
		Samuel Heflybour	1-0-3-7
Jacob Haines	1-0-0-0	John Huply [?]	1-0-0-0

Clarke County, Virginia Personal Property Tax Lists 1836-1853
1840

Geo Heflybour	2-0-3-12	Richard Johnston	1-0-0-0
Edward Handle	1-0-1-0		
Joseph Hesket	1-0-0-7	James Kennan	1-0-0-0
Makes his home at		Samuel Kane	1-0-0-1
Wm Gourley's		This horse is given in and	
John Hay	1-0-3-1	charged to Jas Smith,	
Wm Holtsclaw	2-0-0-1	who claims him and	
Cornelius Hoff	1-0-0-0	says neither Mr. nor	
William Harr	1-0-0-0	Mrs. Kane owns a horse.	
near D. Trislar's		F. J. Kerfoot	1-1-8-12
Blackwell Holtsclaw	1-0-0-0	C. C. Kerby	1-1-5-6
Robert Haney	1-0-0-1	James Keen	3-0-2-5
Mary Howard	0-1-1-0	John Kable	3-0-1-0
Richard Hardesty	1-0-3-10	Thomas Kennerly	2-0-0-0
Benjamin Henry	1-0-0-0	[&] John Brown	
James Henry	1-0-0-0	George Knight	3-2-6-15
Bushrod Hoff	1-0-0-0	Geo Kitchen	1-0-6-10
Joseph Hoff	1-0-0-0	Mary Jane Kneedler	0-0-1-0
Hannah Humphreys	0-0-1-0	John Kerfoot	2-3-14-14
		Wm C. Kerfoot	1-0-9-15
Jeremiah Jordan	1-0-0-0	Geo L. Kerfoot	1-0-11-15
George Johnston	1-0-0-3	Jacob Kennerle	1-0-0-1
Herod Jenkins	1-0-0-0	Benjamin Kent	1-0-0-0
S. R. Jackson	1-1-1-2	Middleton Keeler	1-0-1-0
Mathew Jones	2-0-2-7	Henry Kenniford	1-0-0-0
John Johnston Jr.	1-0-1-1	Thomas Knight	2-0-0-3
Reuben Jordan	1-0-1-2	John N.T.G. Keene	1-0-0-2
John Joliffe	1-1-5-9	Joseph Kirby	1-0-0-0
John J. Johnston	1-0-8-14		
John Johnston	1-0-0-0	Henry Lloyd	1-0-0-3
Elizabeth Jackson	1-0-2-5	James Lanham	1-0-0-0
Thomas Jordan	1-0-0-1	Dr. John Locke	1-0-0-1
Dr. Reubin R. Jordan	1-0-0-2	Charles Lucius	1-0-1-4
Thomas Jackson	1-3-13-10	John Lock	1-0-0-6
Jane Jackson	0-0-1-0	John D. &	
		Jas W. Larue	2-0-5-13
Jacob Isler	3-0-6-9	Wm Littleton	2-1-0-3
		James H. Lee	1-0-0-1
David Jenkins	1-0-0-1	[Margin: F. McC.]	

Clarke County, Virginia Personal Property Tax Lists 1836-1853
1840

Catharine Lock	2-1-0-4	John Maddox	3-0-0-1
William Lock	1-0-0-1-3	Alfred P. Moore	1-0-0-1
Frances Larue	0-2-7-12	Provn McCormick Jr.	1-0-1-2
Sarah Luke	0-0-3-3	James Mitchell	2-1-6-6
Louisa Littleton	0-1-1-1	Wm D. McGuire	1-0-8-12
Washington Lee	1-0-0-1	David H. McGuire	2-0-7-10
Abram Longerbeam &		Otway McCormick	2-0-8-11
John Longerbeam	2-0-0-1	Isaac McCormick	1-1-5-9
Dr. Robert Little	3-0-8-10	William Morgan	1-2-4-9
John Louthan	1-0-2-1	John McCloy	1-0-0-0
Lorenzo Lewis	1-5-32-30	James McCormick	1-0-5-7
James M. Lindsey	1-0-2-3	William McDonald	1-0-0-0
Samuel Larue	1-0-12-13	Francis M. Meade	1-1-4-8
Wm Longerbeam	1-0-0-0	Louisa Meade	0-0-5-2
Sarah Lindsey	0-0-2-0	Richard K. Meade	1-1-1-5
John Lindsey	1-0-0-1	Philip N. Meade	2-0-3-6
Richard Lanham	1-0-0-	Revd. Wm Meade	
John Lloyd	1-0-0-1	Wm Meade Jr.	1-0-0-2
George Longerbeam	1-0-0-1	John N. Meade,	
Samuel Lanham	1-0-0-0	son of David	1-0-0-0
Elizabeth Lanham	0-0-0-1	Miss Mary Meade	0-1-1-0
Edgar Lanham	1-0-0-0	Louis Metcalfe	1-0-0-1
James Lloyd	1-0-0-0	Thomas McCormick	1-1-7-11
Charles Leech Sr.	1-0-0-0	John Marts Sr.	3-0-0-3
Charles S. Leech	1-0-0-1	Thomas L.	
Samuel Lancaster	1-0-0-0	Maccubbin	1-0-0-0
Sarah Longerbeam	0-0-0-1	Geo Moreland	1-0-0-3
John B. Larue	1-1-13-22	Saml & Cy	
Clarissa Larue	0-0-2-1	McCormick	2-2-10-17
Geo S. Lane	1-0-4-9	Geo McCormick	2-1-8-11
Benj B. Lane	1-0-0-1	Levi Marquiss	2-0-0-4
Saml Lloyd	2-0-0-1	Jesse P. Mercer	1-0-0-1
		John Mayers	1-0-0-3
Peter McMurray	2-1-2-7	John & Jas Mitchum	2-0-0-2
Wm McCoy	1-0-0-0	Stephen T. Marlow	1-0-0-1
Albert McCormick	1-0-3-4	Benjamin Morgan	1-2-14-22
Samuel McCormick	1-0-0-1	Elizabeth Morgan	0-0-4-0
Warner Muse	1-0-0-5	Stephen R. Mount	1-3-5-3
John J. Munro	1-0-3-5	Francis McCormick	1-0-10-19

Clarke County, Virginia Personal Property Tax Lists 1836-1853
1840

Charles McCormick	2-2-14-28	Dr. M. Overfield	1-0-0-1
Franklin W. Massy	1-0-0-1	Elizabeth Orear	0-1-7-7
Susan Marshall	0-2-2-6	Enoch Orear	1-1-5-7
John Marshall	1-0-1-2	Jas Aquilla Osbourn	2-0-0-4
James Murphy	1-0-0-1	Mason Oram	1-0-0-0
Jesse McConaha	1-0-0-1	Geo Pultz	1-0-0-1
Lucy Mustin	0-0-1-1	Daniel Powers	1-1-4-6
Edwin Moore	1-0-0-0	John E. Page	1-1-8-2
Sylvanus Moore	1-0-0-0	Est. Wm. B.	
James Murdock	1-0-0-0	Page Dec[d]	0-0-1-0
Thomas Murphy	1-0-0-0	Est. John Page Dec[d]	0-9-38-18
Henry Murphy	1-0-0-0	Eliza M. Page	0-0-1-0
Alexander Marshall	1-0-0-1	Wm B. Page	0-0-2-1
John McPhillin	1-0-0-0	[Margin: J.E.P.]	
Wm Mason	1-0-0-1	John Page of W.B.P.	1-0-3-3
Jacob May	1-0-0-0	Mann R. Page	1-1-9-20
John Morgan	1-2-6-10	Isaac E. Pidgeon	2-0-0-1
Christopher Metcalf	1-0-1-0	Isaac Pidgeon Sr.	2-0-0-6
[Margin: G.H.B.]		James Perrill	1-0-0-0
Wm Mayhew	1-0-0-0	John Pierce Sr.	2-1-3-8
James McDonald	1-1-0-0	Dr. Robt P. Page	1-2-17-17
		James M. Pine	1-0-0-1
Wm Niswanger	2-0-0-4	Mary C. Page	0-2-6-8
Hugh M. Nelson	1-4-20-16	John Page Jr.	3-2-9-7
Ann T. Neile	0-0-3-5	Joseph E. Peyton	2-0-0-2
Geo H. Norris	5-0-13-15	Paul Pierce	1-1-6-8
Philip Nelson	1-5-16-14	Richard E. Parker	2-1-12-13
Thos F. Nelson	1-3-12-13	Judith Page	0-0-3-2
James H. Neville	1-1-1-1	John W. Page	3-1-9-15
Jos Noble	1-0-0-0	Robert Page	1-1-15-15
Abby Nelson	0-1-2-0	McFarland Puller	1-0-0-0
Joseph Neile		Thomas Preston	1-0-0-1
(J. Drake)	0-0-0-4	John Pierce Jr.	1-0-0-2
Wm Nelson	1-1-2-1	John Padget	1-0-0-0
Edward Nash	1-0-0-0		
P. N. Nicholas	0-1-1-0	Jacob Ridgeway	1-0-1-1
Jos M. Nicklin	1-0-1-1	Richard Ridgeway	2-0-0-6
		William Reed	3-0-1-5
John W. Owen	1-0-0-0	Jonas Ridgeway	1-0-0-8

Clarke County, Virginia Personal Property Tax Lists 1836-1853
1840

Thos W. Reynolds	2-0-2-7	E. G. Ships Est.	0-0-4-6
Bennet Russell	1-2-4-8	Jacob Shoop	1-0-0-1
Miss E. Royster	0-0-1-0	James Smith	1-0-0-1
[Margin: J.E.P.]		Horse claimed by Mrs. Kane	
Mathew W. Royston	1-0-1-5	Edward J. Smith	2-3-21-29
Peter Royston	1-0-0-0	Isaac Starkey	2-0-0-1
John Roush	1-0-1-0	& Ishmael _____	
Uriah B. Royston	1-0-0-4	John W. Sowers	1-6-3-10
John Reed	1-0-0-1	Joseph Smith	1-0-1-3
James Russell	1-0-0-1	John Ship	1-0-3-3
Ann Redman	0-0-0-0	Wm Sowers	4-7-5-17
Solomon Redman	1-0-0-3	Including Mr. Whitescarver	
Geo Rutter &		Joseph Shepherd	2-1-5-12
A. Crawford	2-0-0-0	Champ Shepherd	2-0-2-1
Daniel Richards Jr.	2-1-0-1	Benj. F. Seevers	1-1-4-6
Saml B. Redman	1-0-0-2	Edward Sheckles	1-0-0-1
Addison Romine	1-0-0-2	Thomas Shumate	1-1-1-6
Elisha Romine	1-0-0-1	Dr. H. W. Snyder	1-0-1-3
James Ryan	1-1-0-0-	John N. Sowers	3-0-0-3
Robert C.		Wm G. Steel	1-0-1-1
Randolph	1-2-11-15	Daniel W. Sowers	1-1-9-15
Geo R. Robertson	1-0-0-0	Samuel Stype	1-0-3-6
John Peter Riely	1-0-2-2	James Sowers	1-2-3-15
John Russell Sr.	1-0-1-0	Thos Sprint	2-0-0-1
Danl Richards Sr.	1-0-0-1	Emanuel Showers	6-2-0-0
Wm Richardson	1-0-0-0	Adam Shipe	1-0-0-0
Jane Richardson	1-0-2-1	Moses W. Shipe	1-0-0-0
George Reno	1-0-0-1	Barnet Smallwood	1-0-0-1
James Rice	1-0-0-0	Fielding L. Sowers	2-0-7-10
Isaac Ramey Sr.	2-0-0-6	P. D. Shepherd	1-0-1-1
John Rivers	1-0-0-0	Dr. Philip Smith	1-3-18-23
Joseph Robinson	1-0-0-0	Treadwell Smith	2-1-14-12
Mathew Rust	1-0-3-5	Wm R. Seevers	1-0-0-2
Elizabeth Roots	0-0-1-0	Kerfoot Sowers	1-4-4-12
John Richardson	5-1-19-33	John Stewart	4-0-0-4
		Joseph Stewart	1-0-0-0
Margaret Swan	0-0-1-0	James Seevers	2-1-1-6
Col. Jas H. Sowers	1-1-5-12	Daniel A. Sowers	1-0-5-9
Henry Shepherd	1-0-0-1	Enoch Strother	1-1-2-4

Clarke County, Virginia Personal Property Tax Lists 1836-1853
1840

Name	Values	Name	Values
Elizabeth Strother	0-0-5-4	Samuel Taylor	2-2-12-10
James Strother	1-0-0-2	Benjn Thompson Jr.	1-0-0-6
Jacob Shively	1-1-7-7	Joseph Tuley	1-4-22-21
John Strother	1-0-3-9	John Trussel	1-2-2-5
Richard Swift	1-0-0-0	Moses Trussel	1-0-0-3
Alfred Smallwood	1-0-0-0	Wm Thomas	1-0-0-1
Benjamin Starkey	1-0-0-0	Wm Timberlake,	
Edward Street	1-0-0-0	White Post	0-0-2-0
John Shafer	1-0-0-1	Timothy A. Todd	1-0-0-0
Jackson Shafer	1-0-0-1	John B. Taylor	2-2-9-17
Burr Smallwood	1-0-0-0	John Thompson	2-0-3-3
Sarah Smallwood	0-0-0-1	Wm Trenary	1-0-0-1
William Stillions	2-0-0-0	M. R. Throckmorton	2-0-6-12
Simon Stickles	1-0-0-2	W. W. Throckmorton	0-0-3-6
Abram Shipe	1-0-0-0	Wm Tinsman	1-0-0-2
Geo Smedley	2-0-1-1	Snowden Tumblin	1-0-0-0
Conrad Swarts	1-0-0-0	Wm Tumblin	1-0-0-1
David Swarts	1-0-0-0	John Vancleve	2-0-1-4
H. P. Smith's Est.	0-0-1-0	James Violet	2-0-0-2
Susan Smith	0-1-0-0	Jacob Vanmetre	0-0-2-6
		James Valdivear	1-1-3-8
William Turner	1-0-0-1	Jos Vincent	2-1-0-1
Susan B. Taylor	0-1-7-8	Wm Willingham	1-0-0-1
Jesse Taylor	4-0-0-5	Allen Williams	1-2-9-15
Abigail Tanquary	0-0-0-1	James J. Williams	1-0-7-10
Richard M. S.		Timothy Wilcox	1-0-0-0
Timberlake	1-2-8-11	James Wigginton	1-1-0-2
John A. S. Tutt	1-0-0-0	John Wood	2-1-1-9
David Trisler	1-0-0-4	1 free black	
Adam Towner	1-1-0-0	Francis H. Whiting	1-0-3-7
John Tally	1-0-0-0	J. W. Ware &	
Hannah Taylor	0-0-4-2	S. Stribling	1-2-18-25
Greenberry		Lucinda Washington	0-0-2-2
Thompson	1-0-1-3	John H. Watson	1-0-1-4
David Timberlake	2-2-10-11	J. G. Wade & Bros	1-0-0-0
Stephen D.		Jas V. Weir	1-0-6-6
Timberlake	1-0-1-0	Horatea T. Wheat	3-1-1-2
Harrison Thompson	1-0-0-1	Jas Fitzsimons	
Nancy Taylor	1-1-6-8	John Fletcher	

Clarke County, Virginia Personal Property Tax Lists 1836-1853
1840

Hezekiah Wiley	1-0-0-2	Wm Wise	1-0-0-1
Samuel Wiley	1-0-0-1	Sydnor B. Wyndham	1-0-0-1
James Wiley	2-0-0-1	Bennet Wood	2-0-0-0
John Willingham	1-0-0-1	Henry Weaver	1-0-0-0
Alexander Wood	1-0-1-0	Herbert Washington	0-0-2-0
_____ Wright	1-0-0-0	N. Burwell Whiting	1-0-4-10
overseer for P. Nelson		Geo Young	1-0-0-0
E. W. Washington	0-1-1-0	Simeon Yowell	1-0-1-0
Leroy P. Williams	1-1-6-11	S. S. Yeakle	2-1-1-1
William Wood	1-0-0-1	Washn Young	1-0-0-0
Grantham Way	1-0-0-1	T. Smith &	
Wm P. Wigginton	1-1-1-1	S. S. Yeakle	0-0-1-0
Francis B. Whiting	2-4-17-18	Thos Jackson	0-0-1-0
Wm W. Whiting	1-0-0-1	Thos E. Gold	0-0-1-0
Obed Willingham	1-0-0-0		

Free Blacks

Jackson Newman	1-0-0-0	Jacob Adams	1-0-0-1
Thomas Laws	1-0-0-0	John Johnson	1-0-0-0
Henry Green	1-0-0-0	Bristo Smith	1-0-0-0
Kitty Wilkinson	0-0-0-1	Frank Irvin	1-0-0-0
John Williams	1-0-0-2	Billy Butler	1-0-0-0
William Graham	1-0-0-2	Wiley Finch	1-0-0-0
James Murray	1-0-0-2	Mowen Harris	1-0-0-0
Bob Cook	1-0-0-2	John Clifton	1-0-0-0
Burwell Cook	1-0-0-0	Spencer Johnson	1-0-0-0
William Wheeler	1-0-0-0	John Diggs	1-0-0-0
Hannah Robinson	0-0-0-1	Roderick Tribbee	1-0-0-0
Silva Hall	2-0-0-2	Isaac _____	1-0-0-0

Clarke County, Virginia Personal Property Tax Lists 1836-1853

1841

Columns: 1) White males over 16 year of age, 2) Slaves over 12, 3) Slaves over 16, 4) Horses, mares, mules & colts.

Robert Ashby	2-0-0-7		Philip Berlin	2-0-3-7
Thos H. Anderson	1-0-0-5		Wm Berlin	2-0-2-1
Mason Anderson	1-0-1-2		Geo C. Blakemore	1-0-1-1
David H. Allen	4-5-24-4		John Bowlin	1-0-0-0
John Alexander	1-2-8-15		Neille Barnett	1-1-0-1
Wm C. Alexander	1-1-8-12		Thos W. Briggs	1-0-0-3
Augusta Athey	3-0-0-5		Amos A. Bonham	1-1-7-11
Wm Ambrous	1-0-0-4		D. S. Bonham	2-2-5-11
Benjn P. Ashby	2-0-0-3		Jas Boggs	1-0-0-0
John Ambrouse	3-0-0-8		John Brownley	1-3-12-19
John B. Ambrouse	1-0-0-2		Capt. Wm Baker	1-2-5-3
Buckner Ashby	2-2-8-14		Isaac Berlin	3-1-0-3
Joseph Anderson	4-0-2-9		Strother Bell	1-1-3-10
Wm Allen	2-0-3-6		Robt Burchell	1-1-3-9
A. S. Allen	1-3-2-15		Wm Brawner	1-0-0-0
Hathaway Alexander	3-0-0-2		H. W. Brabham	1-0-0-0
Jane Anderson	1-0-0-2		Squire Bell	1-0-1-5
John Ashby	2-0-0-1		Samuel Berlin	1-1-0-0
Westley Ashby	1-0-0-0		Wm Billmyer	2-0-0-0
Robert Ashby Jr.	1-0-0-1		Juliet Boston	2-0-1-1
Martin Ashby	1-0-0-2		Philip Burwell	1-5-24-14
Thomas H. Alexander	3-0-0-1		John D. Barr	1-0-0-0
Nicholas Anderson	2-0-0-1		John H. Berringer	1-0-0-0
David Anderson	1-0-0-1		John W. Byrd	1-0-11-9
Nimrod Ashby	1-0-0-1		Thos Briggs	8-2-3-16
			Lewis Brimley	3-0-0-8
Nathaniel Burwell Jr.	1-0-7-11		James W. Beck	1-0-0-2
Wm C. Benson	1-0-5-6		John C. Bonham	1-1-5-5
John Burchell	1-3-3-9		Nathaniel Burwell Sr.	1-11-40-35
Archibald Bowen	2-0-1-6		Blakemore & Seevers	2-0-0-1
Hiram O. Bell	1-0-4-7		Samuel Bonham	1-0-12-13
Phineas Bowen	2-0-3-11		Col. James Bell	1-3-5-9
F. O. Byrd	1-1-10-10		Wesley Brown	1-0-0-1
John Bourne	1-0-0-3		Robert Ben	1-0-1-4

Clarke County, Virginia Personal Property Tax Lists 1836-1853
1841

Wm Berry	3-1-9-13	John Copenhaver	1-2-1-8
Hector Bell	0-0-2-1	Mariam &	
George H. Burwell	1-6-39-40	Sarah Catlett	1-1-6-13
Jas Bulger	1-0-0-0	Michael Copenhaver	2-0-0-0
Geo Bartlett	1-0-0-0	John Cullerton	1-0-0-0
Jas Boyles	3-0-0-3	Sarah Castleman	0-1-4-6
Christian Bowser	2-0-1-1	Jas H. Clarke	1-1-1-0
Jacob Bowser	1-0-0-0	Wm Castleman	1-1-12-19
James Bell Jr.	1-0-0-1	Thomas H. Crow	1-0-3-2
Thomas H. Burwell	1-0-10-24	John G. Chapman	1-0-0-0
John Blue	1-0-2-6	Wm A. Castleman	1-1-3-12
Samuel Briarly	2-1-7-10	Alfred Clevinger	1-0-2-7
Thos L. Blakemore	0-10-0-0	John Cooper	1-0-0-0
Andutow [sic] Brown	1-1-1-1	Baalis D. Castleman	1-0-0-3
Alexander Baker	1-1-4-6	Elizabeth Crampton	0-0-1-1
John Brown	1-0-0-0	Jas Castleman	2-2-14-26
Napolean Balthop	1-0-0-1	Presley Cooper	1-0-0-0
Docia Billmyer	2-0-0-1	Parkerson Corder	1-0-0-0
George Bolen	1-0-0-0	S. B. T. Caldwell	4-2-2-2
Thos W. Byrne	1-0-0-1	Martha P. Castleman	2-0-9-6
Mrs. Lucy Burwell	0-2-3-0	Thos Carter	1-1-14-19
Ben Barr	1-0-1-0	Fielding Cornwell	1-0-0-0
		John Carrol	2-0-0-3
Alfred Castleman	1-1-4-9	John Carpenter	2-0-1-5
John Campbell	1-0-0-0	Dabney Cauthorn	2-0-0-2
Parkerson Craig	2-1-2-8	Stepehn Cauthorn	1-0-0-1
Osmin Chamberlain	1-0-1-0	Elizth N. Carter	0-0-2-2
John P. Chamberlain	1-0-2-4	Jas Carter	1-0-0-0
Fredk Clopton	1-0-4-8	Geo Castleman	2-0-1-8
Geo F. Calmese	1-0-6-10	David Clevinger	1-0-0-5
Wm Carrington	2-2-3-2	John Cable Jr.	1-0-1-0
Wm Carper	1-0-0-4	Thos Clevinger	1-0-2-7
C. B. Chandler	1-4-12-12	J. W. Casky	1-0-0-0
Elizabeth Carnegy	0-5-18-35	Wm A. Cooper	1-0-0-1
Robt A. Colston	2-0-2-8	Evelina Clark	0-0-0-1
John B. Castleman	1-0-0-1		
Wm H. Colston	1-0-3-7	Peter Dearmont	2-3-5-4
Petre [sic] Crum	1-0-0-1	Andrew R. Davis	1-0-2-2
Elizth K. Carter	2-0-2-6	Dr. H. Dorsey	1-0-0-1

Clarke County, Virginia Personal Property Tax Lists 1836-1853
1841

George Dunn	1-0-0-0	Flore & Keyes	3-0-0-0
John Drish	1-0-0-0	John Furlow	1-0-0-0
Thos G. Dowdle	2-0-2-0	Moses Furr	2-0-0-5
Wm Deakle	2-0-1-0	Martha Foster	0-1-4-7
Samuel Davis	1-0-0-1	Geo Farnsworth	1-0-0-3
Jas Davis	2-0-0-1	Archibald Flemming	2-0-0-3
Michael Dermont	1-1-2-8	John D. Ferguson Sr.	1-2-10-10
Baalis Davis	1-2-1-4	Jas Furr	1-0-0-1
Benj Downing	1-0-0-3	John D. Ferguson Jr.	1-1-2-6
Jas Downing	1-0-0-1	Wm Fowler	2-0-0-4
Thos Duke	2-0-0-1	Benj Franks	1-0-0-3
Jas Doren	1-0-0-1	Henry Franks	1-0-0-0
John E. Dangerfield	1-0-5-9	M. R. Feehrer	2-0-1-1
Saml Dobbins	1-0-0-1	Calvin Fuller	1-0-0-0
John Downing	1-0-0-0	Wash Ferguson	2-0-1-2
John Dow	1-0-0-1	Jas Fuller	1-0-0-0
		Enoch Farnsworth	1-0-0-1
Charles Eckardt	1-0-0-1		
Henry Edward	1-0-0-3	Richard Green Sr.	3-1-2-5
Wm G. Everhart	3-0-2-5	Thomas E. Gold	2-1-4-13
John Eleyett	1-1-0-1	John Greenle	1-2-1-5
John B. Earle	2-2-12-25	Wm Graves	1-0-3-6
Hiram P. Evans	2-1-1-1	Harrison Gordon	1-0-0-6
Jacob Enders	1-0-0-1	Geo Gordon	1-0-0-1
H. Emery	1-0-0-1	Jas Green	1-0-0-5
Wm Elezet [sic]	1-0-0-0	Geo W. Green	1-2-5-10
		John Gant	2-1-5-9
Edward Franks	1-0-0-0	Stephen J. Gant	1-0-3-5
John Furr	1-0-0-0	James L. Grogan	1-0-6-10
Jesse Furr	2-0-0-1	Thos Grubs	1-0-0-0
George Fyst	5-0-1-12	Jos George	1-1-0-2
Danl Feagans	1-0-1-1	Catharine Grove	0-1-0-1
Feagans & Mount	1-0-1-5	John S. Gordon	2-0-0-4
Doct. J. F. Fauntleroy	1-0-3-3	John Gordon	1-0-0-2
Margaret Funston	0-0-4-2	James V. Glass	2-3-6-7
Doct. O. Funston	1-0-1-1	Henry N. Grigsby	1-0-3-5
John Forster	1-0-2-7	Wm Gardner	1-0-0-0
Jane H. Forster	0-0-2-0	Dandridge Garrison	1-0-0-2
Jas Flore	1-1-3-1	Jacob Garter	4-1-1-3

Clarke County, Virginia Personal Property Tax Lists 1836-1853
1841

Jas D. Gibson	1-0-1-1	Cornelius Hooff	1-0-0-0
John Grant	1-1-1-6	Robert Haney	1-0-0-1
Wm Gourley	1-0-1-11	Richard Hardesty	4-0-3-11
Francis Griffin	1-0-0-1	Bushrod Hoff	1-0-0-0
Emanuel Garmong	1-0-0-1	Hannah Humphreys	0-0-1-0
Thornberry Grubs	1-0-0-0	Mary Howard	0-1-1-0
Saml Grubs	1-0-0-0	Henry Hout	1-0-0-0
Nimrod Glasscock	1-0-0-0	Jas Harding	1-0-0-0
Abram Grim	1-0-0-0	Mary Hoff	2-0-0-0
Nancy Galloway	1-0-0-0	Wm H. Hobbs	1-0-0-0
Edwd Gorman	1-0-0-1		
John Graves	1-0-0-1	George Johnston	1-0-1-3
Geo Gardiner	3-0-0-1	Herod Jenkins	1-0-0-0
Richd Green	1-0-4-8	Soln R. Jackson	1-1-1-2
Geo Grubs	1-0-0-0	Mathew Jones	2-0-1-8
		John Johnston Jr.	1-0-0-1
Whiting Hamilton	1-0-0-3	Reuben Jordan	1-0-1-2
Henry D. Hooe	2-0-0-3	John Joliffe	1-1-5-13
Geo D. Harrison	0-0-0-1	John J. Johnston	1-0-2-1
Rudey Hout	1-0-0-3	John Johnston	1-0-0-0
Henry Horner	1-0-1-2	Thos Jordan	1-0-0-1
Edwin Hart	1-0-1-5	Doct. R. R. Jordan	1-0-1-2
Abram Huyet	2-0-0-7	Thos Jackson	1-3-14-9
John Huyet	2-0-0-6	Mrs. Jane Jackson	0-0-1-0
Jas Harris	2-0-4-7	Jacob Isler	5-0-9-10
Doct. James Hay	1-4-12-18	Jeremiah Jordan	1-0-0-0
Thomas Hiett	1-0-1-6	David Jenkins	1-0-0-1
John Hopkins	1-0-2-8	Revd. W. Y. Jones	1-1-3-1
Levi Hiett	2-0-2-11	Chas R. Johnston	1-1-0-2
Isaac J. Hite	1-3-9-11	Wash Johnston	1-0-0-0
Jas M. Hite	1-3-6-6		
Jefferson Hackley	1-0-0-0	Jas C. Kennan	1-0-0-0
Wm T. Helm	5-2-7-13	Saml Kane	2-0-0-1
Wm Hummer	1-0-0-2	F. J. Kerfoot	1-1-8-14
Saml Heflybour	1-0-3-9	C. C. Kirby	1-0-2-8
Geo Heflybour	2-0-4-12	Thomas Kennerly	2-0-0-0
Edwd Handle	2-0-2-1	George Knight	2-2-6-14
John Hay	1-0-3-1	Geo Kitchen	1-0-5-9
Wm Holtsclaw	2-0-0-0	Mary J. Kneedler	2-1-0-0

Clarke County, Virginia Personal Property Tax Lists 1836-1853
1841

John Kerfoot	2-5-9-16		B. B. Lane	1-0-1-2
Wm C. Kerfoot	1-2-8-17		Geo F. Ludwig	3-0-2-3
Geo L. Kerfoot	1-2-9-16		Wash Lock	1-0-0-1
Benjamin Kent	1-0-0-0		Saml Lloyd	1-0-0-1
Henry Kenniford	1-0-0-0		John B. Larue	1-1-13-22
Thos Knight	2-0-0-4		Clarissa Larue	0-0-2-1
John N. Keene	1-0-1-1			
Jos Kirby	1-0-0-0		Peter McMurrey	1-1-2-8
Doct. Kownslar	1-0-2-1		Richd Morgan	1-0-0-0
Wm F. Knight	1-0-0-1		Wm McCoy	1-0-1-0
Arry Kean [?]	0-0-0-2		Albert McCormick	1-0-3-4
			Saml McCormick	1-0-0-1
Henry Lloyd	2-0-0-3		Warner Muse	1-0-0-5
Dr. J. Locke	1-0-0-2		John J. Munroe	1-0-3-5
Chas Lucius	1-1-2-5		John Maddox	4-0-2-4
John Lock	1-0-0-8		Alfred P. Moore	1-0-0-1
John D. Larue	2-0-5-12		Prov McCormick	2-0-1-5
& Jas W. Larue			Jas Mitchell	1-0-5-7
Wm Littleton	3-1-0-4		Wm D. McGuire	1-0-8-14
James H. Lee	1-0-0-1		Ottway McCormick	1-0-11-15
Catharine Lock	2-0-0-4		Isaac McCormick	1-2-3-9
Wm Lock	1-0-0-5		D. H. McGuire	2-0-7-14
Fanny Larue	0-1-7-9		Wm Morgan	1-3-6-10
Sarah Luke	0-0-2-4		John McCloy	1-0-0-1
Louisa Littleton	1-0-1-1		Jas McCormick	0-0-3-1
Wash Lee	1-0-0-1		Wm McDonald	1-0-0-0
Dr. R. H. Little	3-1-9-17		Fras B. Meade	1-1-5-9
John Louthan	1-0-2-1		Mrs. S. W. Meade	1-0-4-5
Lorenzo Lewis	1-5-32-30		P. N. Meade	2-2-4-6
Jas M. Lindsey	1-0-1-3		Wm Meade Jr.	1-0-1-3
Sarah Lindsey	0-0-2-0		Miss Mary Meade	0-1-1-0
Saml Larue	2-0-14-16		Louis Metcalfe	1-0-0-0
Richard Lanham	1-0-0-0		Thos McCormick	1-0-9-12
John Lloyd	1-0-0-1		John Marts Sr.	1-0-0-2
Geo Longerbeam	2-0-0-1		Geo Moreland	1-0-0-3
James Lloyd	1-0-0-0		Saml & Cyrus	
Chas Leech	2-0-0-1		McCormick	3-1-12-20
Sarah Longerbeam	2-0-0-3		Geo McCormick	2-2-7-11
Geo S. Larue	1-1-6-10		Leavi Marquiss	2-0-0-3

Clarke County, Virginia Personal Property Tax Lists 1836-1853
1841

Jesse P. Mercer	1-0-0-1		Jos Noble	1-1-0-0
John Mayers	1-0-0-4		Abby Nelson	0-0-2-0
John & Jas Mitchum	2-0-0-2		Wm Nelson	1-1-2-3
Stephen Marlow	1-0-0-1		P. N. Nicholas	0-1-1-0
Benj Morgan	1-3-15-21		Jos M. Nicklin	1-1-2-1
Chas McCormick	2-2-13-28		Bennet Norris	1-0-0-0
Eliza Morgan	0-0-2-0		Fras Nelson	1-1-1-3
Stephen R. Mount	1-0-3-3			
Fras McCormick	1-0-8-19		John W. Owen	1-0-2-2
Susan Marshall	0-1-3-6		Doct. Overfield	1-0-0-1
John Marshall	1-0-1-34		Eliza Orear	0-1-7-8
Jesse McConaha	1-0-0-1		Enoch Orear	1-1-5-7
Lucy Mustin	0-0-12-1		Mason Oram	2-0-0-5
James Murdock	1-0-0-0			
Alexdr Marshall	1-0-0-2		Geo Pultz	1-0-1-1
Chris Metcalf	1-1-0-0		Daniel Powers	1-2-3-6
John McPhillen	3-0-0-1		John E. Page	1-2-9-15
Wm Mason	1-0-0-1		Wm. B. Page's Est.	0-1-1-0
Jacob May	1-0-0-0		John Pages's [sic]	
John Morgan	1-2-6-11		Est.	0-1-21-5
Wm Mayhuy	1-0-0-0		Eliza M. Page	0-1-1-0
Geo L. McCormick	2-0-0-1		Wm B. Page Jr.	0-1-2-1
John R. Morgan	1-0-0-5		John Page (of Wm)	2-1-4-9
Provn McCormick Sr.	2-0-9-14		Mann R. Page	2-2-9-21
Chas & Saml			Isaac Pidgeon Sr.	1-0-0-2
McCormick	0-0-2-0		John Pierce Sr.	2-1-5-10
Benj F. Mayhue	1-0-0-1		Dr. R. P. Page	1-2-18-18
Alfred Mitchell	1-0-0-1		James M. Pine	1-0-0-1
Isaac J. Manuel	1-0-0-0		Mrs. Mary C. Page	0-0-7-9
W. I. Maxwell			John Page Sr.	3-1-7-12
Taxed in Jefferson County			Jos E. Peyton	1-0-0-2
			Paul Pierce	2-0-4-8
Wm Niswanger	2-0-0-5		Richard E.	
H. M. Nelson	1-1-27-35		Parker's Est.	1-1-10-7
Ann T. Neile	0-0-3-6		John W. Page	3-1-10-16
Geo H. Norris	3-0-12-13		Robert Page's Est.	0-1-10-12
Philip Nelson	1-4-13-20		McFarland Puller	1-0-0-0
Thos F. Nelson	1-2-8-15		John Pierce Jr.	1-0-0-2
Jas H. Neville	1-1-1-1		John Padgett	1-0-0-0

Clarke County, Virginia Personal Property Tax Lists 1836-1853
1841

Name	Values	Name	Values
Saml S. Pidgeon	1-0-0-2	Jas H. Sowers	2-0-5-11
Henry Peters	1-0-1-6	Henry Shepherd	1-0-0-1
Fras N. Page	2-0-0-0	Jacob Seevers	1-1-1-8
Jas Puller	1-0-0-0	Edwd G. Smith	2-4-22-32
		Isaac Starkey	1-0-0-3
Jacob Ridgeway	2-0-1-2	John N. Sowers	5-0-1-2
Rich Ridgeway	2-0-0-8	Jos Smith	1-0-0-3
Wm Reed	2-0-0-4	Wm Sowers	4-6-5-14
Jonas Ridgeway	2-0-1-8	Jos Shepherd	2-0-5-14
Thos W. Reynolds	9-1-6-10	Champ Shepherd	1-0-2-1
Bennett Russell	2-3-3-10	Edwd Sheckles	1-0-0-3
Miss E. Royster	0-0-1-0	Thos Shumate	1-1-1-6
Math W. Royston	1-0-0-8	John W. Sowers	1-3-3-11
Peter Royston	1-0-0-1	Wm G. Steel	2-0-1-2
John Roush	1-0-1-2	Danl W. Sowers	1-2-10-16
Uriah B. Royston	2-0-0-4	Samuel Stipe	1-0-3-5
John Reed	1-0-0-1	Jas Sowers	2-3-11-16
Miss Ann Redman	0-0-1-1	Thos Sprint	2-0-0-1
Solomon Redman	2-0-0-4	Emanl Showers	5-2-0-1
Geo Rutter	1-0-0-0	Adam Shipe	1-0-0-0
Daniel Richard Jr.	1-1-0-2	Barnet Smallwood	1-0-0-1
Saml B. Redman	1-0-0-2	Fielding L. Sowers	2-0-5-13
Addison Romine	2-0-1-1	P. D. Shepherd	2-0-1-1
James Ryan	1-1-0-2	Doct. P. Smith	1-3-21-25
Robt C. Randolph	1-2-11-16	Treadwell Smith	2-1-12-14
John Russell Sr.	1-0-1-0	Kerfoot Sowers Est.	0-1-6-15
Danl Richard Sr.	1-0-0-1	Wm R. Seevers	1-0-0-1
Jane Richardson	2-0-1-1	John Steward	3-1-0-4
George Reno	2-0-0-1	Danl A. Sowers	1-0-4-10
Isaac Ramey	2-0-1-6	Enoch Strother	1-1-2-4
John Rivers	1-0-0-0	Eliz Strother	1-1-5-5
Jos Robinson	1-0-0-0	Jacob Shively	1-1-6-7
Matthew Rust	1-0-3-5	Alfred Smallwood	1-0-0-0
Miss E. Rootes	1-0-2-0	Benjamin Starkey	1-0-0-0
John Richardson	2-1-16-27	Edwd Street	1-0-0-0
Marcus Reed	1-0-0-0	John Shafer	1-0-0-1
Lydia Romine	0-1-0-0	Jackson Shafer	1-0-0-1
Geo W. Reed	1-0-0-0	Burr Smallwood	1-0-0-0
		Sarah Smallwood	0-0-0-1

Clarke County, Virginia Personal Property Tax Lists 1836-1853
1841

Wm Stillions	1-0-0-0		Wm Trenary	1-0-0-1
Simon Stickles	1-0-0-2		Wilson L. Taylor	1-0-0-0
Geo Smedley	1-0-1-1		Warner A. Thompson	1-0-0-1
David Swarts	1-0-0-0		Wm Tomblin	1-0-0-1
H. P. Smith's Est.	0-0-1-0		Wm Tinsman	2-0-0-2
Philip Sherrick	1-0-0-0			
Wm Shieras	1-0-0-1		Jos Vincent	2-0-1-2
Danil H. Sowers	1-0-3-4		John Vanclief	2-0-1-3
H. & C. Shepherd	2-0-0-0		Jas Violet	1-0-0-3
John Scroggin	1-0-5-10		Jacob Vanmetre	1-0-1-10
Wm A. Smith	1-2-7-4		James Voldenear	1-0-4-10
A. J. Sangster	1-1-0-1		Wm Violett	1-0-0-0
John Shell	2-0-0-2			
Jas Smallwood	1-0-0-0		Wm Willingham	1-0-0-1
			Allen Williams	1-1-9-17
Wm Turner	1-0-0-1		Doct. J. Williams	1-0-7-8
Mat R. Throckmorton	2-0-4-7		Timothy Wilcox	1-0-0-0
John A. Throgmorton	1-1-5-7		Jas Wigginton	1-0-1-2
Jesse Taylor	5-0-0-6		John Wood	2-1-2-8
Abigail Tanquary	0-0-1-1		Fras H. Whiting	2-0-3-10
R. M. S. Timberlake	2-1-8-10		Josiah W. Ware	
David Tristler	1-0-1-5		Mrs. Stribling	1-3-18-28
Adam Towner	1-0-0-0		John H. Watson	1-0-0-4
John Tally	1-0-0-0		Mrs. L. Washington	0-0-2-2
Mrs. H. Taylor	0-0-2-2		J. G. Wade & Bros	3-0-0-0
Greenberry			Jas V. Weir	1-3-2-7
Thompson	1-0-1-1		Horatio T. Wheat	3-1-2-2
David Timberlake	2-0-10-10		Hezekiah Wiley	1-0-0-2
Harrison Thompson	1-0-0-1		Saml Wiley	1-0-0-1
Doct. Saml Taylor	1-0-12-13		Jas Wiley	1-0-0-1
Benj Thompson Jr.	2-0-0-6		John Willingham	1-0-0-1
Jos Tuley	1-6-22-21		Alexdr Wood	1-0-1-0
John Trussel	2-2-3-6		Miss E. W.	
Nimrod Trussell	1-0-0-2		Washington	0-0-2-0
Moses Trussel	3-0-0-5		Leroy P. Williams	2-1-6-10
Wm Thomas	1-0-0-0		Wm Wood	1-0-0-0
Wm Timberlake	0-0-2-0		Grantham Way	1-0-0-1
John B. Taylor	3-3-16-22		Wm P. Wigginton	1-2-1-1
Doct. John Thompson	2-2-3-3		Fras B. Whiting	2-3-18-14

Clarke County, Virginia Personal Property Tax Lists 1836-1853
1841

Wm B. Whiting	1-0-0-2	Sydnor B. Windham	1-0-0-0
Obed Willingham	1-0-0-0	Jas W. Wiley	2-0-0-0
Wm Wise	1-0-0-0		
Bennet Wood	1-0-0-0	George Young	1-1-0-0
Henry Weaver	1-0-0-0	Simson Yowell	1-1-0-1
Herbert Washington	0-0-2-0	Saml S. Yeakle	2-0-1-1
Ephraim Watson	2-0-0-6	Washington Young	1-0-0-0
N. B. Whiting	1-0-4-11		

Free Blacks

Columns: 1) free males above 16, 2) slaves over 12, 3) slaves over 16, 4) horses, mares, mules etc.

John Diggs	2-0-0-1	Hannah Robinson	2-0-0-1
Wiley Finch	1-0-0-0	Washington Hall	1-0-0-0
Daniel James	1-0-0-0	Jack Adams	1-0-0-0
Thos Graham	2-0-0-0	Sylvia Hall	1-0-0-1
John Williams	1-0-0-1	John Robertson	1-0-0-0
Nancy Parker	1-0-0-0	Frank Irvin	1-0-0-0
Simeon Parker	1-0-0-0	Geo Green	1-0-0-0
Robt Cooke	1-0-0-2	Priscilla Thornton	1-0-0-0
Bristo Smith	1-0-0-0	Spencer Johnson	1-0-0-0
James Jackson	1-0-0-0		
Geo Ranson	1-0-0-0	Wm Wheeler	1-0-0-0
Geo Wells	1-0-0-0	Kitty Wilkerson	0-0-0-1
Cyrus Davis	1-0-0-0	Gabriel _____	1-0-0-1
John Clifton	1-0-0-0	Ralph _____	1-0-0-0
Jas Thomas	1-0-0-0	Philip Martin	1-0-0-0
Chas Taylor	1-0-0-0	Davy _____	1-0-0-0
Burwell Cook	1-0-0-0	Mowen Harris	1-0-0-0
Jas Butler	1-0-0-0	Jas Thornton	1-0-0-0
Henry Green	1-0-0-0	Roderick Tribee	1-0-0-0

Clarke County, Virginia Personal Property Tax Lists 1836-1853

1842

Columns: 1) White males above 16, 2) Slaves 12-16 years, 3) Slaves over 16 years, 4) Horses, mares, mules, etc.

[The first two pages, names beginning with A & B, are at the end of the 1842 list on the microfilm. They have been placed in the correct position here.]

Name	Values	Name	Values
Robert Ashby	2-0-0-5	John Burchell	1-2-4-10
Thos H. Anderson	1-0-0-6	Archibald Bowen	2-0-1-6
Mason Anderson	0-0-0-0	Hiram O. Bell	1-0-1-6
David H. Allen	4-4-26-44	Phineas Bowen	2-0-3-14
John Alexander	1-3-8-16	Francis O. Byrd	1-1-11-11
Wm C. Alexander	1-4-7-14	Philip Berlin	1-1-3-2
Augusta Athey	3-0-0-6	Wm Berlin	3-0-3-1
Wm Ambrous	1-0-0-4	George C. Blakemore	1-0-1-1
Benjn P. Ashby	2-0-0-2	John Bowlin	1-0-0-0
John Ambrous	3-0-0-9	Neille Barnett	1-1-2-4
John B. Ambrous	1-0-0-1	Thomas W. Briggs	1-0-0-4
Buckner Ashby	1-3-8-15	Amos A. Bonham	1-2-6-13
Joseph Anderson	4-0-2-9	Danl S. Bonham	1-1-6-11
Wm Allen	2-0-3-6	James Bogs	1-0-0-0
A. S. Allen	1-1-8-15	John Brownley	1-4-12-16
Hathaway Alexander	1-0-0-1	Wm Baker	1-2-4-5
John Ashby	2-0-0-4	Isaac Berlin	3-1-0-2
Robert Ashby Jr.	1-0-0-1	Strother Bell	1-2-3-10
Martin Ashby	1-0-0-3	Robert Burchell	1-1-4-9
Thomas H. Alexander	2-1-1-1	H. W. Brabham	1-0-0-0
Nicholas Anderson	2-0-0-2	Squire Bell	1-0-1-5
Nimrod Ashby	1-0-0-1	Saml Berlin	1-0-0-0
George B. Ashby	1-0-0-1	Juliet Boston	1-0-1-1
John E. Anderson	1-0-0-0	Philip Burwell	1-3-27-15
David Anderson	1-0-0-0	John H. Berringer	1-0-0-0
		John W. Byrd	1-0-11-1
Nat Burwell Jr.	1-1-8-14	Thos Briggs	8-2-3-15
Wm C. Benson	1-0-5-7	Lewis Brumley	2-0-0-8

Clarke County, Virginia Personal Property Tax Lists 1836-1853
1842

John D. Barr	1-0-0-0		Wm Carrington	3-2-3-2
James W. Beck	1-0-0-1		Wm Carper	1-0-0-3
John C. Bonham	1-3-6-7		C. B. Chandler	1-4-12-15
Nat Burwell Sr.	1-6-48-37		Elizabeth Carnegy	0-4-19-21
Blackemore &			R. A. Colston	1-0-3-9
Seevers	1-0-0-1		Wm H. Colston	1-0-3-7
Saml Bonham	1-1-12-15		Elizabeth K. Carter	2-0-2-5
T. T. Byrds Est.	0-0-1-1		John Copenhaver	1-0-3-8
Col. James Bell	1-2-6-13		Miriam Catlett	2-1-6-14
Westley Brown	1-0-0-0		John Cillerton	1-0-0-0
Robert Ben	1-0-1-4		Sarah Castleman	0-2-3-6
Wm Berry	3-2-12-13		James H. Clarke	1-1-2-1
George H. Burwell	1-3-40-34		Wm Castleman	1-4-11-17
Jas Bulger	1-0-0-0		Thomas H. Crow	2-0-2-2
James Boyles	2-0-0-4		Wm A. Castleman	1-1-3-12
Saml Briarly	2-1-6-10		Alfred Clevinger	1-0-3-7
Christian Bowser	3-0-1-1		John Cooper	2-0-0-1
Thos H. Burwells Est.	0-0-1-0		Baalis D. Castleman	1-0-0-1
John Blue	1-0-2-7		Elizabeth Crampton	0-0-1-1
Thos L. Blakemore	0-0-1-1		James Castleman	2-1-15-34
Doct. A. Brown	1-1-1-2		S. B. T. Caldwell	4-1-3-6
Alexander Baker	1-0-0-5		Martha P. Castleman	2-0-9-6
John Brown	1-0-0-0		Thomas Carter	1-2-14-13
Napolean Balthop	2-0-0-0		Presley Cooper	1-0-0-1
Docia Billmyer	2-0-0-0		Parkerson Corder	1-0-0-1
George Bolen	1-0-0-0		Fielding Cornwell	1-0-0-0
Lucy Burwell	0-1-3-0		John Carroll	2-0-0-2
Peter Bennet	1-0-0-0		John Carpenter	1-0-3-4
James Brown	1-0-0-1		Dabney Cauthorn	2-0-0-2
Russell Brackett	2-0-0-0		Elizabeth N. Carter	0-0-2-1
Martin Berlin	2-1-2-6		James Carter	1-0-0-0
			David Clevinger	2-0-0-4
Alfred Castleman	1-1-6-9		Thos Clevinger	1-0-2-7
John Campbell	1-0-0-0		George S. Christy	1-0-0-0
Parkerson Craig	2-0-2-7		James N. Corbin	1-0-0-1
Osmin Chamberlain	0-0-0-0		Thomas Cornwell	1-0-0-1
John P. Chamberlain	0-0-0-0		Stephen Cauthorn	1-0-0-1
Frederick Clopton	1-0-5-10		Aaron Chamblin	1-0-0-3
George F. Calmese	1-0-6-14		Michael Copenhaur	2-0-0-1

Clarke County, Virginia Personal Property Tax Lists 1836-1853
1842

Name	Values	Name	Values
Madison Chapman	1-0-0-0	James Flore	1-1-3-1
		Flore & Keyes	2-0-0-2
Peter Dermont	2-3-5-4	John Furlow	1-0-0-0
A. R. Davis	1-1-2-1	Moses Furr	2-0-0-6
Thos G. Dowdle	3-0-1-1	Martha Forster	0-1-1-2
Wm Deakle	2-0-1-0	Geo Farnsworth	1-0-0-3
Saml Davis	1-0-0-0	Archibald Flemming	2-0-3-2
James Davis	2-0-0-1	John D. Ferguson Sr.	1-2-14-12
John Drish	1-0-0-0	James Furr	1-0-0-1
Michael Dermont	1-1-3-7	John D. Ferguson Jr.	1-1-2-8
Baalis Davis	1-1-2-3	James Furr	1-0-0-1
Benj Downing	1-0-0-3	Wm Fowler	2-0-0-6
James Downing	1-0-0-1	Benjamin Franks	1-0-0-2
Thomas Duke	1-0-0-0	Henry Franks	1-0-0-0
James Doren	2-0-1-1	M. R. Feehrer	2-0-2-2
John E. Dangerfield	1-0-4-14	Washington Ferguson	1-0-0-2
Saml Dobbins	1-0-0-1	James Fuller	1-0-0-0
John Dow	1-0-1-2	Allison Fletcher	1-0-0-0
Sarah Douglass	1-0-0-0	McFarland Fuller	1-0-0-0
		Martin Feltner	1-0-0-0
Charles Eckhardt	1-0-0-1		
Henry Edwards	1-0-0-3	Richard Green Sr.	2-0-2-6
Wm G. Everheart	4-0-1-6	Thomas E. & J. Gold	2-2-4-13
John Eleyett	1-0-1-1	John Greenlee	1-0-0-1
John B. Earle	2-2-12-28	Wm Graves	1-0-2-6
Hiram P. Evans	2-1-1-1	Harrison Gordon	1-0-1-4
Jacob Enders	1-1-0-4	George Gordon	2-0-0-0
Henry Emery	1-0-0-0	James Green	1-0-4-5
Wm Eleyett	1-0-0-0	John Gant	2-1-5-9
		Stephen J. Gant	1-0-3-6
Edward Franks	1-0-0-0	James J. Grogan	1-0-5-11
John Furr	1-0-0-0	Edward Gorman	1-0-1-2
Jesse Furr	3-0-0-2	Thomas Grubs	1-0-0-1
George Fyst	4-0-2-10	Joseph George	1-1-0-3
Doct. J. F. Fauntleroy	1-0-3-4	Catharine Grove	0-0-0-1
Margaret Funston	0-0-3-2	John S. Gordon	3-0-0-6
Doct. O. Funston	1-2-11-13	John Gordon	2-0-0-3
John Forster	1-0-2-8	James V. Glass	2-2-6-8
Jane H. Forster	0-0-2-0	Henry N. Grigsby	1-0-4-6

Clarke County, Virginia Personal Property Tax Lists 1836-1853
1842

Wm Gardner	1-0-0-0		Bushrod Hooff	1-0-0-0
Dandridge Garrison	1-0-0-4		Mary Howard	0-1-2-0
Jacob Gaiten [sic]	4-0-3-4		John Holtze	1-0-0-0
John Grant	2-0-2-7		Philip Hansucker	1-0-0-0
James D. Gipson	1-0-0-7		George Harris	1-0-5-6
Wm Gourley	1-0-0-11		Grafton Hellyard	1-0-0-0
Emanuel Garmong	1-0-0-1		Miss Abby Hopkins	0-1-2-0
Saml Grubs	1-0-0-0		Alexander Hillchew	1-0-0-1
Nimrod Glasscock	1-0-0-1			
Abram Grim	2-0-0-0		George Johnson	1-0-0-2
John Graves	1-0-2-3		Herod Jenkins	1-0-0-0
George Gardner	2-0-0-0		Solomon R. Jackson	1-1-1-2
Richard N. Green	1-1-3-8		Mathew Jones	2-1-0-6
George W. Green	1-1-5-10		John Johnston Jr.	1-0-0-1
Branson Goy	1-0-0-0		Reuben Jordan	1-0-1-2
George Gruber	1-0-0-0		John Joliffe	1-1-8-19
Lorenzo D. Gowen	1-0-0-0		John Johnston Sr.	1-0-0-0
John C. Gold	1-0-0-1		Thomas Jordan	1-0-0-1
			Doct. R. R. Jordan	1-0-1-2
Whiting Hamilton	1-0-0-1		Thomas Jackson	1-3-13-10
Henry D. Hooe	2-0-1-3		Jane Jackson	0-0-1-0
Henry Horne	1-1-1-1		Jacob Isler	5-0-5-2
Edwin Hart	2-0-1-3		David Jenkins	1-0-0-0
Abram Huyett	1-0-0-4		Chas R. Johnson	1-0-0-1
John Huyett	2-0-0-6		Washington Johnston	1-0-0-0
Saml Huyett	1-0-0-5		Thomas Jones	1-0-1-1
James Harris	2-0-4-9		Albert Johnson	1-0-0-0
Doct. J. Hay	1-3-15-20			
Thomas Hiett	2-0-0-7		James C. Kennan	1-0-0-0
Levi Hiett	2-0-2-11		Saml Kean	1-0-0-0
Isaac J. Hite	1-0-10-13		Doct. F. J. Kerfoot	1-1-8-16
James M. Hite	1-2-7-7		Mrs. Avry Kean	0-0-0-1
Wm T. Helm	5-2-7-12		Thomas Kennerly	2-0-0-0
Wm Hummer	1-0-0-2		George Knight	2-0-8-15
Saml Heflybour	1-0-3-11		George Kitchen	1-0-6-9
George Heflybour	2-0-4-13		John Kerfoot Est.	1-6-18-12
John Hay	1-0-3-4		Wm C. Kerfoot	1-0-7-16
Wm Holtsclaw	2-0-0-1		George L. Kerfoot	1-2-9-14
Richard Hardesty	4-1-4-11		Benjamin Kent	1-0-0-0

Clarke County, Virginia Personal Property Tax Lists 1836-1853
1842

Thomas Knight	1-0-0-2	Bushrod Longerbeam	1-0-0-0
Doct. Kownslar	1-0-2-1	_____ Leech	1-0-0-0
John T. G. Keene	1-0-0-1	Elizabeth F. Lane	0-1-1-0
John Kable	1-0-2-0		
Wm F. Knight	1-1-2-1	Peter McMurray	1-1-2-8
Nicholas Kriser	1-0-0-0	Wm McCoy	1-0-1-1
		Albert McCormick	1-0-0-5
Henry Lloyd	2-0-0-3	Saml McCormick	1-0-0-0
Charles Lucius	1-0-5-7	Warner Muse	1-0-0-6
John Lock	1-0-0-7	John J. Munroe	1-1-2-3
John & James Larue	2-0-5-11	John Maddox	3-0-3-6
Wm Littleton	3-0-1-4	Province McCormick	2-0-0-2
Catharine Lock	1-0-0-2	James Michell	1-2-4-4
Wm Lock	1-0-0-4	Wm D. McGueir	1-1-7-17
Fanny Larue	0-3-4-11	D. H. McGueer	2-1-9-14
Sarah Luke	1-0-1-0	Otway McCormick	2-0-10-19
Louisa Littleton	1-0-1-0	Isaac McCormick	1-0-0-1
Washington Lee	1-0-0-1	Wm Morgan	1-2-7-10
Dr. R. H. Little	3-1-9-10	John McCloy	1-0-0-1
John Louthan	4-0-2-1	Wm McDonald	1-0-0-0
Lorenzo Lewis	1-5-30-30	Francis B. Meade	1-1-6-9
Doct. James M. Lindsey	1-0-2-3	Mrs. L. W. Meade	0-0-4-5
		Philip N. Meade	2-2-4-9
Saml Larue	3-0-12-16	Wm Meade Jr.	1-0-1-4
John B. Larue	1-1-13-23	John N. Meade	1-0-1-2
Clarisa Larue	0-0-2-1	Miss Mary Meade	0-0-2-0
Sarah Lindsay	0-0-2-0	Thomas McCormick	1-1-7-14
John Lloyd	1-0-0-1	John Marts	1-0-0-2
George Longerbeam	1-0-0-1	Saml & Cy McCormick	3-0-13-19
James Lloyd	1-0-0-0	George McCormick	2-1-6-12
Charles Leech	2-0-0-1	James McBride	1-0-0-1
Sarah Longerbeam	2-0-0-3	Levi Marquess	2-0-0-3
Benjamin B. Lane	1-0-2-6	Jesse P. Mercer	1-0-0-0
George F. Ludwig	2-0-0-2	John Mayers	1-0-0-4
Washington Lock	1-0-0-0	Catharine E. Miller	0-0-0-0
Saml Lloyd	1-0-0-1	John & James Mitchum	2-0-0-2
Doct. Benj Lacey	1-1-3-2		
Miss Sarah Lindsay	1-0-0-0	Benjamin Morgan	1-1-16-23
Edgar Lanham	1-0-0-1	Elizabeth Morgan	0-0-3-0

Clarke County, Virginia Personal Property Tax Lists 1836-1853
1842

Stephen R. Mount	3-0-2-3	Frank Nelson	1-0-0-1
Francis McCormick	2-3-8-17		
Charles McCormick	3-7-22-31	John W. Owen	1-1-4-2
Susan Marshall	0-0-3-6	Elizabeth Orear	0-1-7-7
John Marshall	1-0-1-4	Enoch Orear	1-1-5-7
Jesse McConaha	1-0-0-1	Doct. Overfield	1-0-0-1
Lucy Mustin	0-0-2-1	George Orear	1-0-5-11
James Murdock	1-0-0-0	James A. Osborn	2-0-0-5
Alexander Marshall	1-0-0-1		
John McPhillin	2-0-0-1	George Pultz	1-0-1-2
Wm Mason	1-0-0-1	John E. Page	1-3-9-17
Jacob May	1-0-0-0	John Pages Est.	0-1-21-5
John Morgan	1-1-7-18	Mrs. E. M Page	0-1-1-0
George L. McCormick	2-0-0-1	John Page	1-3-7-12
		Mann R. Page	2-7-10-20
P. McCormick Sr.	2-2-9-17	Isaac Pidgeon	1-0-0-1
Chas & Saml McCormick	0-1-5-8	John Pierce Sr.	1-2-3-8
		Doct. R. P. Page	1-2-18-20
Benj F. Mayhew	1-0-0-0	James M. Pine	1-0-0-1
Alfred Michell	1-0-0-1	Mrs. Mary C. Page	0-1-7-9
Isaac J. Manuel	1-0-0-0	John Page	
W. I. Maxwell	0-0-0-0	of North End	3-1-7-12
James Murphy	1-0-0-1	Joseph E. Peyton	1-0-0-2
Sylvanus More	1-0-0-0	Paul Pierce	1-2-5-6
Travis Miley	1-0-0-1	Richard E. Parkers Est.	1-2-10-8
Revd. Wm Meade	1-0-0-1	John W. Page	4-1-11-14
		McFarland Puller	1-0-0-0
Wm Niswanger	2-0-0-5	John Pierce Jr.	1-2-0-4
Hugh M. Nelson	1-0-7-18	John Padgett	1-0-0-0
Ann T. Neille	1-0-4-6	Saml L. Pidgeon	1-0-0-2
George H. Norris	2-1-12-16	Henry Peters	1-0-1-4
Philip Nelson	1-3-16-15	Francis N. Page	2-0-0-1
Thomas F. Nelson	1-3-10-14	James Puller	1-0-0-0
James H. Neville	1-0-2-2	Michael Pop	3-0-0-0
Joseph Noble	1-1-0-0	Calvin Puller	1-0-0-1
Miss Abby Nelson	0-0-3-0	Peter Mc Pierce	1-0-2-5
Wm Nelson	1-0-2-1	Thornton P. Pendleton	0-0-0-0
P. N. Nicholas	0-0-2-0		
J. M. Nicklin	1-1-2-1	Washington Prichett	1-0-0-1

Clarke County, Virginia Personal Property Tax Lists 1836-1853
1842

Name	Values	Name	Values
		Joseph Smith	1-0-0-2
Jacob Ridgeway	1-0-0-0	Wm Sowers	3-5-7-12
Richard Ridgeway	3-0-0-9	Joseph Shepherd	2-1-5-12
Wm Reed	2-0-0-4	Champ Shepherd	1-0-2-2
Jonas Ridgeway	2-0-0-4	Edwd Sheckles	1-0-0-2
Thos W. Reynolds	4-2-9-6	Thomas Shumate	1-1-3-8
Bennett Russell	1-1-5-8	John W. Sowers	1-3-4-12
Miss E. Royster	0-0-1-0	Wm G. Steeles	2-0-1-2
Mat W. Royston	1-0-1-9	Danl W. Sowers	2-2-10-18
Peter Royston	1-0-1-0	Saml Stipe	1-1-3-6
John Roush	1-0-1-1	James Sowers	1-2-11-16
Uriah B. Royston	2-1-0-6	Thomas Sprint	2-0-0-1
John Reed	1-0-0-1	Emanuel Showers	4-0-2-1
Miss Ann Redman	0-0-0-0	Adam Shipe	2-0-0-1
Solomon Redman	1-0-0-6	Barnet Smallwood	1-0-0-1
George Rutter	1-0-0-0	Fielding L. Sowers	1-2-5-10
Danl Richard Jr.	4-0-1-4	P. D. Shepherd	2-1-3-6
Saml B. Redman	1-0-0-2	Doct. P. Smith	1-3-20-24
Addison Romine	1-1-2-5	Col T. Smith	4-1-11-16
Elisha Romine	1-0-0-2	Wm R. Seevers	1-0-1-2
James Ryan	1-0-1-1	Kerfoot Sowers Est.	0-3-5-15
R. C. Randolph	1-2-11-16	John Stewart	3-0-1-4
John Russell Sr.	1-0-1-0	Danl A. Sowers	1-0-7-9
Jane Richardson	1-0-0-1	Enoch Strothers	0-0-1-0
George Reno	2-0-0-2	Elizabeth Strother	1-0-5-6
Isaac Ramey	2-0-1-6	Jacob Shively	2-2-5-9
Mathew Rust	1-0-3-7	Alfred Smallwood	1-0-0-0
Miss E. Roots	1-0-2-0	Ben Starkey	1-0-0-0
Richardson &		Edward Street	1-0-0-0
Pendleton	2-0-16-23	John Shafer	1-0-0-1
John Richardson	0-0-0-0	Jackson Shafer	1-0-0-1
____ Riely	1-0-0-0	Burr Smallwood	1-0-0-0
____ Russell	1-0-0-	Wm Stillions	1-0-0-0
____ Roberts	0-0-0-0	Simon Stickles	1-0-0-1
		George Smedley	2-0-1-2
James H. Sowers	1-0-6-11	Curad [sic] Swarts	1-0-0-0
James Seevers	1-0-2-9	David Swarts	1-0-0-0
Edward J. Smith	2-5-20-30	Philip Sherick	1-0-0-0
John N. Sowers	7-0-1-1	Revd. A. Shieras	1-0-0-1

Clarke County, Virginia Personal Property Tax Lists 1836-1853
1842

Name	Values	Name	Values
Danl H. Sowers	1-0-4-7	Wm Tansell	1-0-0-0
H. & C. Shepherd	1-0-1-0	Warner A. Thompson	1-0-1-0
Mrs. Scroggins	0-0-1-1	Moses Trussel	3-0-0-5
Wm A. Smith	0-0-5-0	Nimrod Trussell	1-0-0-3
Doct. A. Sangster	1-0-1-1	James Tansell	1-0-0-0
Henry Shepherd	1-0-0-1	John A. Thompson	1-1-3-2
Miss Eliza Smith	0-0-0-1	James Timberlake	2-2-5-11
Wm H. Seevers	1-0-0-0		
Joseph Shipe	1-0-0-0	John Vanclief	2-0-0-4
Heabert Sanders	1-0-0-0	James Violett	1-0-0-4
George Strother	1-0-1-3	Jacob Vanmeter	2-0-1-4
James L. Smith	1-0-0-1	James Voldenear	1-0-4-10
Lewis A. Smith	1-0-0-10	Joseph Vincent	2-0-1-2
Erasmus Shipes Est.	0-0-3-0	Wm Violett	1-0-0-0
James Shackleford	1-0-1-0		
		Wm Willingham	1-0-0-1
Wm Turner	1-0-0-1	Allen Williams	2-0-11-18
Mat R. Throckmorton	1-0-4-9	J. J. Williams	1-0-7-10
John A. Throckmorton	1-0-1-9	Timothy Wilcox	2-0-0-0
		James Wigginton	1-0-1-1
Jesse Taylor	3-0-1-5	John Wood	2-1-2-8
Abigail Tanquary	0-0-1-1	Francis H. Whiting	1-0-3-10
R. M. S. Timberlake	2-2-7-12	Josiah W. Ware	1-3-20-22
David Tristler	1-1-2-4	Mrs. L. Washington	0-0-2-2
Adam Towner	2-0-0-0	John Watsons Est.	0-0-0-1
John Tally	2-0-0-0	J. G. Wade & Bros	3-0-0-0
Mrs. Hannah Taylor	0-0-2-2	James V. Weir	1-3-3-5
Greenberry Tomson	1-0-0-1	H. T. Wheat	1-1-1-2
David Timberlake	1-0-1-1	Hezekiah Weley	2-0-0-3
Harrison Thompson	1-0-0-1	Saml Wely	1-0-0-1
Doct. Saml Taylor	1-1-13-14	James Weeley	1-0-0-0
Benj Thompson Jr.	1-0-0-4	John Willingham	1-0-0-1
Joseph Tuley	1-6-25-22	Alex Wood	1-1--00
John Trussel	2-0-4-6	Miss E. W. Washington	0-0-1-0
Wm Timberlake	0-0-2-0	Leroy P. Williams	2-2-5-11
John B. Taylor	3-0-9-24	Wm P. Wigginton	1-0-1-2
James Thomas	1-0-0-0	Francis B. Whiting	2-3-18-16
Wm Trenary	1-0-0-1	Wm B. Whiting	1-0-1-2
Wm Tinsman	1-0-0-1		

Clarke County, Virginia Personal Property Tax Lists 1836-1853
1842

Obed Willingham	1-0-0-0	Doct. B. Wigginton	1-0-1-0
Wm Wise	1-0-0-0	John Wilson	1-0-0-0
Bennet Wood	1-0-0-0	George B. West	1-0-0-0
Henry Weaver	1-0-0-0	Joseph A. Wiliamson	1-2-7-7
N. B. Whiting	1-1-5-13		
Ephraim Watson	2-1-0-7	George Young	1-0-0-0
Sednor B. Windham	2-0-0-1	Simeon Yowell	1-1-0-1
		S. S. Yeakle	3-1-1-2
James Russell	0-0-0-0	Washington Young	1-0-0-0
Thomas Woods	2-0-0-0	Doct. H. Washington	1-0-1-0

[No Free Blacks in 1842 are on this microfilm.]

Clarke County, Virginia Personal Property Tax Lists 1836-1853

1843

Columns: 1) White males above 16, 2) Slaves 12-16 years, 3) Slaves over 16 years, 4) Horses, mares, mules, etc.

Name	Values	Name	Values
Robert Ashby Senr.	3-0-0-5	Nat Burwell Jr.	1-2-7-16
Thos. H. Alexander	4-0-1-1	Wm C. Benson	1-0-5-5
Thos H. Anderson	1-0-0-6	John Burchell	1-0-5-10
Mason Anderson	1-0-1-1	Archibald Bowen	2-2-1-9
David H. Allen	5-6-24-43	Hiram O. Bell	1-0-1-0
John Alexander	1-4-11-18	Phineas Bowen	3-0-3-13
Wm C. Alexander	1-2-7-11	Francis O. Byrd	1-1-10-11
Augusta Athey	2-0-0-4	Philip Berlin	1-1-2-4
Wm Ambrous	1-0-0-4	George C. Blakemore	1-3-10-15
Benj. P. Ashby	2-0-0-1	John Bowlin	1-0-0-0
John B. Ambrows	2-0-0-1	Neille Barnett	1-0-3-4
Buckner Ashby	1-2-9-17	Thomas W. Briggs	1-0-2-6
Joseph Anderson	3-0-2-7	Amos A. Bonham	1-1-4-12
Wm Allen	2-1-3-6	Danl S. Bonham	1-1-2-10
A. S. Allen	1-2-9-13	James Bogs	1-0-0-0
Hathaway Alexander	2-0-0-0	John Brownley	2-3-14-17
John Ashby	1-0-0-2	Capt. Wm Baker	1-1-4-4
Robert Ashby Jr.	1-0-0-1	Isaac Berlin	3-1-0-3
Martin Ashby	1-0-0-2	Strother Bell	1-1-0-10
Nickolas Anderson	1-0-1-2	Robert Burchell	1-0-4-10
Nimrod Ashby	1-0-0-2	H. W. Brabham	1-0-0-0
George B. Ashby	1-0-0-1	Squire Bell	1-0-1-6
John E. Anderson	1-0-0-1	Juliet Boston	1-0-1-0
John Ambrows	3-0-0-11	Philip Burwell	1-5-24-17
Wm Ashby	1-0-1-0	John W. Byrd	1-0-10-10
Thomas Ashby	1-0-0-1	Thomas Briggs	8-1-4-18
Jefferson Anderson	1-0-0-0	Lewis Brumley	3-0-0-9
John W. Ashby	1-0-0-0	John D. Barr	2-0-0-0
_____ Anderson	1-0-0-1	James W. Beck	1-0-0-2
David T. Armstrons [sic]	1-0-0-0	Nat Burwell Sr.	1-4-46-41
		John C. Bonham	1-0-7-8

Clarke County, Virginia Personal Property Tax Lists 1836-1853
1843

Saml Bonham	1-2-12-15	Elizabeth Carnegy	0-2-19-32
[illegible] Bell	1-2-8-14	Robert A. Colston	1-1-3-12
Robert Ben	1-0-1-5	Wm A. Colston	1-0-3-6
Wm Berry	3-2-9-12	Elizabeth K. Carter	1-0-1-5
George H. Burwell	1-5-40-42	John Copenhaur	1-0-3-8
James Bulger	1-0-0-0	Miriam Catlett	1-2-6-14
Saml Briarly	2-1-6-10	James H. Clarke	1-1-2-1
Christian Bowser	3-0-0-1	Thomas H. Crow	2-0-3-3
John Blue	1-0-2-7	Wm A. Castleman	1-0-5-10
Doct. A. Brown	1-1-1-2	Alfred Clevinger	1-1-3-7
John Brown	1-0-0-0	John Cooper	1-0-0-1
Napolean Balthop	1-0-0-1	Elizabeth Crampton	0-0-1-1
Docia Billmyer	1-0-0-0	James Castleman	4-3-22-30
Lucy Burwell	0-0-3-0	S. B. T. Caldwell	2-1-2-3
James Brown	1-0-0-0	Martha P. Castleman	1-0-8-6
Russell Brackett	1-0-0-0	Thomas Carter	1-2-16-13
Martin Berlin	1-0-3-6	Presley Cooper	1-0-0-2
Jesse Bowen	2-0-0-1	Parkerson Corder	1-0-0-1
Samuel Bowles	1-0-1-5	Fielding Cornwell	1-0-0-0
Abram Beevers	2-0-0-4	John Carroll	1-0-0-2
James Bell	1-0-0-2	John Carpenter	2-0-3-6
Wm Berlin	3-0-3-2	Dabney Cauthorn	2-0-0-1
John Bolen	1-0-0-0	Elizabeth N. Carter	0-0-2-1
John R. Bell	1-1-0-3	James Carter	1-0-0-0
Joseph Bell	1-0-0-0	David Clevinger	2-0-0-6
Catharine Ball	0-1-2-1	Thos Clevinger	1-0-2-8
Saml Bucher	1-1-0-1	George S. Christy	1-0-0-0
Adam Barr	1-0-0-1	James N. Corbin	1-0-0-1
George Barr	1-0-0-1	Thomas Cornwell	1-0-0-0
Benj Barr	1-0-0-0	Aaron Chamblin	1-0-0-4
Wm Brawner	1-0-0-0	Michael Copenhaur	2-0-0-1
		John E. Chapman	1-0-0-0
Alfred Castleman	1-1-5-10	Andrew Cage	1-0-0-0
John Camell	1-0-0-0	Mrs. Ury Castleman	0-1-6-7
Parkerson Craig	1-0-2-7	Wm Corbin	1-0-0-1
Frederick Clopton	1-0-5-9	Joseph L. Carter	1-0-0-0
George F. Calmese	1-3-3-8		
Wm Carrington	2-1-2-1	Doct. H. Dorsey	0-0-0-0
Wm Carper	1-0-0-2	Arthur N. Danley	1-0-0-0

Clarke County, Virginia Personal Property Tax Lists 1836-1853
1843

John Dermont	1-1-4-4		Moses Furr	2-0-0-8
Peter Dermont	1-0-0-0		Mrs. Martha Foster	0-1-1-1
Andrew R. Davis	1-1-1-2		George Farnsworth	1-0-0-3
Thomas G. Dowdle	3-0-2-1		Archibald Flemming	1-1-2-3
Wm Deakle	2-0-1-0		John D.	
Saml Davis	1-0-0-0		Ferguson Senr.	2-1-13-11
James Davis	2-0-0-0		James Furr	1-0-0-2
John Drish	1-0-0-0		John D. Ferguson Jr.	2-2-2-8
Michael Dermont	1-1-3-7		Wm Fowler	2-0-0-6
Baalis Davis	1-0-2-2		Benjamin Franks	1-0-0-2
Benjamin Downing	1-0-0-2		Mrs. K. Feehrer	2-0-2-3
James Downing	1-0-0-2		Washington Ferguson	1-0-1-2
Thomas Duke	1-0-0-0		Martin Feltner	1-0-0-1
James Dorin	1-0-0-1		Joseph Fleming	1-0-0-1
John E. Dangerfield	1-0-5-7			
Saml Dobbins	1-0-0-1		Richard Green	1-0-1-5
George Dunn	1-0-0-0		Thomas E. Gold	2-0-5-14
			John Greenlee	1-0-0-2
Charles Eckhardt	1-0-0-1		Wm Graves	1-0-0-8
Henry Edwards	1-0-0-3		Harrison Gordon	2-0-0-5
Wm G. Everheart	3-0-2-5		George Gordon	2-0-0-1
John Eleyett	1-0-1-2		James Green	1-1-4-7
John B. Earle	2-2-9-25		John Gant	2-3-5-9
Hiram P. Evans	2-1-1-2		Stephen J. Gant	1-0-3-5
Jacob Enders	1-0-2-5		James J. Grogan	1-0-6-10
Jacob W. Everheart	1-0-0-1		Edward Gorman	1-0-0-1
Abram B. Everheart	1-0-0-1		Thomas Grubs	1-0-0-1
			Joseph George	1-1-1-3
Edward Franks	1-0-0-0		John S. Gordon	3-0-1-7
Jesse Furr	0-0-0-2		John Gordon	2-0-1-5
George Fyst	3-0-1-7		James V. Glass	2-2-7-9
Doct. J. F.			Henry N. Grigsby	1-0-3-6
Fauntleroy	1-0-3-4		Dandridge Garrison	1-0-0-2
Margaret Funston	0-0-4-2		John Grant	1-1-1-6
Doct. O. Funston	1-1-6-12		Wm Gourley	2-0-0-10
John Foster	1-0-2-7		Emanuel Garmong	1-0-0-1
Jane H. Foster	0-0-2-0		Saml Grubs	1-0-0-0
James Floore	1-1-2-0		Nimrod Glasscock	2-0-0-2
John Furlow	1-0-0-0		Abram Grim	1-0-0-0

Clarke County, Virginia Personal Property Tax Lists 1836-1853
1843

Name	Values	Name	Values
George Gardner	3-0-0-0	Wm B. Harris	1-0-5-4
Richard N. Green	1-2-3-9	Edward Handle	1-0-0-0
George W. Green	1-0-6-12	Grafton HIllyard	1-0-0-1
Branson Goye	1-0-0-0	James Y. Harris	1-0-0-5
John L. Grant	1-0-1-2	Wm Harris	1-0-0-1
James Gibs	1-0-0-1	Harrison Hooff	1-0-0-0
Nancy Galloway	0-0-1-0	Cornelius Hooff	1-0-0-1
George Gruber	1-0-0-0		
Alcinda Gold	0-0-0-1	George Johnson	1-0-0-3
		Herod Jenkins	1-0-0-1
Whiting Hamilton	1-0-0-2	Sol R. Jackson	1-0-0-1
Henry D. Hooe	2-0-0-3	Mathew Jones	3-0-1-7
Henry Horner	1-0-0-1	Reuben Jordan	1-0-1-3
Edwin Hart	2-0-1-2	John Joliffe	1-1-6-14
Abram Huyett	1-0-0-3	John Johnston	1-0-0-0
John Huyett	2-0-0-7	Thos Jordan	1-0-0-0
Saml Huyett	1-0-3-5	Doct. R. R. Jordan	1-0-1-2
James Harris	2-1-4-12	Thomas Jackson	1-5-14-10
Doct. J. Hay	1-5-15-20	Jane Jackson	0-0-1-0
Thomas Hiett	3-0-0-5	Jacob Isler	5-1-4-2
Levi Hiett	1-0-1-10	David Jenkins	1-0-0-0
Isaac J. Hite	1-1-12-19	Revd. A. Jones	1-1-3-1
James M. Hite	1-2-5-7	Chas R. Johnson	1-0-0-1
Wm T. Helm	1-0-5-8	Washington Johnston	1-0-0-0
Wm Hummer	2-0-0-3	Thomas Jones	1-0-0-1
Saml Heflybour	1-0-3-7	Albert Johnson	1-0-0-0
George Heflybour	2-0-3-13	Dr. J. J. Janey	1-0-2-1
John Hay	1-0-3-1	Thomas Jenkins	1-0-0-4
Wm Holtsclaw	2-0-0-2	Richard Johnson	1-0-0-0
Richard Hardesty	3-0-5-14	Elias Johns	1-0-0-0
Bushrod Hooff	1-0-0-1		
Mary Howard	0-1-2-0	John B. Kerfoot	1-2-4-8
Philip Haunsucker	1-0-0-1	Humphrey Keys	0-0-0-0
George Harris	0-0-7-7	James C. Kennan	1-0-1-0
Abby Hopkins	0-1-1-0	Saml Keane	0-0-0-1
Alexander Holtzclaw	1-0-0-1	Franklin J. Kerfoot	1-0-9-17
Joseph Hoof	1-0-0-0	Thomas Kennerly	1-0-0-0
Levi Hiett & J. Bell	0-1-1-0	George Knight	3-1-7-15
Henry Hunsucker	1-0-0-0	George Kitchen	1-0-6-8

Clarke County, Virginia Personal Property Tax Lists 1836-1853
1843

Wm C. Kerfoot	1-3-8-16	George Longerbeam	1-0-0-0
George L. Kerfoot	1-2-9-14	James Lloyd	1-0-0-0
Benjamin Kent	2-0-0-0	Charles Leech	2-1-0-1
Doct. R. Kownslar	1-1-2-2	Sarah Longerbeam	2-0-0-3
John N. T. G. Keene	1-0-0-1	Benjamin Lane	1-0-0-2
John Kable	2-0-3-1	George F. Ludwick	1-1-2-3
Wm F. Knight	1-1-2-5	Saml Lloyd	1-0-0-1
Nicholas Kriser	1-0-0-0		
Elizabeth Knight	0-0-0-1	Shederick Killion	1-0-0-0
John Kenneford	1-0-0-0		
John Knight	2-0-0-4	Benjamin Lacey	1-0-4-3
George & Wm		Edgar Lanham	1-0-0-1
Kerfoot	0-1-5-8	Bushrod Longerbeam	1-0-0-1
Lydia Kerfoot	0-0-3-2	Squire Lee	1-0-0-1
Middleton Keeler	1-0-0-0	Alfred Logan	1-0-0-4
Wm C. Kennerly	2-1-2-3	Elizabeth Lanham	0-0-0-1
		Enos Lanham	1-0-0-1
George Lowry	1-0-0-0	Saml Lanham	1-0-0-0
Eugene Lynch	1-1-6-7		
Henry Lloyd	1-0-0-3	Peter McMurray	1-1-2-7
Charles Lucius	1-1-3-7	Wm McCoy	1-0-1-1
John Lock	1-0-0-8	Albert McCormick	1-0-0-2
John D. & J. W. Larue	2-0-4-8	Warner Muse	1-0-0-5
Wm Littleton	2-0-1-5	John J. Munroe	1-1-3-8
Catharine Lock	1-0-0-2	John Maddox	2-0-3-5
Wm Lock	1-0-0-6	Prov McCormick Jr.	1-1-0-1
Fanny Larue	0-4-4-7	James Michell	2-0-5-6
Louisa Littleton	2-1-0-2	Wm D. McGuier	1-0-10-15
Saml Larue	2-2-11-17	David H. McGuier	1-0-7-10
Wm Longerbeam	1-0-0-1	Otway McCormick	3-0-10-12
Washington Lee	1-0-0-1	Wm Morgan	1-1-7-11
R. H. Little	6-1-8-17	John McCloy	1-0-0-1
John Louthan	4-0-2-1	Francis B. Meade	1-1-6-9
Lorenzo Lewis	1-5-27-30	Louisa W. Meade	1-0-5-8
James M. Lindsay	4-0-2-0	Philip N. Meade	1-2-4-9
John B. Larue	1-1-13-24	Wm Meade Jr.	1-0-2-6
Clarisa Larue	0-0-2-1	Miss Mary Meade	0-0-1-0
Sarah Lindsay	0-0-2-0	Thomas McCormick	1-0-8-10
John Lloyd	1-0-0-2	John Marts Senr.	1-0-0-2

Clarke County, Virginia Personal Property Tax Lists 1836-1853
1843

Saml & Doct. McCormick	3-0-13-19	Alexander Mason	1-0-0-0
George McCormick	2-0-7-12	John E. McCauley	1-0-0-0
Levi Marquiss	1-0-0-5	Miss Lucy McCormick	0-0-0-1
Jesse P. Mercer	1-0-0-0	Thos W. McCormick	1-0-0-1
John Manes	1-0-0-2	Wm Niswanger	2-0-0-5
John & James Mitchum	2-0-0-2	Hugh M. Nelson	1-2-11-15
Benjamin Morgan	1-1-16-25	Ann T. Neille	1-1-3-8
Elizabeth Morgan	0-1-4-0	George H. Norris	4-1-11-13
Stephen R. Mount	2-0-2-3	Philip Nelson	1-3-16-14
Col. Franck McCormick	1-1-7-17	Thomas F. Nelson	1-3-11-18
Charles McCormick	2-8-25-48	James H. Neville	1-0-2-2
Susan Marshall	0-1-3-8	Joseph Noble	1-1-0-0
John Marshall	1-0-1-3	Miss Abby Nelson	0-0-3-0
Jesse McConaha	1-0-0-1	Wm Nelson	1-0-2-4
Lucy Mustin	0-0-3-1	P. N. Nicholas	0-0-2-0
Alexander Marshall	1-1-0-2	Joseph M. Nicklin	1-0-3-2
John McPhillin	2-0-0-3	Frank Nelson	1-1-1-2
Wm Mason	1-0-0-1	George R. Newman	1-0-1-2
Jacob May	1-0-0-0	John W. Owen	1-0-3-4
John Morgan	1-1-5-17	Elizabeth Orear	0-2-7-8
George L. McCormick	2-0-0-1	Enoch Orear	1-1-5-6
Lawyer P. McCormick Sr.	1-2-8-16	George Orear	1-0-3-10
Charles & Saml McCormick	0-1-5-9	James A. Osborn	2-0-0-3
Benjamin F. Mayhew	1-0-0-0	Wm Orr	1-0-0-1
Isaac J. Manuel	1-0-0-0	George Pultz	1-0-0-1
W. J. Maxwell	2-0-1-4	John E. Page	1-3-13-18
Sylvanus More	1-0-0-0	John Pages Est.	0-1-21-5
James Murphy	1-0-0-1	Mrs. E. M. Page	0-1-1-0
Revd. Wm Meade	1-0-0-1	John Page	1-3-7-13
Wm Marts	1-0-0-0	Mann R. Page	1-1-10-22
Stephen Marlow	1-0-0-1	Isaac Pidgeon	2-0-0-4
Amishadai [sic] More	3-0-2-6	John Pierce Sr.	1-1-3-8
Rebecca S. Meade	0-0-2-2	R. P. Page	1-3-18-20
		James M. Pine	1-0-0-1
		Mary C. Page	0-2-6-8
		John Page of North End	1-0-3-2

Clarke County, Virginia Personal Property Tax Lists 1836-1853
1843

Joseph E. Peyton	2-0-0-3	George Reno	2-0-0-2
Paul Pierce	1-2-5-8	Isaac Ramey	2-0-0-6
Richard E. Parkers Est.	1-0-5-9	Mat Rust	1-0-2-6
		Miss Betty Roots	1-0-1-0
John W. Page	2-1-10-14	Wm Reily	0-0-0-0
John Pierce Jr.	1-2-0-5	James Russell	1-0-1-3
John Padgett	1-0-0-0	Betsy Romine	0-1-0-0
Henry Peters	1-0-1-4	Jacob B. Ritter	1-1-0-1
James Puller	1-0-0-0		
Peter Mc Pierce	1-1-1-6	Richard M. Sydnor	1-0-1-0
Thornton P. Pendleton	2-0-18-31	Carter Shepherd	1-0-0-1
		Mrs. Susan Smith	0-0-1-0
Washington Prichett	1-0-0-2	Joseph Stewart	1-0-0-0
McFarland Puller	1-0-0-0	Col. J. H. Sowers	2-0-0-6
Conrad Pope	1-0-0-0	Edward J. Smith	2-3-19-22
Robert F. Page & Brother	2-0-2-7	Wm D. Smith	1-1-4-10
		Joseph Smith	1-0-0-3
		Wm Sowers	2-3-6-10
Richard Ridgeway	2-0-0-9	Joseph Shepherd	1-2-5-10
Wm Reed	1-0-0-4	Champ Shepherd	1-0-2-2
Jonas Ridgeway	1-0-0-10	Edwd Sheckles	1-0-0-4
Thomas W. Raynolds	8-1-10-6	Thomas Shumate	1-1-2-7
Bennett Russell	1-0-7-9	John W. Sowers	1-3-3-12
Miss E. Royster	0-0-1-0		
Mat W. Royston	1-0-2-7	John Richardson	1-0-0-1
Peter Royston	1-0-0-1		
John Roush	1-0-1-1	Wm G. Steele	1-0-0-0
Uriah B. Royston	1-0-1-6	Danl W. Sowers	2-1-10-17
John Reed	1-0-0-1	Saml Stipe	1-1-3-6
Ann Redman	0-0-0-0	James Sowers	1-2-13-13
Solomon Redman	1-0-0-5	Thomas Sprint	3-0-0-1
George Rutter	1-0-0-0	Emanuel Showers	4-1-1-0
Danl B. Richards Jr.	1-1-0-2	Adam Shipe	1-0-0-0
Saml B. Redman	1-0-0-2	Barnett Smallwood	1-0-0-1
Addison Romine	2-0-1-8	Fielding L. Sowers	1-1-3-10
James Ryan	2-0-1-1	P. D. Shepherd	1-1-4-7
Doct. R. C. Randolph	1-1-13-20	Doct. P. Smith	1-4-18-26
Jane Richardson	2-0-0-1	Col. T. Smith	4-3-13-17
John Russell	1-0-0-0	Wm R. Seevers	1-1-3-3

Clarke County, Virginia Personal Property Tax Lists 1836-1853
1843

Kerfoot Sowers Est.	0-1-6-14	Mrs. H. Taylor	0-0-2-2
John Stewart	3-0-0-4	Greenberry	
Danl A. Sowers	1-1-7-13	Thompson	2-0-0-2
Elizabeth Strother	0-2-5-5	David Timberlake	1-0-0-1
John Shafer	1-0-0-1	Harrison Thompson	1-0-0-1
Jackson Shafer	1-0-0-1	Doct. Saml Taylor	1-1-13-11
Burr Smallwood	1-0-0-1	Ben Thompson Jr.	2-0-0-3
Wm Stillions	2-0-0-1	Col. Joseph Tuley	1-6-25-22
Simon Stickles	1-0-0-3	John Trussell	1-1-4-5
George Smedley	2-0-0-2	Wm Timberlake	0-0-2-0
Conrad Swarts	1-0-0-0	John B. Taylor	7-2-10-22
Revd. A. Shieras	1-0-1-1	[Note:] Add to Mrs. Hannah	
Danl H. Sowers	1-0-5-12	Taylors acct $10.50 for tax on	
H. & C. Shepherd	1-0-1-0	In[tere]st of money Loaned	
Mary Scroggins	0-0-1-1	Wm Trenary	1-0-1-2
Henry Shepherd	1-0-0-1	Wm Tinsman	2-0-0-1
Wm H. Seevers	1-0-0-1	Moses Trussel	2-0-0-5
George Strother	1-0-0-1	Nimrod Trussell	1-0-0-4
James W. Smith	1-0-1-2	James Tansell	1-0-0-1
Lewis A. Smith	1-0-1-2	John A. Thompson	1-0-3-2
Erasmus E. Shipes Est.	0-0-2-0	James W. Timberlake	1-2-5-12
James Shackleford	1-0-1-0	Enoch Triplett	1-0-0-1
Mary E. Shirely	1-2-5-9	Mary Trinary	0-0-0-0
Henry Severs	1-1-0-4	Bushrod Taylor	0-0-4-9
Abram Shipe	2-0-0-0	Robert Tapscott	1-0-1-1
James Strother	1-0-0-1		
Joseph Stickles	1-0-0-3	John Vanclief	2-0-0-6
John Shell	1-0-0-1	Jacob Vanmeter	1-0-0-6
Stephen Shores	1-0-0-0	Joseph Vincent	2-0-1-1
John Shiff	0-0-2-0	Wm Violett	1-0-0-0
Wm Turner	1-0-0-0		
Math R.		Wm Willingham	1-0-0-1
Throckmorton	1-0-0-1	Allen Williams	1-0-11-18
Jesse Taylor	2-0-0-3	J. J. Williams	1-1-7-10
Abigail Tanquary	0-0-1-2	Timothy Wilcox	1-0-0-1
R. M. S. Timberlake	2-2-7-12	James Wigginton	1-0-0-1
David Tristler	1-0-1-4	John Wood	1-0-0-0
Adam Towner	2-0-0-0	Francis H. Whiting	1-0-3-8

Clarke County, Virginia Personal Property Tax Lists 1836-1853
1843

J. W. Ware &		Henry Weaver	1-0-0-0
Mrs. Stribling	1-3-19-24	Nath B. Whiting	1-0-6-13
Lucinda Washington	0-1-2-2	Ephraim Watson	2-0-0-8
J. G. Wade &		Sydnor B. Windham	1-0-0-1
Brothers	3-0-0-1	Thomas Woods	1-0-0-1
H. T. Wheat	2-1-1-2	Benjamin Wigginton	1-0-1-1
Hezekiah Wiely	1-0-0-1	John Wilson	1-0-0-0
Saml Wiely	1-0-0-1	George B. West	1-0-0-0
James Wiely	1-0-0-1	Joseph A. Williamson	1-2-8-14
John Willingham	1-0-0-1	Henry Washington	1-0-2-2
Alexander Wood	1-0-0-2	Wm Wood	1-0-0-1
Miss E. W.		Albert Whittington	1-0-0-0
Washington	0-0-1-0	Thos C. Windham	1-0-0-1
Leroy P. Williams	2-2-6-10	John W. Ware	1-0-0-0
Wm P. Wigginton	1-0-1-1	Wm Willis	1-0-0-0
Francis B. Whiting	3-3-19-14		
Wm W. Whiting	1-0-1-2	George Young	1-0-0-0
Obed Willingham	1-0-0-0	Simeon Yowell	1-1-0-0
Wm Wise	1-0-0-0	S. S. Yeakles Est.	0-0-0-0
Bennet Wood	1-0-0-0		

Clarke County, Virginia Personal Property Tax Lists 1836-1853
1843

Free Negroes in Clarke County

Columns: 1) free males, 2) horses, 3) clocks, 4) watches

John Diggs	1-0-0-0	Nancy at BVille	0-0-0-0
Wily Finch	1-0-0-0	Phil Martin	1-1-0-0
Nancy Mash	0-0-0-0	Sally Fields	0-0-0-0
Mary Parrot	0-0-0-0	Alice Green	0-0-0-0
Tom Gray	1-0-0-0	Sally J. Richardson	0-0-0-0
& 1 slave		Jonathan _____	1-0-0-0
Mariah Dandridge	0-0-0-0	Burwell Cook	1-1-0-0
Nancy Parker	0-0-0-0	M. J. Gray	0-0-0-0
Ann Davis	0-0-0-0	Moses Gray	1-0-0-0
Scimeon Parker	1-0-0-0	Ann Wells	0-0-0-0
Mary Martin	0-0-0-0	Ellen Smith	0-0-0-0
Ann Cook	0-0-0-0	Mowen Harris	1-1-0-0
George Ranson	1-0-0-0	Wm Robertson	1-1-0-0
George Wells	1-0-0-0	to be pd for by Alfred Logan	
John Clifton	2-0-0-0		
Ann Clifton	0-0-0-0	Wm Graham	1-0-1-0
Milly Martin	0-0-0-0	Isaac _____	1-0-0-0
Washington Hall	1-0-0-0	George Lee	1-0-0-0
Jack Adams	1-0-0-0	to be pd for by Wm Reed	
Frank Irvin	2-2-0-0	Charles Thornton	1-1-0-1
to be paid for by		Jacob Johnson	1-0-0-0
S. B. T. Caldwell		to be pd for by	
Spence Johnson	1-0-0-0	John Maddox	
Wm Wheeler	1-0-0-0	John Johnson	2-1-0-0

Add to this for tax on Interest of Money

   Mrs. Margret Funston
   Gold watch of Doct. Nunn & horse
   James W. Raynolas [sic], horse
   A. H. Evans' horse
   John Hay, tax on income
   Wm K. Sowers, tax on income
   Hannah Taylor, tax not charged to her

Clarke County, Virginia Personal Property Tax Lists 1836-1853

1844

[Instead of numbers, some men are referenced with "back of book," although nothing was found for them on the last pages for the year on the microfilm. No lincesses were recorded this year.]

Columns: 1) white males over 16 years, 2) slaves above 12 years, 3) horses

Robert Ashby Senr.	2-0-3	John W. Anderson		
Mason Anderson	1-1-1	Wm Benson &		
David H. Allen	5-31-44	Mat Royston		
John Alexander	1-13-16	H. M. Bowen		
Wm C. Alexander	1-9-11	Margaret Bennett		
Augusta Athey	2-0-4	Nat Burwell Jr.	1-10-14	
Wm Ambrows	2-0-5	Wm C. Benson	1-2-5	
Buckner Ashby	1-11-16	John Burchell	2-4-10	
Joseph Anderson	4-2-8	Archibald Bowen	2-3-10	
Nancy Allen	1-3-6	Hiram O. Bell	1-0-0	
Algernon S. Allen	1-11-15	Phineas Bowen	2-4-12	
John Alexander	2-0-1	Francis O. Byrd	1-11-13	
John Ashby	2-0-4	Philip Berlin	1-3-4	
Robert Ashby Jr.	1-0-1	George C. Blakemore	1-13-15	
Martin Ashby	1-0-2	John Bowlin	1-0-0	
Thos H. Alexander	3-0-3	Neille Barnett	1-3-5	
Nimrod Ashby	1-0-1	Amos A. Bonham	2-5-11	
George B. Ashby	1-0-1	Danl S. Bonham	1-5-9	
John Ambrows	3-0-9	James Bogs	1-0-0	
Wm Ashby	1-2-0	John Brownley	2-15-16	
David F. Armstrong	1-0-1	Wm Baker	1-6-4	
George Aikins	1-0-0	Isaac Berlin	2-1-2	
James Allison	1-0-0	Strother Bell	1-2-0	
Saml Arner [?]	1-0-0	Robert Burchell	1-4-8	
Evan P. Anderson	1-1-0	H. W. Brabham	1-0-0	
		Squire Bell	1-2-5	
[Nothing marked for the next 6 names on this page.]		Philip Burwell	1-30-17	
		John W. Byrd	1-11-10	
Wm T. Allen		Thomas Brigs	8-8-16	
Arthur N. Allen		Lewis Brumley	3-0-8	

Clarke County, Virginia Personal Property Tax Lists 1836-1853
1844

John D. Barr	1-0-1		Thomas Cornwell	1-0-1
James W. Beck	1-0-2		John H. Campbell	0-0-0
John C. Bonham	1-7-7		Alfred Castleman	1-5-10
Nat Burwell Senr.	1-45-39		Frederick Clopton	1-6-10
Saml Bonham	1-14-14		George F. Calmese	1-5-8
Col. James Bell	1-9-18		Wm Carrington	3-2-2
Lewis & James Berlin	2-2-2		Wm Carper	1-0-2
Robert E. Byrd	0-1-1		Ambrows Crawford	1-0-1
Robert Ben	1-1-4		Robert A. Colston	1-4-13
Wm Berry	3-13-12		Wm H. Colston	1-2-6
George H. Burwell	2-45-33		Elizabeth K. Carter	1-1-6
James Bulger	1-0-0		John Copenhaur	2-3-9
Saml Briarly	2-7-10		Miriam & Sarah	
Christian Bowser	3-0-1		Catlett	1-7-14
John Blue	1-2-7		James H. Clarke	1-3-1
Doct. A. Brown	1-4-2		Thomas H. Crow	3-6-3
Napolean Balthop	1-0-1		Wm A. Castleman	1-4-10
Russell Brackett	1-0-0		Alfred Clevinger	1-4-7
Martin Berlin	1-0-8		John Cooper	1-0-0
Jesse Bowen	1-0-0		Elizabeth Crampton	0-3-3
Samuel Bowles	1-0-4		James Castleman	
Abram Beevers	1-0-3		back of book	
James Bell	1-0-2		S. B. T. Caldwell	3-2-2
Wm Berlin	2-2-2		Martha P. Castleman	2-8-5
John R. Bell	2-1-0		Thomas Carter	1-18-12
Adam Barr	1-0-1		Presley Cooper	1-0-2
Benjamin Barr	1-0-0		Parkerson Corder	1-0-2
Wm Brawner	1-0-0		Fielding Cornwell	0-0-0
Andrew Billmyre	1-0-1		John Carroll	2-0-3
Richard Billmyre	1-0-0		John Carpenter	2-3-6
Jesse Butler	1-0-0		Dabney Cauthorn	1-0-0
George Bowlen	1-0-0		Elizabeth N. Carter	1-2-1
Danl Butler	1-0-1		James Carter	1-0-0
John S. Burns	1-2-6		Edward Cornwell	2-0-1
Juliet Boston	1-1-0		John Coleman	1-0-2
Emily Boston	0-0-0		Frederick Carper [?]	1-0-3
Nancy Boston	0-0-0		Robert Y. Conrad	0-0-0
T. T. Byrds Est.	0-1-1		David Clevinger	1-0-5
			Thos Clevinger	1-3-8

Clarke County, Virginia Personal Property Tax Lists 1836-1853
1844

George S. Christy	2-0-1		John B. Earle	2-10-20
James N. Corbin	2-0-1		Hiram P. Evans	2-1-2
Aaron Chamblin	1-0-4		Jacob Enders	1-2-5
Michael Copenhaur	1-0-1		Jacob W. Everheart	1-0-1
John G. Chapman	1-0-0		John Evans	1-0-1
Andrew Cage	1-0-0			
Mrs. Ury Castleman	0-9-7		Edward Franks	1-0-0
Elisha Carver	1-0-0		Jesse Furr	0-0-2
Jacob Clink	1-0-0		George Fyst	2-2-8
Daniel Coleman	1-0-1		Doct. John	
Stephen D.			Fauntleroy	1-4-3
Castleman	1-7-9		Doct. Allen Funston	1-11-14
Wm Cooper	1-0-0		John Forster	1-1-7
James Carper	2-2-6		Jane H. Forster	0-2-0
			John Furlow	1-0-0
John Dermont	1-3-5		Moses Furr	4-0-8
Peter Dermont	1-4-0		Mrs. Martha Forster	0-3-1
Thomas G. Dowdle	2-1-1		George Farnsworth	1-0-4
Wm Deakle	3-2-0		Archibald Flemming	1-3-3
Saml Davis	1-0-0		John D. Furgerson Sr.	2-11-8
James Davis	2-0-0		James Furr	1-0-1
John Drish	1-0-0		John D. Furgerson	1-0-1
Michael Dermont	1-5-7		Wm Fowler	1-0-5
Baalis Davis	1-3-1		Benjamin Franks	1-0-2
Benjamin Downing	1-0-2		Washington	
James Downing	1-0-2		Furgerson	1-1-8
Thomas Duke	1-0-0		Martin Feltner	1-0-1
James Dorin	1-0-1		Joseph Fleming	1-0-1
Saml Dobbins	1-0-0		John Furr	1-0-0
George W.			Thomas Fowler	1-0-1
Diffendaffer	1-0-0		Miss Ann Funston	
Davis & G. W.			Minor Furr	2-0-4
Gilkerson	0-0-0		Ann Farnsworth	
Harrison Dorsey	0-0-0			
			Richard Green	1-3-5
Charles Eckhardt	1-0-1		Thomas E. Gold	2-9-15
Henry Edwards	1-0-2		Wm Graves	3-0-6
Wm G. Everheart	2-1-5		Harrison Gordon	1-0-4
John Eleyett	1-1-2		George Gordon	2-0-1

Clarke County, Virginia Personal Property Tax Lists 1836-1853
1844

James Green	1-5-7		Thomas Hiett	3-1-6
John Gant	1-7-8		Levi Hiett	1-1-1
Stephen J. Gant	1-2-6		Isaac J. Hite	1-14-19
Mrs. Rebecca Grogan	0-3-3		James M. Hite	2-6-7
Edward Gorman	1-0-1		Wm T. Helm	1-2-5
Thomas Grubs	1-1-0		Wm Hummer	1-0-3
Joseph George	1-1-3		Saml Heflybour	1-2-9
John S. Gordon	3-1-7		John Hay	1-1-1
John Gordon	2-0-5		George Heflybour	1-2-5
James V. Glass	2-8-10		John Hay	1-1-1
Henry N. Grigsby	1-3-11		Wm Holtsclaw	2-0-1
Dandridge Garrison	1-0-1		Richard Hardesty	3-5-13
John Grant	1-2-5		Bushrod Hooff	1-0-1
Wm Gourley	0-0-5		Mary Howard	0-3-0
Emanuel Garmong	1-0-1		Philip Host	0-0-0
Saml Grubs	1-0-0		George Hunsucker	0-0-0
Nimrod Glasscock	2-0-3		Philip Haunsucker	2-1-1
Abram Grim	1-0-0		George Harris	1-3-8
Richard N. Green	1-5-9		Miss Abby Hopkins	0-2-0
George W. Green	1-7-10		Alexander Holtzclaw	1-0-0
John L. Grant	1-2-5		Levi Hiett & J. Bell	0-2-7
James Gibs	1-0-0		Wm B. Harris	1-6-5
Nancy Galloway	1-1-0		Edward Handle	2-1-0
Martin Gant	1-2-4		Grafton Hillyard	1-0-1
George W. Grubs	1-1-0		James Y. Harris	1-2-6
Wm B. Grubs	1-1-1		Wm Harris	1-0-1
Danl Gold	0-0-0		Cornelious Hooff	1-0-0
G. W. Gant	0-0-0		James Hummer	1-0-0
			Richard S. Hardesty	1-2-4
Lucy Harrison	0-0-0		Thomas Hughes	1-1-0
Whiting Hamilton	1-0-2		Robert Haney	1-0-1
Henry D. Hooe	2-0-2		John Hillyard	1-0-1
Henry Horner	1-0-0			
Edwin Hart	2-1-5		George Johnson	2-0-3
Abram Huyett	2-0-4		Herod Jenkins	1-0-1
John Huyett	2-0-6		Solomon R. Jackson	1-1-2
Saml Huyett	1-4-6		Mathew Jones	3-2-8
James Harris	2-2-9		Reuben Jordan	1-2-3
Doct. James Hay	1-18-20		John Joliffe	1-6-11

Clarke County, Virginia Personal Property Tax Lists 1836-1853
1844

John Johnston	1-0-0	George & Wm	
Thomas Jordan	1-0-1	Kerfoot	0-7-8
Doct. R. R. Jordan	1-1-2	Mrs. Lydia Kerfoot	0-2-3
		Middleton Keeler	1-0-0
Jacob Isler	4-7-5	Wm C. Kennerly	2-2-1
		Joseph Kline	1-1-0
Rev. Wm G. H. Jones	1-4-1	John B. Kerfoot	1-4-9
Charles R. Johnson	1-0-1		
Washington Johnson	1-0-1	Franklin Littleton	0-1-0
Thomas Jones	2-1-2	George Lowry	1-0-0
Albert Johnson	1-0-0	Henry Lloyd	2-0-3
Dr. J. J. Janey	1-2-2	Charles Lucius	1-2-5
Thomas Jenkins	1-0-2	John Lock	1-0-6
Richard Johnson	1-0-1	J. D. & J. W. Larue	2-4-8
Elias Johns	1-0-0	Wm Littleton	2-2-6
Joseph M. Joliffe	2-0-3	Catharine Lock	1-0-3
Abraham Jeter	1-2-2	Wm Lock	1-0-5
		Fanny Larue	0-8-7
George H. Isler	0-0-0	Washington Lee	1-0-2
		Charles Littleton	1-2-2
Saml G. Kneller	0-0-0	Charles Leech Jr.	1-0-1
James C. Kennan	1-1-0	Doct. R. H. Little	3-9-11
Doct. F. J. Kerfoot	1-11-15	John Louthan	4-2-1
Avry Keane	0-0-1	Lorenzo Lewis	1-34-30
Revd. Thomas		Saml Larue	2-14-15
Kennerly	1-22-33	John B. Larue	1-15-26
George Knight	1-10-15	Mrs. Clarisa Larue	0-1-1
George Kitchen	1-5-9	John Lloyd	1-0-2
Wm C. Kerfoot	1-10-17	George Longerbeam	1-0-1
Benjamin M. Knight	1-0-2	James Lloyd	1-0-0
George L. Kerfoot	2-12-14	Benjamin B. Lane	1-0-1
Benjamin Kent	1-0-0	George F. Ludwig	2-3-3
Doct. R. Kownslar	1-3-2	Saml Lloyd	1-0-1
John N. T. G. Keane	2-1-2	Edgar Lanhan	1-0-1
John Kable	2-2-1	Charles Leech Senr.	1-0-1
Wm F. Knight	1-3-6	Alfred Logan	1-0-4
Nicholas Kriser	1-0-0	Enos Lanham	2-0-2
Mrs. Elizabeth Knight	0-0-0	Saml Lanham	1-0-0
John Kenneford	1-0-0-0	Abram Longerbeam	1-0-2

Clarke County, Virginia Personal Property Tax Lists 1836-1853
1844

Elizabeth Lanham	0-0-1		Jesse McConaha	1-0-1
James Lanham	1-0-1		Lucy Mustin	0-1-1
Wm Longerbeam	1-0-1		Alexander Marshall	1-0-2
John Lewis	0-0-0		John McPhillin	2-1-4
Fisher A. Lewis	0-0-0		Wm Mason	1-0-1
			John Morgan	1-6-11
Peter McMurray	1-2-7		George L.	
Saml McCormick	1-0-0		McCormick	2-0-2
John J. Munroe	1-2-5		Province	
John Maddox	1-4-8		McCormick Sr.	1-10-13
Province McCormick	1-2-3		Charles & Saml	
Albert McCormick	1-0-2		McCormick	0-6-12
James Michell	1-6-7		Benjamin F. Mayhew	1-0-0
Wm D. McGuire	2-9-13		John N. Meade	1-0-4
Otway McCormick	2-11-14		Mrs. Catharine	
John McCloy	1-0-1		Milton	0-0-0
Francis B. Meade	1-7-10		Isaac J. Manuel	1-0-0
Mrs. L. W. Meade	1-0-6-5		Wm J. Maxwell	1-2-4
Philip N. Meade	1-8-10		James Murphy	1-0-2
Wm Meade Jr.	0-0-0		Revd. Wm. Meade	1-0-1
Miss Mary Meade	0-2-0		Wm Marts	1-0-0
Thomas McCormick	1-9-11		Stephen Marlow	1-0-1
John Marts Senr.	1-0-1		Amishadai More	2-4-7
Doct. & Saml			Rebecca S. Meade	Back
McCormick	4-12-20			of Book
George McCormick	2-8-12		Alexander Mason	1-0-0
Levi Marquess	2-0-4		John G. McCauley	1-0-1
Jesse P. Mercer	1-0-1		Thomas W.	
John & James			McCormick	1-0-0
Mitchum	2-0-3		Violett Mayers	1-0-2
Col. B. Morgan	1-18-28		Saml Moreland	1-0-3
Mrs. Elizabeth			David H. McGuire	1-7-10
Morgan	0-9-9		Alfred P. Moore	1-0-0
Stephen R. Mount	1-2-2		Thomas Murphy	1-0-0
Col. Franck				
McCormick	1-8-12		Wm Niswanger	3-0-6
Charles McCormick	2-32-48		Hugh M. Nelson	1-10-16
Susan Marshall	0-4-9		Ann T. Neille	0-5-10
John Marshall	1-1-5		Philip Nelson	1-18-13

Clarke County, Virginia Personal Property Tax Lists 1836-1853
1844

Thomas F. Nelson	3-17-22	Peter Mc Pierce	1-4-7
James H. Neville	1-2-1	Thornton P.	
Joseph Noble	1-1-0	Pendleton	2-17-25
Miss Abby Nelson	0-3-0	Farland Puller	1-0-0
Doct. Wm Nelson	1-2-3	Conrad Pope	2-0-0
Joseph M. Nicklin	1-3-2	Calvin Puller	1-0-1
George R. Newman	1-1-1	Richard L. Page	
Revd. Cleveland R. Nelson	1-3-2	Richard Ridgeway	2-1-10
Doct. John M. Nunn	1-0-2	Wm Reed	1-0-6
George W. Norris	0-0-0	Thomas W. Raynolds	5-10-7
Wm Norris	2-11-14	Bennet Russell	1-8-9
		Miss E. Royster	0-1-0
John W. Owen	1-2-4	Mat W. Royston	4-0-5
Elizabeth Orear	0-9-7	Peter Royston	1-0-1
Enoch Orear	1-7-7	John Roush	1-0-1
George Orear	2-3-12	Uriah B. Royston	1-0-6
Wm Orr	1-1-0	John Reed	1-0-1
David Osborn	2-0-3	Ann Redmon	0-0-0
Mason Olliver	1-0-1	Solomon Redmon	1-1-5
		George Rutter	1-0-1
George Pultz	1-1-1	Danl B. Richards Jr.	2-0-1
John E. Page	1-10-23	Saml B. Redmon	1-1-2
John Pages Est.	0-22-5	Addison Romine	1-2-11
Mrs. E. M. Page	0-2-0	James Ryan	2-1-1
John Page	1-3-15	Doct. R. C.	
John Page Jr.	0-0-0	Randolph	1-14-20
Mann R. Page	2-11-21	John Russell	1-1-0
Isaac Pidgeon	2-0-5	Jane Richardson	1-0-1
John Pierce Sr.	1-4-8	George Reno	2-0-2
Doct. R. P. Page	1-21-19	Isaac Ramey	2-0-6
James M. Pine	1-0-1	Matthew Rust	1-3-5
Mrs. Mary C. Page	2-8-8	Miss Betty Roots	0-1-0
Joseph E. Peyton	2-0-3	Elizabeth Reily	0-3-1
Paul Pierce	1-6-9	Conrad Ringman	1-0-0
John W. Page	3-11-13	John Russell	1-0-1
John Pierce Jr.	2-3-7	John Richardson	0-0-0
John Padgett	1-0-0	John Rust	0-0-0
James Puller	1-0-0		

Clarke County, Virginia Personal Property Tax Lists 1836-1853
1844

Richard M. Sydnor	1-1-0	James Shackleford	1-0-0
Mrs. Susan Smith	0-1-0	Mary E. Shirely	3-9-10
Edward J. Smith	2-22-22	Henry Severs	1-1-6
Wm D. Smith	1-4-9	Abram Shipe	2-0-1
Joseph Smith	1-0-2	James Strother	1-0-1
Wm Sowers	1-9-10	Joseph Stickles	1-0-2
Joseph Shepherd	2-8-12	John Shell	2-0-3
Champ Shepherd	1-3-1	Henry Shepherd	1-0-1
Edwd Sheckles	1-0-4	Erasmus G. Ships Est.	0-1-0
Thomas Shumate	1-2-8	Robert Sowers	1-0-1
John W. Sowers	1-7-12	Wm H. Seevers	1-0-0
Wm G. Steele	1-0-0	Wm T. Storrow [?]	1-0-0
Danl W. Sowers	2-14-17	Thomas Shearman	0-0-0
Saml Stipe	1-4-7	David Shaul	1-3-8
James Sowers	1-12-14	Edward Street	1-0-0
Thomas Sprint	2-0-1		
Emanuel Showers	3-1-0	Timothy A. Tord [?]	1-0-0
Barnett Smallwood	1-0-1	Sarah Timberlake	1-12-12
Fielding L. Sowers	1-3-11	Wm Turner	1-0-1
P. D. Shepherd	1-5-7	Mat R. Throckmorton	1-0-1
Doct. Philip Smith	1-20-26	Abigail Tanquary	0-1-2
Col. T. Smith	4-15-16	David Tristler	1-1-7
Wm R. Seevers	1-4-4	Adam Towner	1-1-0
Kerfoot Sowers Est.	0-6-11	Mrs. Hannah Taylor	0-2-2
John Stewart	3-1-4	Greenberry Thompson	2-0-3
Danl A. Sowers	1-6-11	David Timberlake	1-0-1
Elizabeth Strother	0-8-6	Harrison Thompson	1-0-0
John Shafer	1-0-1	Doct. Saml Taylor	1-13-10
Jackson Shafer	1-0-1	Benjamin Thompson Jr.	1-0-4
Burr Smallwood	1-0-1	Col. Joseph Tuley	1-31-22
Wm Stillions	1-0-1	John Trussell	1-4-6
Simon Stickles	1-0-2	Wm Timberlake	0-2-0
George Smedley	2-0-2	Wm G. Taylor	3-12-15
Revd. A. Shieras	0-0-0	Wm Trinary	1-1-2
Danl H. Sowers	1-5-13	Wm Tinsman	1-0-1
~~Champ Shepherd~~		Moses Trussel	2-0-4
R. Sowers	1-0-1	James Tansell	1-0-3
George Strother	1-1-1		
James W. Smith	3-0-4		

Clarke County, Virginia Personal Property Tax Lists 1836-1853
1844

John A. Thompson	1-5-2	John Willingham	1-0-1
James W. Timberlake	1-7-12	Miss E. W.	
Mary Trinary	0-0-0	Washington	0-2-0
Robert Tapscott	1-1-0	Leroy P. Williams	1-8-9
Thomas W. Tinsman	1-0-1	Wm P. Wigginton	1-2-2
Monteval Tinsman	1-0-1	Francis B. Whiting	3-21-14
Ludwell Tinsman	1-0-2	Wm W. Whiting	1-1-2
Saml Tinsman	1-0-2	Obed Willingham	1-0-0
Coleman Thompson	1-0-0	Wm Wise	1-0-0
		Bennet Wood	1-0-0
John Vanclief	2-0-5	Henry Weaver	1-0-0
Jacob Vanmeter	0-0-1	Nathaniel B. Whiting	1-6-12
Joseph Vincent	1-0-1	Ephraim Watson	2-1-7
Wm Violett	2-0-0	Sidnor B. Windham	2-0-1
John Vincent	1-1-2	Thomas Wood	1-0-1
		Doct. B. Wigginton	1-2-1
A. S. Tidball	1-6-9	John Wilson	2-0-1
R. M. S. Timberlake		Joseph A. Williamson	1-10-13
Est.	0-0-0	Doct. H. Washington	1-2-2
Joseph Tidball	0-0-0	Wm Wood	1-0-1
		Albert Whittington	1-0-0
Wm Willingham	1-0-1	Thos C. Windham	1-0-1
Allen Williams	1-12-16	Thomas E.	
Timothy Wilcox	2-0-1	Woodward	1-0-2
James Wigginton	1-0-1	James W. Ware	1-0-1
John Wood	1-0-1	James Wright	1-0-0
Francis H. Whiting	1-3-9	James V. Wier	1-3-2
J. W. Ware &		Harrison White	0-0-0
Mrs. Stribling	1-26-22	Charles W. Wood	0-0-0
Lucinda Washington	0-3-2	P. Williams	0-0-0
J. G. Wade &		Lydia Williams	0-0-0
Brothers	2-0-1		
H. T. Wheat	1-2-2	George Young	1-0-0
Hezekiah Wiley	1-0-1	Simeon Yowell	1-0-0
Saml Wiley	1-0-1		
James Wiley	1-0-1	Jacob Hefflybour	1-1-6

Clarke County, Virginia Personal Property Tax Lists 1836-1853
1844

Free Negroes in Clarke County, Owners of Property

Columns: 1) slaves, 2) horses, 3) common silver watches, 4) clocks, wood

John Diggs	1-0-0-0	~~Gabriel Williams~~		
Frank Irvin	0-2-0-0	Slaves hiring themselves	4	
Philip Martin	0-1-0-0	Owners of Property		
Burwell Cook	0-1-0-0	Thomas Whiting	0-1-1-0	
Mowen Harris	1-1-0-0	John Fenin	0-0-0-1	
Wm Graham	0-0-1-0	Alfred Fox	0-0-0-1	
John Jackson	0-1-0-0			

[After recapitulation, at the bottom of page]

James Castlemam	3-20-21	W. W. Meade	1-2-3
R. S. Meade	0-3-0		

Clarke County, Virginia Personal Property Tax Lists 1836-1853

1845

Columns: 1) white males above 16 years, 2) slaves above 16 years, 3) slaves 12-16 years, 4) horses, mares, mules & colts.

Name	Values	Name	Values
Robert Ashby Senr.	1-0-0-2	Nathaniel Burwell Jr.	1-10-1-16
Mason Anderson	1-1-0-1	Wm C. Benson	1-3-0-5
David H. Allen	4-22-6-44	John Burchell	2-5-0-9
John Alexander Senr.	0-0-0-0	Archibald Bowen	2-2-1-7
Wm C. Alexander	0-0-0-0	Hiram O. Bell	1-0-0-0
Augusta Athey	1-0-0-3	Phineas Bowen	2-3-2-10
Wm Ambrows	2-1-0-4	Francis O. Byrd	1-1-9-13
Buckner Ashby	1-10-2-14	Philip Berlin	1-3-0-3
Joseph Anderson	4-2-0-9	George C. Blakemore	1-7-3-15
Nancy Allen	1-2-0-5	John Bowlin	1-0-0-0
Algernon S. Allen	1-10-1-15	Neille Barnett	1-3-0-5
John Ashby	2-0-0-3	Danl S. Bonham	1-3-1-8
Robert Ashby Jr.	1-0-0-1	James Bogs	1-0-0-0
Martin Ashby	1-0-0-1	John Brownley	2-14-1-15
Thomas H. Alexander	3-0-0-2	Wm Baker	1-4-2-3
Nimrod Ashby	1-0-0-1	Isaac Berlin	2-1-0-2
George B. Ashby	1-0-0-2	Strother Bell	1-0-0-0
John Ambrows	4-0-0-11	Robert Burchell	1-3-1-9
Wm Ashby	1-1-0-0	H. W. Brabham	1-0-0-0
Thomas Ashby	1-0-0-1	Squire Bell	1-1-0-5
John W. Ashby	1-0-0-1	Philip Burwell	1-25-5-15
David F. Armstrong	1-0-0-1	John W. Byrd	1-10-0-10
George Aikins	1-0-0-3	Thomas Briggs	9-5-1-20
James Allison	1-0-0-0	John Brumley	3-0-0-7
Saml Armer	1-0-0-0	John D. Barr	1-0-0-1
Evan P. Anderson	1-1-0-1	James W. Beck	1-0-0-3
John W. Anderson	1-0-0-1	John C. Bonham	1-4-0-6
Austin C. Ashby	1-0-0-2	Nathaniel Burwell Senr.	1-39-3-41
John Alexander Jr.	1-0-0-1	Saml Bonham	2-11-3-16
John Allison	1-0-0-0	Col. James Bell	1-7-5-18
Eli Anderson	1-0-0-0	Lewis Berlin	1-3-0-1

Clarke County, Virginia Personal Property Tax Lists 1836-1853
1845

Name	Values	Name	Values
Isaac Bowles	1-0-0-0	Ambrows Crawford	1-0-0-1
Robert Ben	1-1-0-4	Robert A. Coltson	1-5-0-11
Wm Berry	1-13-1-10	Wm. H. Coltson	1-1-1-5
George H. Burwell	2-42-3-36	Elizabeth K. Carter	2-1-0-7
James Bulger	1-0-0-0	John Copenhaur	2-3-0-11
Saml Briarly	2-8-0-9	Miriam Catlett	1-6-0-13
Christian Bowser	3-0-1-1	James H. Clarke	2-3-0-1
John Blue	1-2-0-6	Thomas H. Crow	2-2-1-3
Doct. C. Brown	1-3-1-3	Wm A. Castleman	1-4-0-7
Napoleon Baltrip	0-0-0-0	Alfred Clevenger	1-3-1-7
Russell Brackett	1-0-0-0	John Cooper	1-0-0-2
Martin Berlin	1-0-0-7	Elizabeth Crampton	0-4-0-4
Jesse Bowen	1-0-0-1	James Castleman	3-14-4-24
Saml Bowles	1-1-0-4	Martha P. Castleman	2-8-0-4
Abram Beevers	1-0-0-3	Thomas Carter	1-4-1-7
James Bell	1-0-0-1	Presley Cooper	1-0-0-1
Wm Berlin	3-2-1-3	Parkerson Corder	1-0-0-1
Adam Barr	1-0-0-1	John Carroll	3-0-0-3
Ben Barr	1-1-0-0	John Carpenter	2-4-0-6
Richard Billmyre	2-0-0-2	Dabney Cauthorn	2-0-0-1
Jesse Butler	1-0-0-1	Elizabeth N. Carter	1-2-0-1
George Bowlin	1-0-0-0	James Carter	1-0-0-0
Jehu S. Burns	1-4-1-9	Edward Cornwell	1-0-0-1
Juliet Boston	0-0-0-0	John Coleman	1-0-0-1
Emily Boston	0-0-0-0	David Clevinger	1-0-0-7
Nancy Boston	1-1-0-1	Thomas Clevinger	1-2-1-8
T. T. Byrds Est.	1-1-0-2	George S. Christy	1-0-0-0
John R. Bell	1-3-0-7	James N. Corbin	2-0-0-4
Strother Bowen	1-1-0-0	Thomas Cornwell	1-0-0-1
Mahlon Blakley	5-4-1-3	Aaron Chamblin	1-0-0-6
Thomas W. Briggs	1-2-0-9	Michael Copenhaver	1-0-0-1
Thomas W. Burns	1-0-0-1	John G. Chapman	1-0-0-0
George W. Bartlett	1-0-0-2	Andrew Cage	1-0-0-0
		Mrs. Ury Castleman	0-9-1-8
Alfred Castleman	2-5-1-12	Elisha Carver	2-0-0-2
Frederick Clopton	1-5-0-8	Jacob Clink	1-0-0-0
George F. Calmese	1-5-0-8	Daniel Coleman	1-0-0-1
Wm Carrington	3-1-0-1	Stephen D. Castleman	1-6-1-7
Wm Carper	1-0-0-1		

Clarke County, Virginia Personal Property Tax Lists 1836-1853
1845

Wm Cooper	1-0-0-0		
James Carper	1-2-0-8	John D. Furgerson	1-4-0-6
Peter Cain	2-0-0-3	Wm Fleming	1-1-0-1
James Chapman	1-0-0-0	Farlan Fuller	1-0-0-0
Henry Crosby	1-0-0-1	James Fuller	1-0-0-0
Hugh B. Camell	1-0-0-0	Edward Franks	1-0-0-0
Stephen Cauthorn	1-0-0-1	Jesse Furr	0-0-0-2
Wm. H. Corbin	1-0-0-0	George Fyst	2-2-0-8
Miss Eloesa		Doct. John Fauntleroy	1-3-1-3
Castleman	0-0-0-0	Doct. Oliver Funston	1-7-2-15
		Jane H. Forster	0-3-0-3
John Dermont	1-3-0-2	John Furlon [?]	1-0-0-0
Peter Dermont	1-1-0-2	Moses Furr	3-0-0-7
Wm Deakle	3-1-1-1	Martha Forster	0-3-0-1
Saml Davis	1-0-0-0	George Farnsworth	1-0-0-3
James Davis	3-0-0-1	Archibald Fleming	1-2-1-3
John Drish	1-0-0-0	James Furr	1-0-0-2
Michael Dermont	2-1-2-1	Wm Fowler	1-0-0-5
Baalis Davis	1-2-1-1	Benjamin Franks	1-0-0-2
Benjamin Downing	1-0-0-0	Washington	
James Downing	1-0-0-2	Furgerson	1-3-1-7
Thomas Duke	1-0-0-0	Martin Feltner	1-0-0-1
James Dorin	1-0-0-1	Joseph Fleming	1-0-0-3
Saml Dobbins	1-0-0-0	John Furr	1-0-0-1
George W.		Thomas Fowler	1-0-0-2
Diffenderfer	1-0-0-0	Danl Furr	1-0-0-0
Reuben K. Dinkle	1-0-0-0	Minor Furr	1-0-0-4
Thos Duke Jr.	1-0-0-0	Marcus R. Feehrer	2-1-0-2
Wm Davis	2-0-0-2	Miss Jane Forster	0-0-0-1
		John Fox	0-3-0-0
Charles Eckhardt	1-0-0-1	Benjamin Ford	1-0-0-2
Henry Edwards	1-0-0-3	Ephraim Furr	1-0-0-1
Wm G. Everheart	0-0-0-0	Thomas Finnell	1-0-0-0
John Eleyett	1-1-0-2	Josiah Furgerson	1-2-1-4
Alexander M. Earle	1-3-1-9		
Hiram P. Evans	2-1-1-2	Richard Green	1-1-1-6
Jacob Enders	1-2-0-5	Thomas E. Gold	2-7-1-15
Jacob Everheart	2-0-0-1	Wm Graves	3-0-0-5
John Evans	0-0-0-0	Harrison Gordon	1-0-0-1

Clarke County, Virginia Personal Property Tax Lists 1836-1853
1845

George Gordon	2-1-0-1		James Harris	2-3-1-11
James Green	1-4-1-6		Doct. James Hay	1-13-5-20
John Gant	1-5-1-8		Thomas Hiett	2-1-1-8
Stephen J. Gant	1-2-0-5		Levi Hiett	1-3-0-7
Mrs.Rebecca Grogan	0-3-0-3		Isaac J. Hite	1-11-0-19
Edward Gormon	1-0-0-1		James M. Hite	2-4-0-7
Thomas Grubs	1-1-0-0		Wm Hummer	1-0-0-2
Joseph George	1-2-0-8		Saml Heflybour	1-2-0-9
John S. Gordon	4-1-0-7		John Hay	1-0-0-1
John Gordon	2-0-0-6		Jacob Heflybour	1-3-1-6
James __[?] Glass	2-7-1-11		Wm Holtsclaw	2-0-0-1
Henry N. Grigsby	1-4-0-10		Richard Hardesty	1-5-0-15
Dandridge Garrison	1-0-0-1		Mary Howard	0-2-1-0
John Grant	1-0-2-5		Philip Hunsucker	3-0-1-1
Wm Gourley	1-0-0-8		George Harris	1-4-0-8
Emanuel Garmong	1-0-0-1		Miss Abby Hopkins	0-8-0-4
Saml Grubs	1-0-0-1		Wm B. Harris	1-4-0-6
Nimrod Glasscock	1-0-0-0		Edward Handle	2-0-0-0
Abram Grim	1-0-0-0		Grafton Hillyard	1-0-0-1
Richard N. Green	1-6-0-7		James G. Harris	1-1-0-7
George W. Green	1-6-1-7		Cornelius Hooff	1-0-0-0
John L. Grant	1-1-1-4		Richard S. Hardesty	1-1-0-6
James Gibs	1-0-0-1		Robert Haney	1-0-0-2
Martin Gant	1-2-0-4		Philip Host	1-0-0-0
George W. Grubs	1-0-0-0		George Heflybour	1-0-0-1
Wm B. Grubs	1-0-0-0		John Hughes	1-1-0-1
G. G. Grove	1-1-0-1		John Hughes for 1844	1-0-0-1
Wm. Gardner	1-0-0-0		Francis W. Heskit	1-0-0-1
Charles Grubs	1-0-0-1		John F. Hogans	1-0-0-0
Alexander C. Grove	1-0-0-0		Armistead Hooff	1-1-1-1
Wm. Grubs	1-0-0-1			
			George Johnson	1-1-0-3
Whiting Hamilton	1-0-0-2		Herod Jenkins	1-0-0-0
Henry D. Hooe	2-0-0-2		Solomon R. Jackson	1-0-0-1
Henry Horner	1-0-0-1		Matthew Jones	3-1-1-9
Edwin Hart	1-1-0-4		Reuben Jordan	1-1-1-3
Abram Huyett	2-0-0-4		John Joliffe	1-7-2-9
John Huyett	2-0-0-5		John Johnson Senr.	0-0-0-0
Saml Huyett	1-3-0-7		Thomas Jordan	1-0-0-1

Clarke County, Virginia Personal Property Tax Lists 1836-1853
1845

Name	Values	Name	Values
Doct. R. R. Jordan	1-1-0-1	George Lowry	1-0-0-0
Jacob Isler	3-7-1-9	Henry Loyd	2-0-0-4
Revd. M.[?] Jones	1-4-0-1	Charles Lucius	1-1-0-5
Charles R. Johnson	1-0-0-1	John Lock	2-0-0-8
Washington Johnson	1-0-0-1	James W. Larue	1-4-0-7
Thomas Jones	2-0-0-4	Catharine Lock	2-0-0-5
Albert Johnson	1-0-1-0	Fanny Larue	0-6-2-9
Doct. J. J. Janney	1-2-1-2	Wm Longerbeam	1-0-0-1
Thomas Jenkins	1-0-0-2	Washington Lee	1-0-0-2
Richard Johnson	1-0-0-1	Charles Littleton	1-1-0-1
Elias Johns	1-0-0-0	Charles Leach Jr.	1-0-0-2
Joseph M. Joliffe	2-0-0-3	Doct. R. H. Little	3-8-2-8
George H. Isler	1-0-0-1	John Louthan	3-2-0-1
John Johnson Jr.	1-0-0-0	Lorenzo Lewis	1-29-5-26
John Jenkins	1-0-0-0	Saml Larue	2-11-3-16
		John B. Larue	1-12-3-27
James C. Kenan	1-0-0-0	Clarissa Larue	0-1-0-1
Doct. F. J. Kerfoot	2-11-0-14	John Loyd	1-0-0-1
Revd. Thomas Kennerly	1-19-2-30	George Longerbeam	1-0-0-1
		James Loyd	1-0-0-1
George Knight	1-7-1-14	Benjamin B. Lane	1-0-0-0
George Kitchen	1-4-0-9	George F. Ludwig	1-0-2-3
Wm C. Kerfoot	2-7-5-18	Saml Loyd	2-0-0-0
Benjamin M. Knight	1-1-0-2	Edgar Lanham	1-0-0-1
George L. Kerfoot	1-9-3-14	Charles Leech Senr.	1-0-0-1
Benjamin Kent	1-0-0-0	Alfred Logan	2-1-0-4
Doct. R. Kownslar	1-3-0-2	Richard Lanham	1-0-0-1
John Kable	2-2-0-1	Saml Lanham	1-0-0-0
Wm F. Knight	1-1-1-5	Abram Longerbeam	1-0-0-2
Nickolas Kroeser	1-0-0-1	Elizabeth Lanham	0-0-0-1
Mrs. Elizabeth Knight	0-0-0-0	James Lanham	1-0-0-0
John Kenneford	1-0-0-0	A. L. P. Larue	1-0-0-2
Geo & Wm Kerfoot	0-7-1-10	Wm D. Littleton	2-1-0-5
Middleton Keeler	1-1-0-0	Harrison Loyd	1-0-0-1
Joseph Kline	1-0-0-1	Alfred Lee	1-0-0-0
		Doct. J. M. Lindsay	1-0-0-0
John D. Larue	1-0-0-1	John Longerbeam	1-0-0-1
John T Lindsay	1-0-0-3	Ben Longerbeam	1-0-0-0
Franklin Littleton	2-1-0-2	Minor Lanham	1-0-0-0

Clarke County, Virginia Personal Property Tax Lists 1836-1853
1845

Peter McMurray	1-1-0-7	Wm Mason	1-0-0-1
Saml McCormick	1-0-0-0	John Morgan	1-7-1-11
J. J. Monroe	1-2-2-5	George L. McCormick	2-0-0-3
John Maddex	2-3-0-8	P. M. McCormick Senr.	2-11-0-11
Province McCormick	2-1-0-4	Charles & Saml McCormick	1-7-2-16
Albert McCormick	1-0-0-2	Benjamin F. Mayhew	2-0-0-0
James Michell	1-2-0-7	John N. Meade	0-0-0-0
Doct. Wm D. McGuire	2-8-0-11	Mrs. Catharine Milton	0-0-1-0
Otway McCormick	1-6-1-19	Isaac J. Manuel	1-0-0-0
John McCloy	1-0-0-1	Wm J. Maxwell	1-2-0-3
Francis B. Meade	1-5-0-12	James Murphy	1-0-0-3
Mrs.Louisa W. Meade	1-4-0-6	Sylvanus Moore	1-0-0-1
Philip N. Meade	1-6-1-8	Revd. Wm Meade	1-0-0-1
Wm Meade Jr.	1-0-0-4	Wm Marts	1-0-0-1
Miss Mary Meade	0-1-1-0	Stephen Marlow	0-0-0-0
Thomas McCormick	1-10-2-10	Amishadai Moore	3-3-0-7
John Marts Senr.	1-0-0-1	Mrs. Rebecca S. Meade	0-2-0-2
Doct. C. McCormick	1-8-1-10	Alexander Mason	1-0-0-1
George McCormick	1-7-1-10	John G. McCauley	2-1-0-2
Levi Marquess	2-0-0-3	Thomas W. McCormick	1-0-0-1
Jesse P. Mercer	1-0-0-1	Mrs. Violett Mayers	0-2-0-2
John & James Michum	2-0-0-3	Saml Moreland	1-0-0-3
Col. Benjamin Morgan	1-15-3-32	David H. McGuire	1-6-1-10
Mrs. Elizabeth Morgan	0-9-2-8	Alfred P. Moore	1-0-0-0
Col. Francis McCormick	1-8-2-14	Thomas Murphy	1-0-0-0
Charles McCormick	3-27-7-53	Stephen R. Mount	1-2-1-2
Miss Susan Marshall	0-4-1-8	Edward W. Massey	2-1-0-2
John Marshall	1-1-0-5	Isaac McCormick	1-0-0-1
Jesse McConaha	1-0-0-1	John McClur [?]	1-0-0-1
Miss Lucy Mustin	0-1-0-1		
Alexander Marshall	1-0-0-2	Wm Niswanger	3-0-0-6
John McPhillin	3-2-0-7	Hugh M. Nelson	1-9-3-14

Clarke County, Virginia Personal Property Tax Lists 1836-1853
1845

Name	Values	Name	Values
Mrs. Ann T. Neille	0-3-0-7	Thornton P. Pendleton	2-16-2-28
Wm Norris	0-0-0-0	Wm B. Page	0-2-1-0
Philip Nelson	1-16-2-12		
Thomas F. Nelson	0-0-0-0	Washington F. Padgett	1-1-0-1
James H. Neville	1-2-0-1	Richard L. Page	0-0-0-1
Joseph Noble	1-0-0-0		
Miss Abby Nelson	0-3-0-0	Richard Ridgway	2-1-0-8
Doct. Wm Nelson	1-2-0-3	Wm Reed	1-0-0-6
P. N. Nickolas	0-3-0-0	Thomas W. Raynolds	0-10-1-6
Joseph M. Nicklin	1-3-0-2	Bennet Russell	2-9-0-10
George R. Newman	2-1-0-1	Miss Elizabeth Royster	0-1-0-0
Doct. J. M. Nunn	1-3-0-2	Mat W. Royston	1-0-2-6
John W. Owen	1-3-0-4	Peter Royston	1-0-0-1
Mrs. Elizabeth Orear	0-8-2-7	John Roush	1-0-0-1
Enoch Orear	1-6-0-7	Uriah B. Royston	1-0-0-4
George Orear	2-4-1-12	John Reed	1-0-0-1
Wm Orr	1-0-1-0	Miss Ann Redmon	0-1-0-0
David Osbourn	1-0-0-4	Solomon Redmon	1-0-0-5
Mason Olliver	1-0-0-1	George Rutter	2-0-0-1
George Pultz	1-0-0-1	Danl B. Richards	2-1-0-2
John E. Page	1-15-2-20	Saml B. Redmon	1-0-0-2
Mrs.E. M. Page	0-1-1-0	Addison Romine	1-2-0-12
John Page	1-9-2-15	James Ryan	2-1-0-2
Mann R. Page	2-8-2-17	Doct. R. C. Randolph	1-12-2-18
Isaac Pidgeon	2-0-0-5	John Russell	1-1-1-1
John Pierce Senr.	1-3-1-8	Jane Richardson	1-1-0-2
Doct. R. P. Page	1-18-3-19	George Reno	1-0-0-2
James M. Pine	1-0-0-1	Isaac Ramey	2-0-0-4
Mrs.Mary C. Page	1-8-0-9	Mathew Rust	1-4-0-5
Joseph E. Peyton	2-0-0-5	Miss Betty Roots	0-2-0-0
Paul Pierce	1-6-0-9	Mrs. Elizabeth C. Riley	0-2-1-2
John W. Page	2-8-1-13	John Russell	1-0-1-1
John Pierce Jr.	2-2-1-8	James Russell	1-2-0-3
John Padgett	1-0-0-0	Luster Riley	1-0-0-0
James Puller	1-0-0-0		
Calvin Puller	1-0-0-1		
Peter Mc Pierce	1-3-1-7		

Clarke County, Virginia Personal Property Tax Lists 1836-1853
1845

Stephen Reed	1-0-0-1		
Kemp Royston	1-0-0-0	Burr Smallwood	1-0-0-1
Betsy Romine	0-0-1-0	Wm Stillions	0-0-0-0
		Simon Stickles	1-0-0-2
Alfred Smallwood	1-0-0-0	George Smedley	1-0-0-1
Joseph Stewart	1-0-0-0	Danl H. Sowers	1-3-0-14
Richard M. Sydnor	1-1-0-0	Robert Sowers	1-0-0-2
Mrs. Susan Smith	0-2-1-0	George Strother	1-0-0-3
Edward L. Smith	1-18-3-22	James Shackelford	1-0-0-0
Wm D. Smith	1-6-1-9	Mrs. Mary E. Shirely	0-7-2-10
Joseph Smith	1-0-0-1	Henry Seevers	1-0-2-7
Wm Sowers	2-4-3-9	Abram Shipe	2-0-0-1
Joseph Shepherd	2-6-2-10	James Strother	1-1-0-1
Champ Shepherd	1-2-0-2	Joseph Stickles	0-0-0-0
Edward Shickles	1-0-0-3	John Shell	1-0-0-2
Thomas Shumate	1-2-1-9	Erasmus G. Ships Est.	0-1-0-0
John W. Sowers	1-5-1-12	Jerry Shay	0-0-0-1
Wm G. Steele	1-0-0-0		
Danl W. Sowers	1-10-4-18	[More names beginning with S	
Saml Stipe	1-3-0-7	and T were recorded or filmed	
James Sowers	1-10-1-14	out of order. See page 95].	
Thomas Sprint	2-0-0-1		
Emanuel Showers	3-1-0-1	Thomas W. Tinsman	1-0-0-2
Adam Shipe	0-0-0-0	Montreval Tinsman	1-0-0-1
Barnett Smallwood	1-0-0-1	Ludwell Tinsman	1-0-0-1
Fielding L. Sowers	1-3-1-10	Saml Tinsman	1-0-0-1
Parkerson D.		Coleman Thompson	0-0-0-0
Shepherd	2-4-1-7	A. S. Tidball	1-5-2-13
Doct. Philip Smith	1-19-4-24	Wm Tomblin	1-0-0-1
Col. Tredwell Smith	3-14-2-14	Harrison [?]	
Wm K. Sowers	1-3-1-3	Thompson	1-0-0-0
Kerfoot Sowers Est.	0-7-0-12	Saml Tinsman	1-0-0-0
[Next 5 names are very faint.]		John Vanclief	1-0-0-4
John Stewart	2-0-1-2	Jacob Vanmeter	0-0-1-2
Danl A. Sowers	1-4-0-10	Wm Violett	1-0-0-0
Elizabeth Strother	0-5-4-6	John Vincent	1-0-0-2
John Shafer	1-0-0-1		
Jackson Shafer	1-0-0-1	Wm Willingham	1-0-0-2

Clarke County, Virginia Personal Property Tax Lists 1836-1853
1845

Allen Williams	1-10-2-14		Greenberry	
Timothy Wilcox	1-0-0-1		Thompson	2-0-0-3
James Wigginton	1-0-0-1		David Timberlake	1-0-0-0
Francis H. Whiting	1-3-1-9		Harrison Thompson	1-0-0-1
J. W. Ware &			Doct. Saml Taylor	1-12-2-11
Mrs. Stribling	1-21-4-24		Benjamin Thompson	1-0-0-1
Mrs. Lucinda			Col. Joseph Tuley	1-27-6-25
Washington	0-3-0-2-		John Trussell	2-3-1-7
J. G. Wade &			Wm Timberlake	0-2-0-0
Brothers	2-1-0-1		Wm G. Taylor	2-8-1-14
H. T. Wheat	2-2-1-2		Wm Trinary	1-1-0-2
Hezekiah Wiley	1-0-0-1		Wm Tinsman	2-0-0-1
Saml Wiley	1-0-0-1		Moses Trussell	2-0-0-5
James Wiley	1-0-0-1		James Tansell	1-0-0-5
John Willingham	1-0-0-1		James W.	
Miss E. W.			Timberlake	1-5-1-10
Washington	0-1-0-0		Mrs. Mary Trinary	0-0-0-0
Leroy P. Williams	2-7-3-10		Robert Tapscott	1-1-1-1
Wm P. Wigginton				
back of book			Francis B. Whiting	2-18-3-15
			Wm W. Whiting	1-1-0-3
David Shaull	1-2-1-9		Obed Willingham	1-0-0-0
Edward Street	1-0-0-0		Wm Wise	1-0-0-1
Shepherd & Sowers	1-1-0-0		Bennet Wood	1-0-0-0
Nathaniel Seevers	1-0-0-0		Henry Weaver	1-0-0-0
David Swarts	1-0-0-0		N. B. Whiting	1-5-0-9
Elisha Smallwood	1-0-0-1		Ephraim Watson	2-0-1-7
Wm H. Shores	1-0-1-0		Sydnor B. Windham	2-0-0-1
Joseph Shipe	1-0-0-1		Thomas Woods	1-0-0-1
Hezekiah Shisker	1-0-0-0		John Wilson	2-0-1-1
			Joseph A. Williamson	2-8-0-17
Timothy R. Toad [?]	1-0-0-0		Doct. H. Washington	1-2-0-2
Mrs. Sarah			Albert Whittington	1-0-0-0
Timberlake	1-9-1-12		Thomas C. Windham	1-0-0-0
Wm Turner	1-0-0-1		Thomas E.	
Abigail Tanquary	0-1-0-2		Woodward	1-0-0-1
David Tristler	1-1-0-3		Francis Whittington	1-0-0-0
Adam Towner	1-0-1-0		James W. Ware	1-0-0-1
Mrs. Hannah Taylor	0-2-0-2		James V. Wier	1-2-0-3

Clarke County, Virginia Personal Property Tax Lists 1836-1853
1845

Wm Willis	1-0-0-0	George Young	1-0-0-1
Revd. Richard H. Wilmer	1-2-1-1	Scimeon Yowell	1-1-0-0
Jacob Wagely	1-1-1-1	Jacob Zackarias	1-0-0-2
Wm Wagely	2-1-0-1	[Additional names at end of recapitulation]	
Wm H. Whiting	1-1-0-5		
Alexander Wood	1-0-0-0	Wm P. Wigginton	
Laban Whitaker	1-0-0-1	George Flecher	1-0-0-1
John Wiley	1-0-0-0	Charles H. Milton	1-0-0-0
James Wiley Jr.	1-0-0-1	Wm H. Saunders	1-0-0-0
Laban Whittington	1-0-0-1	C. Hennis	1-0-0-0

Property owned by Free Negroes

Columns: 1) free people, 2) slaves above 16 years, 3) slaves above 12 years, 4) horses, mules, etc.

John Diggs	1-1-0-0	Jack Adam	1-0-0-0
Spencer Johnson	1-0-0-0	Johnathan ____	1-0-0-0
Philip Martin	1-0-0-1	Moses Gray	1-0-0-0
Burwell Cook	1-0-0-1	Wm Davis	1-0-0-0
Mowen Harris	1-1-0-0	George Davis	1-0-0-0
Wm Grayham	1-0-0-0	Wat Howard	1-0-0-0
Jacob Johnson	1-0-0-1	Gusty Howard	1-0-0-0
John Jackson	1-0-0-4	Wm Howard	1-0-0-0
Alfred Fox	1-0-1-0	John Ranson	1-0-0-0
Bennet Taylor	1-0-0-0	Volny Lucas	1-0-0-0
Wiley Finch	1-0-0-0	John Robertson	1-0-0-0
Thomas Gray	1-0-0-0	Henson ____	1-0-0-0
Scimeon Parker	1-0-0-0	Jacob Gains	1-0-0-0
George Wells	1-0-0-0	Danl Gracen	1-0-0-0
John Clifton	1-0-0-0	Bennet Taylor	1-0-0-0
Washington Hall	1-0-0-0		

Clarke County, Virginia Personal Property Tax Lists 1836-1853

1846

Columns: 1) white males above 16 years, 2) slaves above 16 years, 3) slaves 12-16 years, 4) horses, mares, mules & colts.

Name	Values	Name	Values
Robert Ashby Senr.	1-0-0-2	Francis O. Byrd	1-10-1-9
Mason Anderson	1-1-0-0	Philip Berlin	1-3-1-6
David H. Allen	4-27-2-39	George C. Blakemore	1-8-1-9
John Alexander Senr.	1-11-4-17	John Bowlin	1-0-0-0
Wm C. Alexander	1-8-2-12	Neille Barnett	1-3-0-5
Augusta Athey	1-0-0-2	Thomas W. Briggs	1-2-1-8
Joseph Anderson	3-2-0-8	Danl S. Bonham	1-5-0-7
Nancy Allen	1-2-0-5	James Bogs	1-0-0-0
Algernon S. Allen	1-8-2-13	John Brownley	2-12-0-14
John Alexander Jr.	1-0-0-0	Wm Baker	1-4-1-3
John Ashby	1-0-0-2	Isaac Berlin	2-0-0-1
Robert Ashby Jr.	1-0-0-1	Strother Bell	1-0-0-0
Martin Ashby	1-0-0-1	Robert Burchell	1-3-1-8
Thomas H. Alexander	1-0-0-2	H. W. Brabham	1-0-0-0
Nimrod Ashby	11-0-0-1	Squire Bell	1-1-0-4
George B. Ashby	11-0-0-2	Philip Burwell	1-28-4-15
John Ambrows	1-0-0-9	John W. Byrd	1-9-1-11
Wm Ashby	1-1-0-1	Thomas Briggs	8-5-2-17
David F. Armstrong	1-1-0-1	John Brumley	3-0-0-7
George Aikins	1-0-0-2	John D. Barr	1-0-0-1
James Allison	1-0-0-0	James W. Beck	1-0-0-2
Saml Armour	1-0-0-0	John C. Bonham	1-5-0-7
Evan P. Anderson	1-1-0-2	Nathaniel Burwell Senr.	1-43-3-46
Austin C. Ashby	1-0-0-2	Saml Bonham	3-12-14
Thomas Ashby	1-0-0-1	Col. James Bell	1-7-4-16
		Lewis Berlin	1-3-0-1
Nathaniel Burwell Jr.	1-10-2-15	George W. Berlin	1-0-0-1
Wm C. Benson	1-3-0-4	Strother H. Bowen	1-0-1-0
John Burchell	2-4-3-9	Robert Ben	1-1-0-3
Archibald Bowen	2-3-0-7	Wm Berry	3-13-0-8
Hiram O. Bell	1-0-0-0	George H. Burwell	2-40-5-36
Phinehas Bowen	2-3-2-11		

Clarke County, Virginia Personal Property Tax Lists 1836-1853
1846

Saml Briarly	2-7-0-8	Robert A.	
Christian Bowser	2-1-0-1	Coltson [sic]	1-5-0-11
John Blue	1-2-0-7	D° in possession of	
Napoleon Baltrip	1-0-0-1	W. H. Coltson	0-2-0-4
Russell Brackett	1-0-0-0	Wm. H. Coltson	1-0-0-0
Martin Berlin	1-0-0-0	Elizabeth K. Carter	1-1-0-5
Jesse Bowen	1-1-0-3	John Copenhaver	1-3-1-12
Abram Beevers	1-0-0-3	Miriam Catlett	1-6-0-13
James Bell	1-0-0-1	James H. Clarke	1-3-0-0
Wm Berlin	3-2-1-4	Thomas H. Crow	2-3-1-3
Adam Barr	1-0-0-1	Wm R. Castleman	1-4-0-7
Ben Barr	1-1-0-0	Alfred Clevenger	1-5-0-7
Richard Billmyre	1-0-0-0	John Cooper	1-0-0-1
Andrew Billmyre	1-0-0-1	Elizabeth Crampton	0-5-2-3
Jesse Butler	1-0-0-1	Martha P. Castleman	1-5-0-2
George Bowlin	1-0-0-0	Thomas Carter	2-5-1-10
John S. Burns	1-5-1-9	Parkerson Corder	1-0-0-3
Juliet Boston	0-1-0-0	John Carroll	3-0-0-2
Nancy Boston	0-0-0-0	John Carpenter	2-4-0-7
T. T. Byrds Est.	0-1-0-1	Dabney Cauthorne	1-0-0-0
John R. Bell	1-3-0-6	Elizabeth N. Carter	1-2-0-1
Thomas W. Burns	1-0-0-1	James Carter	2-0-0-0
Charles Blake	1-0-0-1	David Clevinger	1-0-0-7
Peter Bennet	1-0-0-1	Thomas Clevinger	1-0-0-8
Henry W. Bayliss	1-0-0-0	James N. Corbin	2-0-0-4
Jacob Bowser	1-0-0-0	Thomas Cornwell	1-0-0-1
Lewis D. Ball	1-0-0-1	Bushrod Crawford	1-0-0-0
Thomas Boteler	2-0-0-0	George W. Cooper	1-0-0-0
Nancy Brown	0-0-0-0	John P. Carrigan	1-0-0-0
George W. Bartlett	1-1-0-2	Aaron Chamblin	2-0-0-6
		Michael Copenhaver	2-0-1-1-
Shederick Crouse	1-0-0-0	John G. Chapman	1-0-0-0
Alfred Castleman	3-5-1-11	Andrew Cage	1-0-0-0
Frederick Clopton	1-5-0-8	Ury Castleman	0-6-1-6
George F. Calmese	1-5-0-8	Jacob Clink	1-0-0-0
Wm Carrington	3-1-0-1	Daniel Coleman	1-0-0-1
Wm Carper	1-0-0-2	Stephen D.	
Ambrows Crawford	1-0-0-1	Castleman	1-4-0-7
		James Carper	1-2-0-7

Clarke County, Virginia Personal Property Tax Lists 1836-1853
1846

Peter Cain	2-0-0-5	Henry Edwards	1-1-0-1
Joseph Chapman	1-0-0-0	Wm G. Everheart	2-1-0-4
Henry Crosby	1-0-0-1	John Eleyett	1-1-0-2
Stephen Cauthorn	1-0-0-1	Alexander M. Earle	1-4-0-8
Wm H. Corbin	1-0-0-1	Hiram P. Evans	1-1-1-2
Wm G. Cole	2-1-0-1	Jacob Enders	1-2-1-6
Wm K. Carter	1-2-0-1	Jacob Everheart	1-0-0-0
John S. Crim	1-0-0-0	Christopher Elliott	1-0-0-1
John R. Corbin	1-0-0-2	Franklin Ellis	1-0-0-0
Eloesa Castleman	0-0-0-0	Edward Eno	0-3-0-1
Philip P. Cooke	1-2-0-1		
Edwin Cauthorn	1-0-0-0	Edward Franks	1-0-0-0
John Cooper	2-0-0-2	Jesse Furr	0-0-0-2
Wm G. Carter	1-1-0-0	George Fyst	2-2-1-7
Elisha Carver	1-0-0-1	Doct. John Fauntleroy	1-3-2-3
James Carver	1-0-0-1	Doct. Oliver Funston	1-9-1-14
		Jane H. Forster	1-4-0-3
John Dermont	1-7-0-3	Moses Furr	3-0-0-6
Peter Dermont	1-0-0-1	Martha Forster	0-3-0-1
Wm Deakle	3-1-0-2	George Farnsworth	3-0-0-4
Saml Davis	2-0-0-1	Archibald Fleming	4-2-1-3
James Davis	2-0-0-1	James Furr	1-0-0-1
John Drish	1-0-0-1	John D. Furgerson Jr.	1-2-0-5
Michael Dermont	2-4-2-9	John Fowler	1-0-0-5
Baalis Davis	1-2-1-1	Benjamin Franks	1-0-0-2
James Downing	1-0-0-0	Washington	
Thomas Duke	1-0-0-0	Furgerson	1-2-1-6
James Dorin	1-0-0-1	Martin Feltner	1-0-0-1
Saml Dobbins	1-0-0-0	Joseph Fleming	1-0-1-3
George W.		Thomas Fowler	1-0-0-2
Diffenderfer	1-0-0-1	Minor Furr	1-0-0-4
Thos Duke Jr.	1-0-0-0	Marcus R. Feehrer	2-1-0-3
Wm Davis	1-0-0-2	Jane Forster	0-0-0-1
Hugh Davis	1-0-0-0	John Fox	0-2-0-0-
John Dow	1-1-0-2	Benjamin Ford	1-0-0-2
George Dunn	1-0-0-0	Thomas Finnell	1-0-0-0
John Davis	1-0-0-0	Josiah Furgerson	1-3-1-4
		John Fletcher	1-0-0-1
Charles Eckhardt	1-0-0-1	H. B. Farrow	1-0-0-1

Clarke County, Virginia Personal Property Tax Lists 1836-1853
1846

		Whiting Hamilton	1-0-0-2
Richard Green	1-2-0-5	Henry D. Hooe	2-0-0-2
Thomas E. Gold	2-9-2-15	Henry Horner	1-0-0-1
George Gordon	1-0-0-1	Edwin Hart	1-2-0-7
James Green	2-5-0-7	Abram Huyett	2-0-0-4
Stephen J. Gant	1-2-0-5	John Huyett	3-1-0-6
Rebecca Grogan	0-3-0-3	Saml Huyett	1-2-0-8
Edward Gormon	1-0-0-1	James Harris	1-2-2-8
Thomas Grubs	1-0-0-0	Doct. James Hay	1-13-1-9
Joseph George	1-1-0-3	Levi Hiett	1-3-0-7
John S. Gordon	4-1-0-7	Isaac J. Hite	1-11-3-19
Lewis Glass	1-1-3-5	James M. Hite	2-4-0-3
Dandridge Garrison	1-0-0-1	Wm Hummer	1-0-0-2
John Grant	1-1-1-5	C. Haney,	
Wm Gourley	1-1-0-9	alias Hennis	1-0-0-0
Emanuel Garmong	1-0-0-1	Thomas Harris	1-0-0-1
Saml Grubs	1-0-0-0	Saml Heflybour	1-2-0-10
Nimrod Glasscock	1-0-0-0	John Hay	1-0-0-0
Abram Grim	1-0-0-0	Jacob Heflybour	1-4-0-9
Richard N. Green	1-3-1-7	Wm Holtsclaw	1-0-0-0
George W. Green	1-7-1-9	Blackwell Holtsclaw	1-0-0-2
John L. Grant	1-1-0-4	Richard Hardesty	2-5-0-15
James Gibs	1-0-0-0	Mary Howard	0-2-0-0
Martin Gant	1-3-1-5	Philip Hunsucker	3-0-1-1
Wm B. Grubs	1-0-0-1	George Harris	1-5-0-8
G. G. Grove	2-1-0-0	Abby Hopkins	1-3-0-6
~~Wm. Gardner~~		Wm B. Harris	1-6-0-7
A. C. Grove	1-0-0-0	Edward Handle	1-1-0-0
Wm Grubs	1-0-0-1	Grafton Hillyard	1-0-0-0
Catharine Grove	1-0-0-0	James G. Harris	1-1-0-7
John Grayham	1-0-0-0	Cornelius Hoof	1-0-0-0
James Gavins	1-0-0-1	Richard S. Hardesty	1-2-0-6
Isabella Glass	0-1-1-0	Robert Haney	1-0-0-2
Adam Greenwall	1-0-0-0	Philip Host	1-0-0-0
		George Heflybour	1-0-0-1
Henry Huntsberry	1-0-0-0	John Hughes	3-0-0-2
Frederick D.		Francis W. Heskit	1-0-0-1
Harryman	1-0-0-0	John F. Hogans	1-0-0-0
Joseph Hull	1-0-0-1	Armistead Hoof	2-2-0-1

Clarke County, Virginia Personal Property Tax Lists 1836-1853
1846

John Hodge	1-0-0-0	Wm F. Knight	1-1-0-1
Wm G. Hardesty	1-2-0-6	Nickolas Krocser	1-0-0-1
		Elizabeth Knight	0-0-0-0
George Johnson	1-1-0-3	Geo & Wm Kerfoot	0-7-1-11
Herod Jenkins	1-0-0-1	Middleton Keeler	1-1-0-0
Solomon R. Jackson	1-0-0-1	Wm C. Kennerly	2-0-0-2
Matthew Jones	2-1-1-7	Joseph Kline	1-0-0-1
Reuben Jordan	1-1-1-2	Saml G. Kneller	1-1-0-1
John Joliffe	1-7-2-9	Doct. Olliver B.	
Doct. R. R. Jordan	1-0-1-1	Knode	1-0-0-1
Jacob Isler	3-7-2-10	John B. Kerfoot	1-0-0-1
Revd. Wm. G. H.			
Jones	1-3-0-1	James Loyd Jr.	1-0-0-1
Charles R. Johnson	1-0-0-2	John T. Lindsay	1-0-0-0
Thomas Jones	2-1-1-5	Franklin Littleton	2-0-0-2
Albert Johnson	1-0-1-0	George Lowry	1-0-0-0
Doct. J. J. Janey	1-2-0-2	Henry Loyd	0-0-0-3
Thomas Jenkins	1-0-0-2	Charles Lucius	1-1-1-6
Richard Johnson	1-0-0-1	John Lock	2-0-0-10
Elias John	1-0-0-0	James W. Larue	1-4-0-6
John Johnson Jr.	1-0-0-0	Catharine Lock	0-0-0-0
John Jenkins	1-0-0-0	Wm Longerbeam	1-0-0-1
John Johnson Senr.	1-0-0-1	Washington Lee	2-0-0-1
Alfred Jackson	1-3-0-4	Charles Littleton	1-1-0-2
Leonard Jones	1-0-0-0	Charles Leach Jr.	1-0-0-2
Richardson Janey	1-0-0-0	Doct. R. H. Little	3-7-2-9
Jeremiah Jenkins	1-0-0-0	John Louthan	4-2-0-1
James C. Kenan	2-0-0-0	Lorenzo Lewis	1-14-5-26
Doct. F. J. Kerfoot	2-9-0-15	Saml Larue	1-13-0-12
Revd. Thomas		John B. Larue	1-10-4-27
Kennerly	1-18-2-25	John Loyd	1-0-0-1
George Knight	1-7-1-15	George Longerbeam	1-0-0-1
George Kitchen	1-4-1-9	James Loyd	1-0-0-0
Wm C. Kerfoot	1-9-3-17	B. B. Lane	1-0-0-0
Benjamin M. Knight	1-1-0-1	Saml Loyd	1-0-0-1
George L. Kerfoot	1-9-1-13	Edgar Lanham	1-0-0-0
Ben Kent	1-0-0-0	Charles Leech Senr.	1-0-0-1
Doct. R. R. Kounslar	1-3-0-2	Alfred Logan	1-0-0-5
John Kable	1-2-0-1	Richard Lanham	1-0-0-1

Clarke County, Virginia Personal Property Tax Lists 1836-1853
1846

Saml Lanham	1-0-0-1		George McCormick	1-8-1-9
Abram Longerbeam	1-0-0-1		Levi Marquess	1-0-0-1
Elizabeth Lanham	0-0-0-1		N. C. Mason	1-0-0-0
James Lanham	1-0-0-0		Jesse P. Mercer	1-0-0-1
A. L. P. Larue	1-0-0-2			
Wm D. Littleton	2-2-0-4		John & James	
Harrison Loyd	1-0-0-1		Michum	2-0-0-3
Alfred Lee	1-0-0-0		Col. B. Morgan	2-14-5-31
Doct. J. M. Lindsay	1-0-0-1		Elizabeth Morgan	0-8-1-8
John Longerbeam	0-0-0-1		Col. Frank	
Ben Longerbeam	1-0-0-0		McCormick	2-8-2-10
Minor Lanham	1-0-0-0		Charles McCormick	1-29-2-43
Sally Longerbeam	0-0-0-1		Susan Marshall	0-4-1-7
Ben Lock	1-0-0-3		John Marshall	1-1-0-5
Rice W. Levi	2-0-0-2		Jesse McConaha	1-0-0-0
James Larue's heirs	0-1-0-1		Lucy Mustin	0-2-0-1
Squire Lee	2-0-0-2		Alexander Marshall	1-0-0-1
John Littleton	1-0-0-1		John McPhillin	2-3-1-8
George Lanham	1-0-0-0		Wm Mason	1-0-0-1
Wm Lee	1-0-0-0		John Morgan	1-7-1-7
			George L.	
Peter McMurray	1-2-0-8		McCormick	3-0-0-4
Saml McCormick	1-0-0-0		Province McCormick	2-10-0-12
J. J. Monroe	1-1-2-5		Charles & Saml	
John Maddex	1-4-0-9		McCormick	2-7-2-14
Albert McCormick	1-0-0-2		Ben F. Mayhew	1-0-0-1
James Michell	1-3-0-6		John N. Meade	1-3-0-6
Doct. Wm D.			Isaac J. Manuel	1-0-0-0
McGuire	2-9-1-12		James Murphy	1-0-0-2
Otway McCormick	1-6-1-8		Sylvanus Moore	1-0-0-0
John MCloy	1-0-0-2		Revd. Wm Meade	1-0-0-1
Francis B. Meade	1-6-2-13		Wm Marts	1-0-0-0
Louisa W. Meade	0-4-0-2		Stephen Marlow	1-0-0-1
Philip N. Meade	1-5-2-9		Amishadai Moore	1-3-0-5
Wm Meade Jr.	1-2-0-4		Rebecca Meade	0-3-1-0
Mary Meade	0-1-1-0		Alexander Mason	1-0-0-0
Thomas McCormick	1-9-2-10		John G. McCauley	1-0-0-1
John Marts Senr.	1-0-0-1		Violet Mayers	1-0-0-2
Doct. C. McCormick	1-8-1-9		David H. McGuire	1-6-2-9

Clarke County, Virginia Personal Property Tax Lists 1836-1853
1846

Alfred P. Moore	1-0-0-0	David Osbourn	1-0-0-3
~~Thomas Murphy~~		Mason Olliver	1-0-0-0
George D. Morse	2-2-0-3	George Osbourn	1-0-2-3
Stephen R. Mount	1-1-1-1	Jesse Orear	1-1-0-2
Edward W. Massey	2-1-0-2		
Isaac McCormick	1-0-0-1	George Pultz	1-0-0-1
Charles Milton	1-0-0-1	John E. Page	1-15-2-20
Abram Mark	1-0-0-0	Eliza M. Page	0-1-0-0
Elijah Milton	1-0-1-0	John Page	1-6-5-14
Ben B. Miley	1-0-0-4	Mann R. Page	2-9-2-18
MClain MClingon	1-0-0-1	Isaac Pidgeon	2-0-0-5
Jacob Messmore	0-1-0-0	John Pierce Senr.	1-3-1-8
John McDonald	1-0-0-0	Doct. R. P. Page	1-18-3-18
Wm McCormick	1-0-0-2	James M. Pine	1-0-0-0
Thomas Y. Michell	1-0-0-0	Mary C. Page	1-4-0-5
Micale Moranghan	1-0-0-0	Joseph E. Peyton	2-0-0-5
		Paul Pierce	1-6-1-9
Doct. S. S. Neale	1-0-0-1	John W. Page	3-8-1-13
Wm Niswanger	2-0-0-6	John Pierce Jr.	2-2-0-8
Hugh M. Nelson	1-13-2-17	John Padgett	1-0-0-0
Ann T. Neille	0-3-0-4	James Puller	1-0-0-0
Philip Nelson	1-14-2-17	Calvin Puller	1-0-0-1
Thomas F. Nelson	2-12-5-18	Peter Mc Pierce	1-3-1-7
James H. Neville	1-1-1-1	Thornton P.	
Joseph Noble	1-0-1-0	Pendleton	2-18-4-27
Abby Nelson	0-3-0-0	Washington F.	
Doct. Wm Nelson	1-2-1-3	Padgett	1-0-0-0
Joseph M. Nicklin	2-3-0-2	Richard L. Page	0-3-0-1
George R. Newman	3-1-0-2	McFarland Puller	1-0-0-0
Doct. J. M. Nunn	1-3-0-2	John Patterson	1-0-0-2
Lewis Neale	1-0-0-0	James Payne	1-0-0-1
L. B. & B. T. Norris	1-8-0-14		
		Richard Ridgeway	2-1-0-6
Doct. Mat Page	0-2-0-0	Wm Reed	1-0-1-5
		Thomas W. Raynolds	2-7-1-6
John W. Owen	1-2-1-3	Bennet Russell	2-9-0-10
Mrs. Elizabeth Orear	0-9-2-7	Elizth Royster	0-1-0-0
Enock Orear	1-6-0-7	Mat W. Royston	1-3-0-7
George Orear	2-3-1-8	Peter Royston	1-0-1-1

Clarke County, Virginia Personal Property Tax Lists 1836-1853
1846

John Roush	1-0-0-1	Joseph Shepherd	2-6-2-10
Uriah B. Royston	1-0-0-6	Champ Shepherd	1-3-0-4
Peter R. Royston	1-1-1-0	Edward Shickles	1-0-0-3
John Reed	1-0-0-1	Thomas Shumate	1-4-0-8
Nancy Redmon	0-1-0-0	John W. Sowers	1-6-1-11
Solomon Redmon	1-0-0-2	Wm G. Steele	1-0-0-0
George Rutter	1-0-0-1	Danl W. Sowers	1-10-2-16
Danl B. Richards	2-1-0-2	Saml Stipe	1-3-0-8
Saml B. Redmon	1-0-1-2	James Sowers	1-11-0-13
Addison Romine	1-2-0-9	Thomas Sprint	2-0-0-1
James Ryan	2-1-0-2	Emanuel Showers	4-1-0-1
Doct. R. C. Randolph	1-13-0-16	Barnett Smallwood	1-0-0-1
John Russell	1-1-0-0	Fielding L. Sowers	1-5-2-11
Jane Richardson	1-0-0-1	P. D. Shepherd	2-4-1-8
George Reno	1-0-0-2	Doct. Philip Smith	2-20-4-26
Isaac Ramey	3-0-0-4	Col. T. Smith	2-16-1-16
Mathew Rust	2-3-0-5	Kerfoot Sowers Est.	1-7-1-10
Betty Roots	0-2-0-0	John Stewart	3-0-0-3
E. C. Riley	1-3-0-4	Danl A. Sowers	1-3-1-8
John Russell	1-0-0-1	Elizabeth Strother	0-6-1-6
James Russell	1-2-0-6	John Shafer	1-0-0-0
Stephen Reed	1-0-0-2	Jackson Shafer	1-0-0-1
John Rowland	1-0-0-5	Bur Smallwood	1-0-0-1
James W. Raynolds	1-0-0-2	Simon Stekles	1-0-0-1
Thompson Ritt	1-0-0-1	George Smedley	1-0-0-0
Wm Riley	1-0-0-1	Danl H. Sowers	1-1-1-12
D° as guardian for		Robert Sowers	1-0-0-0
Wm. M. T__[illegible]		Joseph Shipe	1-0-0-0
John Raynolds	1-0-0-0	George Strother	1-0-0-2
James Reed	1-0-0-0	James Shackelford	1-0-0-0
		Mary E. Shirely	0-7-2-10
George Smith	1-0-0-1	John Sharp	2-0-0-2
Joseph Stewart	1-0-0-	Wm B. Sowers	1-0-0-0
Richard M. Sydnor	2-1-0-0-	Henry Shepherd	2-3-1-1
Susan Smith	0-1-1-0	Henry Seevers	1-1-1-4
Edward L. Smith	1-11-1-16	Abram Shipe	1-0-0-0
Wm D. Smith	1-15-2-15	James Strother	1-0-0-1
Joseph Smith	1-0-0-0	John Shell	1-0-0-1
Wm Sowers	2-4-3-9	David Shaul	1-1-0-8

Clarke County, Virginia Personal Property Tax Lists 1836-1853
1846

Name	Values	Name	Values
Edward Street	1-0-0-	Doct. Geo Wm Taylor	1-3-1-3
Wm H. Shores	1-0-0-0		
Alexander Saunders	1-0-0-0	Peter Umbenhaur	1-0-0-0
Stephen Shores	1-0-0-0		
Jerry Shay	1-0-2-1	John Vanclief	1-0-0-6
Jonathan S. Smith	1-2-0-1	Jacob Vanmeter	0-4-1-9
Wm L. Smith	1-0-0-0	Wm Violett	1-0-0-0
Richard Swift	1-0-0-0	John Vincent	1-0-0-1
Mountjoy Shell	1-0-0-1	Thomas Vaughan	1-0-0-0
John Wm Shell	1-0-0-1		
		Jacob P. Wagely	1-0-11
Sarah Timberlake	1-8-1-14	Wm Willingham	1-0-0-2
Wm Turner	1-0-0-1	Allen Williams	1-9-2-9
Abigail Tanquery	0-1-0-1	Timothy Wilcox	1-0-0-1
David Tristler	1-1-0-04	James Wigginton	1-0-0-1
Adam Towner	1-0-1-0	Francis H. Whiting	1-3-1-11
Hannah Taylor	0-2-0-2	J. W. Ware &	
Greenberry		Mrs. Stribling	1-19-4-25
Thompson	3-0-0-3	Lucinda Washington	0-3-1-2-
David Timberlake	1-0-0-0	J. G. Wade &	
Harrison Thompson	1-0-0-0	Brothers	2-2-0-2
Doct. Saml Taylor	1-12-2-12	H. T. Wheat	2-2-1-2
Ben Thompson Jr.	1-0-0-3	Hezekiah Wiley	1-0-0-0
Col. Joseph Tuley	1-22-5-21	Saml Wiley	1-0-0-0
Richard Timberlake	0-2-0-0	James Wiley	2-0-0-1
Wm G. & Charles		Thornton O.	
Taylor	3-3-0-5	Windham	1-0-0-0
Wm Trinary	1-1-0-5	John Willingham	1-0-0-1
Wm Tinsman	1-0-0-0	E. W. Washington	0-0-0-0
James Tansell	1-0-0-4	Leroy P. Williams	2-6-1-10
James W.		Wm P. Wigginton	0-0-0-0
Timberlake	1-6-2-13	Francis B. Whiting	2-17-3-15
Robert Tapscott	1-0-0-0	Wm W. Whiting	1-1-0-3
Montreval Tinsman	1-0-0-1	Obed Willingham	1-0-0-0
Saml Tinsman	2-0-0-1	Wm Wise	1-0-0-0
A. S. Tidball	1-7-1-15	Bennet Wood	1-0-0-0
Wm Tomblin	1-0-0-1	N. B. Whiting	1-3-2-10
Saml Tinsman	1-0-0-0	Ephraim Watson	1-0-0-8
John B. Taylor	1-13-1-21	Sidnor B. Windham	1-0-0-1

Clarke County, Virginia Personal Property Tax Lists 1836-1853
1846

Thos Woods	1-0-0-3	Wm Wood	1-0-0-0
John Wilson	2-0-0-0	John Wiley	1-0-0-0
Joseph A. Williamson	2-7-0-14	David Whittington	1-0-0-2
Doct. H. Washington	1-1-0-2	James W. Wiley	1-0-0-2
Albert Whittington	1-0-0-0	Jacob Welch	2-0-0-4
Thos C. Windham	1-0-0-0	David H. Wilcox	1-0-0-1
Thos E. Woodword	1-0-0-1	Wm Wells	1-0-0-0
James E. Ware	1-0-1-0	George Woodward	1-0-0-0
James V. Wier	1-4-0-4		
Wm Willis	1-0-0-0	George Young	1-0-0-1
Revd. R. H. Wilmer	1-2-1-1	Scimeon Yowell	1-1-0-0
Wm Wagely	1-0-0-1		
Wm H. Whiting	1-4-0-7	Jacob Zacerias	1-0-0-1
Alexander Wood	1-0-0-0		

Property owned by Free Negroes

John Diggs	0-1-0-0	John Jackson	0-0-0-2
Spencer Johnson	0-0-0-1	Wm Davis	0-0-0-1
Mowen Harris	0-1-0-2	Peter Coates	0-0-0-1
Wm Grayham	0-0-0-1	Ellen Taylor	0-1-0-1

[Additional names written after recapitulation.]

Joseph Shepherd	2-6-2-10	Lorenzo Lewis	0-0-0-0
E. L. Smith	0-0-0-0	George G. Gore	0-0-0-0
Doct. R. Kownslaw	0-0-0-0	Wm P. Wigginton	2-2-0-2

Clarke County, Virginia Personal Property Tax Lists 1836-1853

1847

Columns: 1) white males above 16 years, 2) slaves above 16 years, 3) slaves 12-16, 4) horses, mares, mules & colts.

Robert Ashby	1-0-0-3	Nat Burwell	1-9-1-13
Mason Anderson	1-1-0-0	Wm C. Benson	1-1-0-1
David H. Allen	4-25-3-40	John Burchell	2-4-2-11
John Alexander	1-16-2-18	Archibald Bowen	1-4-0-6
Wm C. Alexander	1-8-2-14	Hiram O. Bell	1-0-0-0
Augusta Athey	1-0-0-2	Phinehas Bowen	1-4-0-10
Wm Ambrows	2-0-0-6	Francis O. Byrd	1-10-2-10
Joseph Anderson	3-1-0-7	Philip Berlin	2-3-2-5
Nancy Allen	1-1-0-6	George C. Blakemore	17-1-9
Algernon S. Allen	2-9-1-12	D° as guardians for	
John Alexander	1-0-0-1	Leonidas Enders	
Joel Alexander	1-0-0-0	John Bowlin	1-0-0-0
John Ashby	1-0-0-1	Neille Barnett	1-2-1-5
Robert Ashby Jr.	1-0-001	D° as guardian [for]	
Martin Ashby	1-0-0-1	J. B. & J. W. Carter	
Thomas H. Alexander	1-0-012	Thomas W. Briggs	1-2-0-8
Nimrod Ashby	1-0-0-1	Danl S. Bonham	1-5-1-7
George B. Ashby	1-0-0-2	James Bogs	1-0-0-0
John Ambrows	2-2-0-9	John Brownly	1-11-1-15
Wm Ashby	1-1-0-1	Wm Baker	1-5-0-4
David F. Armstrong	1-1-0-1	Isaac Berlin	2-0-0-1
George Aikins	1-0-0-0	Strother Bell	1-0-0-0
James Allison	1-0-0-0	Robert Burchell	1-3-1-7
Saml Armour	1-0-0-0	H. W. Brabham	1-0-0-0
James Allison	1-0-0-0	Squire Bell	2-3-0-3
Saml Armour	1-0-0-0	Philip Burwell	1-27-4-1415
Evan P. Anderson	1-1-0-1	John W. Byrd	1-8-1-11
Austin C. Ashby	1-0-0-2	Thomas Briggs	9-4-1-20
John Allison	1-0-0-0	John Brumley	3-0-0-5
Jeremiah Ashby	1-0-0-1	John D. Barr	1-0-0-0
John Anderson	1-0-0-0	James W. Beck	2-0-0-2
		John C. Bonham	1-6-0-7

Clarke County, Virginia Personal Property Tax Lists 1836-1853
1847

Nathaniel Burwell Senr.	1-42-3-44	Adam Barr Senr.	1-0-0-0
Col. James Bell	1-7-4-14	Wm Barley	1-0-0-0
Lewis Berlin	1-2-0-1	James Berlin	1-0-0-0
George W. Berlin	1-0-0-0	Richard Billmyre	1-0-0-0
Strother H. Bowen	3-0-0-1	Shederick Crouse	1-0-0-1
Robert Ben	1-1-0-3	Alfred Castleman	3-5-1-12
Wm Berry	2-12-2-8	Frek Clopton	1-5-0-7
George H. Burwell	2-40-5-36	George F. Calmese	1-4-1-6
Saml Briarly	2-8-0-7	Wm Carrington	3-1-0-1
Christian Bowser	2-0-2-1	Wm Carper	1-0-0-2
John Blue	1-2-0-6	Ambrows Crawford	1-0-1-1
Napoleon Baltrip	1-0-0-1	Robert A. Coltson [sic]	1-4-0-10
Russell Brackett	1-0-0-0	Wm. H. Coltson	1-0-0-0
Jesse Bowen	1-1-0-3	Elizabeth K. Carter	2-1-0-5
Abram Beevers	1-0-0-2	John Copenhaver	2-3-1-10
James Bell	1-0-0-1	Miriam Catlett	1-6-0-14
Wm Berlin	3-4-1-2	James H. Clarke	1-2-2-1
Adam Barr	1-0-0-0	Thomas H. Crow	3-4-1-5
Ben Barr	1-1-0-0	Wm A. Castleman	1-4-0-7
Saml Bonham	2-13-0-14	Alfred Clevenger	1-4-0-5
Andrew Beillmyre	1-0-0-1	John Cooper	1-0-0-3
Jesse Butler	1-0-0-1	Elizabeth Crampton	0-5-1-3
George Bowlin	1-0-0-0	James Castleman	2-12-4-25
Juliet Boston	0-1-0-0	Thomas Carter	0-9-0-8
Nancy Boston	0-0-0-0	Patterson Corder	1-0-0-3
T. T. Byrd's Est.	0-1-0-1	John Carroll	2-0-0-2
John R. Bell	1-3-0-5	John Carpenter	2-3-0-6
Charles Blake	1-0-0-1	Dabney Cauthorn	1-0-0-0
Jacob Bowser	1-0-0-0	Elizabeth N. Carter	1-2-0-2
Butler & Johnson	3-0-0-1	James Carter	1-0-0-0
George W. Bartlett	1-0-0-1	David Clevinger	2-0-0-6
Ephraim Bloxon	1-0-0-0	James N. Corbin	1-0-1-4
James Brown	1-0-0-1	Thomas Cornwell	1-0-0-1
Thomas Bolon	1-0-0-0	George W. Cooper	1-0-0-0
		Aaron Chamblin	2-0-0-5
Charles Castleman	1-0-0-1	Michael Copenhaver	2-0-0-1
Henry Castleman	1-0-0-1	John G. Chapman	1-0-0-0
		Andrew Cage	1-0-0-0

Clarke County, Virginia Personal Property Tax Lists 1836-1853
1847

Mrs. Ury Castleman	0-6-1-7	John D. Davis	1-0-0-1
Jacob Clink	1-0-0-0		
Stephen D. Castleman	2-6-1-6	Charles Eckhardt	1-0-0-0
		Henry Edwards	1-1-0-2
James Carper	1-4-0-7	Wm G. Everheart	1-1-0-5
Peter Cain	2-0-0-5	John Eleyett	1-1-0-2
Stephen Cauthorn	1-0-0-1	Alexander M. Earle	1-4-0-9
Wm. H. Corbin	1-0-0-1	Hiram P. Evans	2-1-2-2
Wm. K. Carter	1-2-0-5	Jacob Enders	1-5-0-8
John R. Corbin	1-0-0-2	Jacob W. Everheart	1-0-0-1
Miss Eloesa Castleman	0-0-0-0	Edward Eno	1-4-0-3
P. P. Cooke	1-0-0-2	Edward Franks	1-0-0-0
Wm G. Carter	1-1-0-1	Jesse Furr	0-0-0-3
Joseph Chapman	1-0-0-0	Ephraim Furr	1-0-0-0
Doct. Chunn	1-0-1-1	George Fyst	1-3-0-7
McClain Clingon	1-0-0-0	Doct. J. Fauntleroy	1-3-2-3
Taylor Cole	1-0-0-0	Doct. O. Funston	1-11-1-15
		Jane H. Forster	1-4-0-4
John Dermont	1-5-0-3	Moses Furr	2-0-0-4
Peter Dermont	1-0-0-0	Martha Forster	0-3-0-1
Wm Deakle	2-0-1-2	George Farnsworth	2-0-0-3
Saml Davis	2-0-0-1	Archibald Fleming	1-1-0-3
James Davis	2-0-0-1	James Furr	1-0-0-1
John Drish	1-0-0-1	Wm Fowler	1-0-0-4
Michael Dermont	2-7-1-12	Ben Franks	1-0-0-2
Baalis Davis	1-2-1-1	Washington Furgerson	1-3-2-5
Thomas Duke	1-0-0-0	Martin Feltner	1-0-0-1
James Dorrin	1-0-0-1	Joseph Fleming	1-0-1-3
Saml Dobbins	1-0-0-0	Thomas Fowler	1-0-0-2
George W. Diffenderfer	1-0-0-1	Marcus R. Feehrer	1-3-0-2
Thos Duke Jr.	1-0-0-0	Jane Forster	0-0-0-1
Wm Davis	1-0-0-2	John Fox	0-1-0-0
Hugh Davis	1-0-0-0	Allen Williams to pay	
John Dow	1-1-0-2	Josiah Furgerson	1-2-0-4
Aaron Duble	1-0-0-1	John W. Friese	1-0-0-0
James T. Danley	1-0-1-2	Kemp Furr	1-0-0-1
Newton Danley	1-0-0-0		

Clarke County, Virginia Personal Property Tax Lists 1836-1853
1847

Charles Furr	1-0-0-1	Jesse Green	1-0-0-0
Ben F. Fuller	1-0-0-0	Jemima Gant	0-4-0-0
Thomas J. Forster	1-0-0-0	George W. Gant	1-0-0-0
Johnson Furr	1-1-1-6	Patrick Gilmer	1-0-0-0
Miss Finch	0-0-0-0	Henry Huntsberry	1-1-0-0
D° for 1846		Joseph Hiett	1-0-0-1
		Whiting Hamilton	1-0-0-2
Richard Green	1-0-0-0	Henry D. Hooe	2-0-0-1
Thomas E. Gold	2-7-1-13	Henry Horner	1-0-0-1
George Gordon	1-1-0-1	Edwin Hart	1-2-0-7
James Green	2-5-1-7	Abram Huyett	2-0-0-5
Stephen J. Gant	1-2-0-4	John Huyett	2-0-0-3
Rebecca Grogan	0-2-1-3	Saml Huyett	1-3-1-6
Edward Gormon	1-0-0-1	James Harris	1-6-1-8
Thomas Grubs	1-1-0-0	Doct. J. Hay	1-14-1-20
Joseph George	1-2-0-3	Levi Hiett	1-3-0-8
John S. Gordon	4-1-0-8	J. M. Hite	1-0-0-2
Henry N. Grigsby	1-4-1-7	Wm Hummer	1-0-0-2
Dandridge Garrison	1-0-0-1	Charles Hennis	1-0-0-0
John Grant	1-0-0-4	Thomas Harris	1-0-0-1
Wm Gourley	1-0-1-7	James H. Hooe	1-0-0-2
Emanuel Garmong	1-0-0-1	Saml Heflybour	1-2-0-10
Saml Grubs	1-0-0-0	John Hay	1-1-0-0
Nimrod Glasscock	1-0-0-0	Jacob Heflybour	1-3-3-9
Abram Grim	1-0-0-0	Wm Holtsclaw	1-0-0-0
Richard N. Green	1-6-1-7	Blackwell Holtsclaw	1-0-0-2
George W. Green	1-9-0-11	Richard Hardesty	2-3-0-12
John L. Grant	1-1-1-4	Mary Howard	0-3-0-0
James Gibs	1-0-0-0	Philip Hunsucker	2-0-0-1
Martin Gant	1-2-2-6	George Harris	0-5-0-11
G. G. Grove	1-1-0-0	Abby Hopkins, nothing,	
George Gardner	1-0-0-0	left County	
Catharine Groves	0-0-0-0	Edward Handle	1-0-1-0
Isabella Glass	0-1-1-0	Grafton Hillyard	1-0-0-0
Adam Greenwall	1-0-0-0	Cornelius Hoof	1-0-0-0
Nathaniel Grubs	1-0-0-0	Richard S. Hardesty	2-0-0-5
Madison Grubs	1-0-0-0	Robert Haney	1-0-0-2
Jefferson Grubs	1-0-0-1	Philip Host	1-0-0-0
John Grayham	1-0-0-0	John Hughes	1-1-0-1

Clarke County, Virginia Personal Property Tax Lists 1836-1853
1847

Thomas Hughes	1-0-0-0	F. J. Kerfoot		
Armistead Hoof	2-2-0-1	See back of book or		
John Hodge	1-0-0-0	end of recapitulation		
Wm G. Hardesty	1-3-0-8	Revd. Thos Kennerly	2-20-3-20	
Thornton Hummer	1-0-0-1	George Knight	1-6-1-14	
James W. Hummer	1-0-0-0	George Kitchen	1-8-1-12	
George Hunsucker	1-1-0-0	Wm C. Kerfoot	1-10-3-17	
Wm Hefflin	1-0-0-0	Ben M. Knight	1-1-0-1	
Henry Huyett	1-0-0-3	Geo L. Kerfoot	1-10-5-17	
Geo W Harris	1-2-0-2	Doct. R. Kownslar	1-3-0-2	
Robert L. Horner	1-0-0-0	John Kable	1-2-0-1	
		Wm F. Knight	1-1-0-1	
		Nickolas Kriser	1-0-0-1	
George Johnson	1-0-1-1	Elizabeth Knight	0-0-0-0	
Herod Jenkins	1-0-0-0	Geo & Wm C. Kerfoot	0-8-1-9	
Solomon R. Jackson	1-0-0-0	Middleton Keeler	1-0-0-0	
Matthew Jones	2-2-0-8	Wm C. Kennerly	1-5-2-5	
Reuben Jordan	1-2-6-2	Joseph Kline	1-0-0-1	
John Joliffe	1-7-1-14	Saml G. Kneller	1-1-0-1	
Thomas Jordan	1-1-0-1	Doct. O. B.Knode	1-0-1-1	
Jacob Isler	4-7-2-11	John B. Kerfoot	1-0-0-1	
Revd. Wm G. H. Jones	1-4-1-1	James M. Kiger	1-2-0-4	
Charles R. Johnson	1-0-0-2	D° for 1846	1-0-0-4	
Thomas Jones	3-1-0-6	Ben Kent	1-0-0-0	
Albert Johnson	1-0-0-1			
Doct. J. J. Janey	1-1-0-5	Wm Lee	1-0-0-0	
Thomas Jenkins	1-0-0-4	Doct. J. M. Lindsay	1-0-0-0	
Elias Johns	1-0-0-0	Franklin Littleton	2—0-2	
Joseph M. Joliffe	1-0-0-4	George Lowry	1-0-0-0	
John Johnson Jr.	1-0-0-0	Henry Loyd	0-0-0-3	
John Johnson Senr.	1-0-0-1	Charles Lucius	1-3-0-8	
Joseph Johnson	2-1-1-7	John Lock	2-0-0-6	
Alfred Jackson	1-3-0-4	James W. Larue	1-4-0-6	
Leonard Jones	1-0-0-1	Wm Longerbeam	1-0-0-1	
Jeremiah Jenkins	1-0-0-0	Washington Lee	1-0-0-1	
		Charles Littleton	1-2-0-4	
		Doct. R. H. Little	2-7-4-10	
James Knight	1-0-0-0	John Louthan	4-2-0-1	
James C. Kenan	1-0-0-0	Lorenzo Lewis	1-14-5-26	

Clarke County, Virginia Personal Property Tax Lists 1836-1853
1847

Saml Larue	1-12-2-12		Mary Meade	0-1-0-0
John B. Larue	2-10-5-29		Thomas McCormick	1-9-1-11
John Loyd	1-0-0-1		John Marts Senr.	1-0-0-1
George Longerbeam	1-0-0-1		Doct. C. McCormick	1-8--8
James Loyd	2-0-0-1		Levi Marquess	3-0-0-0
Saml Loyd	1-0-0-0		N. C. Mason	1-0-0-0
Edgar Lanham	1-0-0-0		Jesse P. Mercer	1-0-0-1
Alfred Logan	1-0-0-3		John & James	
Saml Lanham	1-0-0-1		Michum	2-0-0-3
Abram Longerbeam	3-0-0-3		Col. B. Morgan	1-17-2-29
Elizabeth Lanham	0-0-0-1		Elizabeth Morgan	0-8-2-8
James Lanham	1-0-0-0		Col. F. McCormick	2-10-2-10
A. L. P. Larue	1-0-0-1		Charles McCormick	1-25-3-40
Wm D. Littleton	2-2-0-6		Susan Marshall	0-3-1-7
Harrison Loyd	1-0-0-0		John Marshall	1-1-0-3
Alfred Lee	1-0-0-0		Jesse McConaha	1-0-0-0
John T. Lindsay	1-0-0-3		Alexander Marshall	1-0-0-1
Minor Lanham	1-0-0-0		John McPhillin	3-3-2-10
Ben Lock	1-0-0-3		Wm Mason	1-0-0-1
Rice W. Levi	1-0-0-1		John Morgan	1-7-0-7
James Larues heirs	0-1-0-1		George L. McCormick	3-0-0-4
Squire Lee	2-0-0-2		Province McCormick	1-2-0-3
John Littleton	1-0-0-1		Charles & Saml	
Alfred Lyons	1-0-0-1		McCormick	1-7-3-15
Franklin Little	1-1-0-0		Ben F. Mayhew	1-0-0-0
B. B. Lanes Est.	0-0-0-1		John N. Meade	1-2-1-8
George Lanham	2-0-0-2		Isaac S. Manuel	1-0-0-1
			James Murphy	1-0-0-3
Peter McMurray	1-1-0-8		Sylvanus Moore	1-0-0-1
Saml McCormick	1-0-0-0		Revd. Wm Meade	1-0-0-1
J. J. Monroe	1-2-1-4		Stephen Marlow	1-0-0-1
John Maddex	2-2-0-7		Amishadai Moore	2-2-0-10
James Michell	1-3-1-5		Rebecca S. Meade	0-2-0-0
Wm D. McGuire	2-9-1-12		Alexander Mason	1-0-0-0
Otway McCormick	2-6-2-7		John McCauley	1-0-0-0
Francis B. Meade	1-6-2-13		Violett Mayers	1-0-0-2
Louisa W. Meade	0-2-0-3		David H. McGuire	1-6-1-4
Philip N. Meade	1-6-1-8		Alfred P. Moore	1-0-0-0
Wm Meade Jr.	1-3-0-5		Stephen R. Mount	1-1-1-1

Clarke County, Virginia Personal Property Tax Lists 1836-1853
1847

Edmund W. Massey	2-1-0-1	Elizabeth Orear	0-9-2-6
I. McCormick,		Enock Orear	1-7-0-9
exr L. Glass	2-7-1-9	George Orear	1-4-0-6
Elijah Milton	1-0-0-1	David Osbourn	1-0-0-3
B. B. Miley	1-1-0-3	Mason Olliver	1-6-0-1
Henry J. Messmore	1-3-1-2	George Osbourn	1-2-0-3
John Marple	1-0-0-0	Jesse Orear	1-1-0-2
John McDonald	1-0-0-0	Hugh Orouk	1-0-0-0
Thomas Y. Michell	1-0-0-0	Landon O. Reed	1-0-0-
Province McCormick	1-8-0-12	Elias Overall	1-2-0-1
Micale Moranghan	1-0-0-1		
George Marple	1-0-0-1	George Pultz	1-0-0-1
John Martin	2-0-0-1	John E. Page	1-13-2-18
Saml McCormick	1-0-0-1	Eliza M. Page	0-3-1-0
As guardian of Wm Taylor		John Page	1-7-3-12
Seth Mason	1-5-1-7	Mann R. Page	2-9-2-17
Geo W. McCormick	1-0-0-2	Isaac Pidgeon	2-0-0-5
Harrison McCormick	1-0-0-1	John Pierce Senr.	1-4-0-8
James Murphy	1-0-0-1	R. P. Page	1-18-3-19
		James M. Pine	1-0-0-1
		Mary C. Page	1-6-1-7
Doct. S. S. Neale	1-0-0-1	Joseph E. Peyton	2-0-0-5
Wm Niswanger	3-0-0-5	Paul Pierce	1-5-1-9
Hugh M. Nelson	1-10-1-15	John W. Page	2-7-0-5
Ann T. Neille	0-3-0-2	John Pierce Jr.	2-3-0-8
Philip Nelson	1-14-3-12	John Padgett	1-0-0-0
Thomas F. Nelson	2-13-5-17	James Puller	1-0-0-1
James H. Neville	1-1-0-1	Calvin Puller	1-0-0-1
Joseph Noble	1-0-1-0	Peter McPierce	1-4-0-6
Abby Nelson	0-2-0-0	Thornton P.	
Doct. Wm Nelson	1-2-2-3	Pendleton	2-18-3-27
Joseph M. Nicklin	2-2-2-2	Washington F.	
George R. Newman	3-1-0-2	Padgett	1-0-1-0
Elizabeth Nunn	0-2-1-0	Richard L. Page	0-3-0-1
L. B. & B. T. Norris	1-10-3-12	McFarland Puller	1-0-0-0
		John Patterson	1-0-0-2
Mat Page	0-1-0-0	James Payne	1-0-0-0
Wm Pete [?]	1-0-1-0	Barnett Prichett	1-0-0-1
		L. W. Palmer	1-0-0-1

Clarke County, Virginia Personal Property Tax Lists 1836-1853
1847

Alfred Prescott	1-0-0-0		Wm Riley	1-0-0-1
M. Page of Carolina	0-1-0-0		D° as guardian for	
B. Harrison	1-2-1-4		young Furgerson	
			John Riley	1-0-0-0
Richard Ridgeway	2-1-0-6		Michael Russell	1-0-0-0
Wm Reed	1-1-0-4		Luster Riley	1-0-0-0
Thomas W. Raynolds	1-6-0-3			
Bennet Russell	2-8-1-10		George Smith	1-0-0-0
Elizth Royster	0-1-0-0		Joseph Stewart	1-0-0-0
Mat W. Royston	1-3-2-8		Richard M. Sydnor	1-1-1-1
Peter Royston	1-0-1-1		Susan Smith	0-1-0-0
John Roush	1-0-0-1		Edward L. Smith	1-13-2-10
Uriah B. Royston	1-0-0-6		Wm D. Smith	1-19-3-23
Peter K. &			Joseph Smith	1-0-0-0
M. W. Royston	1-3-0-4		Wm Sowers	2-4-2-8
John Reed	1-0-0-1		Joseph Shepherd	1-7-1-9
Nancy Redmon	0-1-0-0		Champ Shepherd	1-3-0-4
Solomon Redmon	1-0-0-1		Edward Shickles	1-0-0-2
George Rutter	2-0-0-0		Thomas Shumate	1-2-2-13
Danl B. Richards	2-1-0-2		John W. Sowers	1-6-1-11
Saml B. Redmon	1-0-0-1		Wm G. Steele	1-0-0-0
Addison Romine	1-2-0-7		Danl W. Sowers	1-11-2-17
James Ryan	2-1-0-0		Saml Stipe	1-3-1-7
Doct. R. C.			James Sowers	1-11-0-15
Randolph	1-12-1-16		Thomas Sprint	1-0-0-1
John Russell	1-0-0-1		Emanuel Showers	4-1-0-1
Jane Richardson	1-0-0-1		Barnett Smallwood	1-0-0-1
George Reno	2-0-0-2		Fielding L. Sowers	2-4-2-8
Isaac Ramey	2-0-0-3		P. D. Shepherd	2-4-1-8
Mathew Rust	2-3-1-5		P. Smith	2-20-4-24
Joseph Ryan	1-0-0-4		Col. T. Smith	1-13-1-18
Betty Roots	0-1-0-0		Kerfoot Sowers Est.	1-5-0-16
Elizabeth C. Riley	1-4-0-5		John R. Stewart	1-0-0-3
John Russell	1-1-1-1		Wm Stewart	1-0-0-1
James Russell	1-2-0-5		Daniel A. Sowers	2-3-1-7
Stephen Reed	1-0-0-3		Elizabeth Strother	0-6-2-6
John Rowland	1-0-0-7		John Shafer	1-0-0-0
James W. Raynolds	1-0-0-2		Jackson Shafer	1-0-0-1
Thompson Ritt	1-0-0-2		Burr Smallwood	1-0-0-1

Clarke County, Virginia Personal Property Tax Lists 1836-1853
1847

Simon Stickles	1-0-0-1	Saml Taylor	1-12-2-10
George Smedley	1-0-0-0	Ben Thompson Jr.	1-0-0-7
Danl H. Sowers	1-2-0-9	Col. Joseph Tuley	1-21-5-20
Joseph Shipe	1-0-0-0	John Trussell	2-3-0-5
George Strother	1-2-0-1	Charles Taylor	2-5-0-3
James Shackelford	1-0-0-0	Wm Trinary	1-1-0-3
Mary E. Shirely	0-7-3-10	Wm Tinsman	1-0-0-0
John Sharp	1-0-0-1	James Tansell	1-0-0-1
Henry Shepherd	1-0-1-2	James W. Timberlake	1-7-0-10
Henry Seevers	1-1-1-4	Mary Trinary	
Abram Shipe	1-0-0-0	Robert Tapscott	1-0-0-0
John Shell	1-0-0-1	Montreval Tinsman	1-0-0-1
David Shaul	1-2-0-8	Saml Tinsman	1-0-0-1
Wm H. Shores	1-0-0-0	A S. Tidball	1-8-2-13
Stephen Shores	1-0-0-0	Wm Tomblin	1-0-0-0
Jerry Shay	1-2-0-2	George W. Taylor	1-3-1-2
Jonathan S. Smith	1-2-0-1	George Tinsman	1-0-0-2
Wm L. Smith	1-0-0-0	Saml Tinsman Jr.	1-0-0-0
Ben Stonestreet	1-0-0-0	Enoch Triplett	1-0-0-0
Emanuel Shackelford	2-0-0-1	Warner A. Thompson	1-2-1-1
B. H. Sinnot	1-0-0-0	Isaac Tally	1-0-0-0
Henry Stickles	1-0-0-0		
Charles Showers	2-0-0-0	Peter Umbenhaur	1-0-0-0
Robert Seavur	1-0-0-0		
Carter Shepherd	1-0-0-1	John Vanclief	2-0-0-4
Saml Schooler	1-0-0-0	Jacob Vanmeter	0-3-0-9
Dennis Sheehan	1-0-0-1	Wm Violett	1-0-0-0
James W. Smith	1-0-0-1	John Vincent	1-0-0-1
Sarah Timberlake	2-10-0-12	Wm Willingham	1-0-0-1
Wm Turner	2-0-0-1	Allen Williams	1-8-2-13
Abigail Tanquery	0-0-0-1	Col. James Wigginton	1-0-0-1
David Tristler	1-1-0-7	Francis H. Whiting	1-3-0-11
Adam Towner	1-0-0-0	J. W. Ware &	
Hannah Taylor	0-2-0-2	Mrs. Stribling	1-18-3-20
Greenberry		J. G. Wade & Brother	2-2-0-1
Thompson	4-0-0-3	H. T. Wheat	2-1-1-2
David Timberlake	1-0-0-0	Hezekiah Wiley	1-0-0-0
Harrison Thompson	1-0-0-0	Saml Wiley	1-0-0-1

Clarke County, Virginia Personal Property Tax Lists 1836-1853
1847

James Wiley	1-0-0-1	James V. Wier	1-4-0-9
John Willingham	1-0-0-0	Wm Willis	2-0-0-0
E. W. Washington	0-0-0-0	Revd. R. H. Wilmer	1-3-1-1
Leroy P. Williams	3-7-1-10	Wm H. Whiting	1-4-1-7
Wm P. Wigginton	1-2-0-2	Alexander Wood	1-0-1-0
Francis B. Whiting	2-17-3-15	John Wiley	1-0-0-0
Wm W. Whiting	1-1-1-1	David Whittington	1-0-0-2
Obed Willingham	1-0-0-0	James W. Wiley	1-0-0-2
Bennet Wood	1-0-0-0	Jacob Welch	2-0-0-4
N. B. Whiting	1-5-0-10	David H. Wilcox	1-0-0-0
Ephraim Watson	1-1-0-8	Wm Wells	1-0-0-0
Sidnor B. Windham	1-0-1-2	Beverly Washington	1-0-0-0
Thomas Woods	1-0-0-2	James Wood	1-0-0-0
John Wilson	1-0-0-0	Franklin Wilson	1-0-0-1
Joseph A. Williamson	1-8-3-11	Lewis Weaver	1-0-0-0
Henry Washington	1-1-0-1		
Albert Whittington	1-0-0-0	George Young	1-0-0-1
Thomas C. Windham	1-0-0-0	Simeon Yowell	1-1-0-1
Thomas E. Woodword	2-0-0-1	Wm Young	1-0-0-0
James E. Ware	1-0-1-0		

Clarke County, Virginia Personal Property Tax Lists 1836-1853
1847

Free Negroes over 16 years old

John Diggs	1-1-0-0	Peter Coates	1-0-0-2
Thomas Gray	1-0-0-0	Wat Howard	1-0-0-0
Scimeon Parker	1-0-0-1	Wm Richardson	1-0-0-0
George Ransom	1-0-0-0	Wm Howard	1-0-0-0
George Wells	1-0-0-0	Frederick _____	1-0-0-0
John Clifton	1-0-0-0	Lewis Clifton	1-0-0-0
Washington Hall	1-0-0-0		
Jack Adams	1-0-0-0	Nick Voss	1-0-0-1
Spencer Johnson	1-0-0-1	Frank _____	1-0-0-0
Wm Wheeler	1-0-0-0	George Gray	1-0-0-0
Philip Martin	1-0-0-0	Richard Lee	1-0-0-0
Burwell Cook	1-0-0-0	Saml Ransom	1-0-0-0
Mowen Harris	1-0-0-1	Frederick Cook	1-0-0-1
Wm Grayham	1-0-0-3	Lewis Toliver	1-0-0-0
George Lee	1-0-0-0	Wm Henry	1-0-0-0
Jacob Johnson	1-0-0-0	Bennet Taylor	1-0-0-2
Nathan Johnson	1-0-0-0	Billy Butler	1-0-0-0
John Jackson	1-0-0-0	John _____	1-0-0-1
George Davis	1-0-0-0	Alfred _____	1-0-0-0

[Additional names a few pages later.]

J. Dow to pay
Henry Akins to pay
Joseph M. Joliffe to pay
Page Brook
   A. Moore to pay

[After recapitulation]

1 Gold watch, charge Miss Harriet McCormick
Wm Grubs, 1 horse
Franklin J. Kerfoot, 1 white tithable, 9 slaves, 15 horses
Edward McCormick, 1 white tithe, 9 slaves, 9 horses
Wm G. Taylor, 2 white Levies, 10 slaves over 16, 1 over 12, 17 horses

Clarke County, Virginia Personal Property Tax Lists 1836-1853

1848

Columns: 1) white males over 16, 2) slaves over 16 years, 3) slaves 12-16, 4) horses, etc.

Robert Ashby Senr.	1-0-0-1		Phinehas Bowen	2-3-0-9
Mason Anderson	1-1-0-2		Francis O. Byrd	1-10-2-9
David H. Allen	1-18-3-20		Philip Berlin	2-3-2-5
John Alexander	1-16-1-20		George C. Blakemore	1-8-0-8
Wm Alexander	1-9-3-13		D° as guardian for	
Augusta Athey	1-0-0-1		Leonidas Enders	
Buckner Ashby	2-10-1-18		John Bowlin	not in county
Joseph Anderson	3-2-0-8		Neille Barnett	1-3-1-5
Nancy Allen	2-1-1-6		D° as guardian for	
Algernon S. Allen	2-9-1-12		young Carters	
John Alexander Jr.	1-0-0-1		Thomas W. Briggs	1-2-2-7
John Ashby	1-0-0-1		Danl S. Bonham	1-6-0-7
Robert Ashby Jr.	1-0-0-0		James Bogs	1-0-0-0
Martin Ashby	1-0-0-1		John Brownly	0-9-2-11
Thomas H. Alexander	2-1-0-2		Wm Baker	1-5-1-5
Nimrod Ashby	1-0-0-1		Isaac Berlin	2-0-1-1
John Ambrows	2-1-0-7		George Berlin	1-0-0-1
David T. Armstrong	1-1-0-0		Strother Bell	1-0-0-0
Saml Armour	1-0-0-1		Robert Burchell	1-3-2-6
Evan P. Anderson	1-1-0-1		H. W. Brabham	1-0-0-0
Austin C. Ashby	1-0-0-3		Squire Bell	2-0-0-5
Hathaway Alexander	0-1-0-0		Philip Burwell	1-26-3-13
Jeremiah Ashby	1-0-0-1		John W. Byrd	1-10-2-10
John Anderson	1-0-0-0		Thomas Briggs	9-4-1-20
James Allison	1-0-0-0		John Brumley	4-0-0-11
Wm T. Allen	1-3-0-2		John D. Barr	1-0-0-0
Thomas Ashby	1-0-0-1		James W. Beck	2-0-0-1
David Armstrong	1-0-0-0		John C. Bonham	1-6-0-7
			Nat Burwell Senr.	1-41-4-42
Nathaniel Burwell Jr.	1-8-2-12		Col. James Bell	1-7-4-8
Wm C. Benson	1-1-0-0		Lewis Berlin	1-2-0-1
John Burchell	2-4-3-101		George H. Burwell	2-44-3-39
Archibald Bowen	1-4-0-5		Wm Berlin	3-3-1-4
Hiram O. Bell	1-0-0-0		Juliet Boston	0-1-0-0

Clarke County, Virginia Personal Property Tax Lists 1836-1853
1848

Name	Values	Name	Values
Nancy Boston	0-0-0-0	Wm Carrington	5-1-0-1
George W. Berlin	1-0-0-1	Wm Carper	1-0-0-2
Strother H. Bowen	3-1-0-1	Ambrows Crawford	2-0-1-1
Robert Ben	2-1-0-3	Robert A. Coltson	1-4-1-9
Wm Berry	2-13-1-11	Wm. H. Coltson	1-0-0-0
George Bolen	1-0-0-0	Elizabeth K. Carter	2-2-0-5
Saml Briarly	2-8-0-9	John Copenhaur	2-2-1-10
Christian Bowser	2-0-1-2	Elizabeth Crampton Est.	0-1-0-0
John Blue	1-2-0-8	Miriam Catlett	1-6-0-12
Jacob Bowser	1-0-0-0	James H. Clarke	1-3-1-1
Napoleon Baltrip	1-0-0-1	Thomas H. Crow	2-3-2-5
Jesse Bowen	1-2-0-1	Wm. A. Castleman	1-3-0-8
Abram Beevers	1-0-0-2	John Cooper	2-0-0-3
James Bell	1-0-0-1	James Castleman	1-15-4-28
Adam Barr	1-0-0-0	Thomas Carter	2-11-2-10
Ben Barr	1-1-0-0	Parkerson Corder	1-0-0-2
Saml Bonham	2-15-0-15	John Carroll Sr.	1-0-0-0
Andrew Billmyre	1-0-0-1	John Carroll Jr.	1-0-0-1
Jesse Butler	1-0-0-1	John Carpenter	1-4-0-6
T. T. Byrd's Est.	0-1-0-1	Dabney Cauthorn	1-0-0-0
John R. Bell	1-2-0-5	Elizabeth N. Carter	1-2-0-2
Charles Blake	1-0-0-1	James Carter	2-0-0-0
James Berlin	1-1-0-1	David Clevinger	1-0-0-3
Thomas Botelor	1-0-0-0	James N. Corbin	2-0-1-5
George W. Bartlett	1-0-0-1	Thomas Cornwell	1-0-0-1
Ephraim Bloxon	1-0-0-0	Stephen Cauthorn	1-0-0-0
James Brown	1-0-0-1	George W. Cooper	not found
Thomas Bolen	1-0-1-0	Aaron Chamblin	3-0-0-6
Adam Barr Sr.	1-0-0-0	Michael Copenhaur	2-0-0-1
Wm Bailey	1-0-0-0	John G. Chapman	1-0-0-0
Richd Billmyre	1-0-0-0	Andrew Cage	1-0-0-0
Henry W. Bayliss	1-0-0-0	Mrs. Ury Castleman	0-6-1-7
James Bukheimer	1-0-0-0	Stephen D. Castleman	3-2-2-1
Isaac Berlin Jr.	1-0-0-0	John N. Collier	1-0-0-1
Shederick Crouse	1-0-0-1	James Carper	2-2-0-7
Alfred Castleman	2-4-1-12	Jacob Crim	1-0-0-0
Frederick Clopton	1-5-0-6	Stephen B. Cook	1-0-0-5
George F. Calmese	1-5-2-9		

Clarke County, Virginia Personal Property Tax Lists 1836-1853
1848

John B. Carter	1-2-0-2		Elijah Dulen	1-0-0-0
Peter Cain	2-0-0-5		Henry F. Dixon	1-2-1-1
Wm. H. Corbin	1-0-1-0		Revd. George	
Wm. K. Carter	1-2-0-4		Dunham	1-0-0-1
John R. Corbin	1-0-0-0			
Miss Eloesa			Charles Eckhardt	1-0-0-1
Castleman	0-0-0-0		Henry Edwards	1-0-0-2
Philip P. Cooke	1-1-0-2		Wm G. Everheart	1-2-0-6
Wm G. Carter	1-1-0-1		John Eleyett	1-1-0-1
Joseph Chapman	1-0-0-0		Alexander M. Earle	1-5-0-8
Doct. Chunn	1-2-1-1		Hiram P. Evans	2-1-0-1
McClain Clingon	1-0-1-0		Jacob Enders	1-5-1-9
Charles M.			Jacob W. Everheart	1-0-0-1
Castleman	1-0-0-1		Edward Eno	2-3-0-2
Henry W. Castleman	1-0-0-1			
John W. Carter	1-0-0-0		Edward Franks	1-0-0-0
John A. Carter	1-1-0-4		Wm Franks	1-0-0-0
David Carper	1-1-0-6		Jesse Furr	0-0-0-2
Danl Carroll	1-0-0-1		Ephraim Furr	1-0-0-1
Andrew Collins	1-0-0-1		George Fyst	1-3-2-8
			Doct. J. Fauntleroy	1-2-1-3
John Dermont	1-3-1-2		Doct. O. Funston	1-10-0-16
Peter Dermont	1-2-0-1		Jane H. Forster	1-1-1-5
Wm Deakle	2-0-2-2		Moses Furr	1-0-1-5
Saml Davis	2-0-0-1		Martha Forster	0-3-0-1
James Davis	1-0-0-1		George Farnsworth	1-0-0-3
John Drish	1-0-0-1		Archibald Fleming	1-2-0-3
Michael Dermont	2-8-1-13		James Furr	1-0-0-1
Baalis Davis	1-3-0-1		Wm Fowler	1-0-0-3
Thomas Duke	1-0-0-0		Ben Franks	1-3-0-4
James Dorin	1-0-0-1		Washington	
Saml Dobbins	1-0-0-2		Furgerson	1-1-1-2
George W.			Martin Feltner	1-0-0-1
Diffenderfer	1-0-0-1		Joseph Fleming	1-0-1-2
Hugh Davis	1-0-0-0		Thomas Fowler	1-0-0-1
John Dow	1-2-1-5		Marcus R. Feehrer	1-2-0-3
Aaron Duble	1-0-0-1		John Fox	0-1-0-0
John D. Davis	1-0-0-1		Allen Williams to pay	
James Danley	1-0-0-2		Josiah Furgerson	1-1-0-2

Clarke County, Virginia Personal Property Tax Lists 1836-1853
1848

John W. Friese	1-0-0-0		Thornberry Grubs	1-0-0-0
Kemp Furr	1-0-0-1		Doct. J. Hays Est.	0-18-0-17
Ben F. Fuller	1-0-0-0		A. C. Grove	1-0-0-0
Thomas L. Forster	1-0-0-0			
Johnson Furr	1-1-0-6		Henry Huntsberry	1-1-0-0
Matthew Frier	1-0-0-1		Joseph Hiett	1-0-0-6
Ebin Frost	1-0-0-0		Whiting Hamilton	1-0-0-2
Thomas E. Gold	2-6-2-14		Henry D. Hooe	2-1-0-1
George Gordon	2-0-0-1		Henry Horner	1-0-0-1
James Green	2-4-1-7		Edwin Hart	1-2-0-7
Stephen Gant	1-2-0-3		Abram Huyett	1-0-0-5
Rebecca Grogan	0-3-1-3		John Huyett	1-0-0-2
Edward Gormon	1-0-0-1		Saml Huyett	1-3-0-9
Thomas Grubs	1-1-0-0		James Harris	1-9-1-8
Joseph George	1-2-0-5		Levi Hiett	1-3-0-8
John S. Gordon	4-1-0-9		J. M. Hite	1-0-0-2
Henry N. Grigsby	1-0-4-8		Wm Hummer	1-0-0-1
Dandridge Garrison	1-0-0-1		Charles Hennis	1-0-0-1
John Grant	1-1-2-4		Thomas Harris	1-0-0-2
Wm Gourley	2-1-0-6		James H. Hooe	1-0-0-3
Emanl Garmong	1-0-0-1		Saml Heflybour	1-3-2-9
Saml Grubs	1-0-0-0		John Hay	see back of book
Nimrod Glasscock	1-0-0-0		Jacob Heflybour	1-3-2-10
Abram Grim	1-0-0-0		Wm Holtsclaw	1-0-0-1
Richd N. Green	1-6-0-9		Blackwell Holtsclaw	1-0-0-1
George W. Green	1-8-0-10		Mary Howard	0-3-0-0
John L. Grant	1-2-0-4		Philip Hunsucker	2-0-0-1
James Gibs	1-0-0-0		George Harris	1-6-0-7
Martin Gant	1-3-1-6		Wm B. Harris	1-6-1-7
Jemima Gant	0-1-0-1		Edward Handle	1-1-0-0
George G. Grove	1-1-0-1		Grafton Hillyard	1-0-0-0
George Gardner	1-0-0-0		Cornelius Hoof	1-0-0-0
Catharine Grove	0-0-0-0		Richard S. Hardesty	1-3-0-6
Isabella Glass	0-1-1-0		Robert Haney	1-0-0-2
Adam Greenwall	1-0-0-0		Philip Host	1-0-0-0
Jefferson Grubs	1-0-0-0		John Hughes	1-1-0-1
Wm Grubs	1-0-0-1		Thomas Hughes	1-0-0-1
Jesse Green	1-0-0-1		Armistead Hoof	2-0-0-0
Joseph B. Gourley	1-0-0-1		John Hodge	1-0-0-1

Clarke County, Virginia Personal Property Tax Lists 1836-1853
1848

Wm G. Hardesty	2-2-1-7	James C. Kenan	1-0-0-0
Thornton Hummer	1-0-0-1	Doct. L. J. Kerfoot	1-10-1-16
Sarah Hardesty	1-3-0-12	Revd. T. Kennerly	2-20-2-20
John R. Hooper	1-0-0-1	George Knight	1-7-0-12
Wm Heskit	1-0-0-0	Mariah L. Kitchen	0-2-0-3
George Hunsucker	1-1-0-0	Wm P. Kerfoot	1-9-4-18
Wm Hefflin	1-0-0-0	Ben M. Knight	1-1-0-1
Henry Huyett	1-0-0-5	George L. Kerfoot	1-11-5-17
George W. Harris	1-0-0-2	Ben Kent	1-0-0-0
Robert L. Horner	1-0-0-0	Doct. R. Kownslar	1-3-0-3
Doct. B. Harrison	1-4-1-7	John Kable	1-2-0-1
Frank Helison [?]	1-0-0-0	Wm F. Knight	1-0-0-1
John W. Hart	1-0-0-0	Nickolas Kriser	1-0-0-1
Theobald B. Himes	2-0-0-0	Elizabeth Knight	0-0-0-0
Revd. L. T. Hoof	1-4-0-1	Geo & Wm C. Kerfoot	0-6-0-12
		Middleton Keeler	1-1-0-0
George Johnson	1-0-1-1	Wm C. Kennerly	1-5-1-7
Herod Jenkins	1-0-0-0	Joseph Kline	1-0-0-1
Solomon R. Jackson	1-0-0-0	Saml G. Kneller	1-1-0-1
Matthew Jones	2-1-0-8	Doct. O. B. Knode	1-0-0-2
Reuben Jordan	1-2-0-2	John B. Kerfoot	1-0-0-2
John Joliffe	1-6-1-12	James M. Kiger	1-1-0-4
Doct. R. R. Jordan	1-0-0-1	Augustus L. Knight	1-0-0-0
Jacob Isler	2-6-2-13	Edward V. Kercheval	1-0-0-0
Albert Johnson	1-0-0-1	Franklin Kenneford	1-0-0-0
Doct. J. J. Janey	1-2-1-4	Isaac Kiger	2-0-0-0
Thomas Jenkins	1-0-0-5	Jacob Kriser	1-0-0-1
Joseph M. Joliffe	2-0-0-5		
John Johnson Jr.	1-0-0-0	Wm Lee	1-0-0-0
John Johnson Senr.	1-0-0-1	Doct. J. M. Lindsay	1-0-0-0
Joseph Johnson	1-1-2-6	Franklin & Wm	
Alfred Jackson	1-2-0-4	Littleton	2-1-0-3
Leonard Jones	1-0-0-1	Henry Lloyd	1-0-0-3
Harrison Jones	1-0-0-1	Charles Lucius	1-4-0-8
George W. Joy	1-0-0-0	John Lock	2-0-0-5
James W. Johnson	1-0-0-1	James W. Larue	1-4-1-5
Edward Jackson	1-5-0-1	Wm Longerbeam	1-0-0-1
Elizabeth Iden	0-0-0-3	Washington Lee	1-0-0-1
Ransall Johnson	1-0-0-1	Charles Littleton	1-0-0-3

Clarke County, Virginia Personal Property Tax Lists 1836-1853
1848

Name	Values	Name	Values
Doct. R. H. Little	1-8-3-8	J. J. Monroe	1-2-1-4
John Louthan	4-3-0-1	John Maddex	1-1-0-6
Lorenzo Lewis Est.	0-22-5-27	James Michell	1-2-1-6
John D. Lanham	1-0-0-1	Doct. Wm D.	
Saml Larue	1-12-2-12	McGuire	2-10-2-9
John B. Larue	2-10-5-29	Otway McCormick	2-4-2-8
John Lloyd	1-0-0-1	Francis B. Meade	1-6-2-13
George Longerbeam	1-0-0-1	Mrs. L. W. Meade	0-2-1-1
James Lloyd	1-0-0-1	Philip N. Meade	1-6-1-8
Saml Lloyd	1-0-0-0	Wm Meade Jr.	1-2-0-5
David Lloyd	1-0-0-0	Miss Mary Meade	0-1-0-1
Edgar Lanham	1-0-0-0	Thomas McCormick	1-1-0-0
Saml Lanham	1-0-0-2	John Marts Senr.	1-0-0-1
Abram Longerbeam	1-0-0-0	Doct. C. McCormick	1-8-1-8
Elizabeth Lanham	0-0-0-1	Levi Marquess	3-0-0-2
A. L. P. Larue	1-0-0-1	Jesse P. Mercer	1-0-0-1
Wm D. Littleton	2-2-0-6	John & James	
Harrison Lloyd	1-0-0-1	Michum	2-0-0-3
Alfred Lee	1-0-0-0	Col B. Morgan	1-15-3-28
John T. Lindsay	1-3-0-3	Col F. McCormick	1-9-2-9
Minor Lanham	1-0-0-1	Charles McCormick	1-27-5-41
Ben Lock	1-0-0-4	Susan Marshall	0-5-0-6
Rice W. Levi	1-0-0-1	John Marshall	1-1-2-5
James Larues heirs	0-1-0-1	Jesse McConaha	1-0-0-0
Squire Lee	2-0-0-2	Alexander Marshall	1-0-0-1
Alfred Lyons	1-0-0-0	John McPhillin	4-4-2-10
Joseph Shipe	1-0-0-0	Wm Mason	1-0-0-0
George Lanham	1-0-0-1	John Morgan	2-7-1-12
James Lloyd Jr.	1-0-0-1	George L.	
John Longerbeam	1-0-0-0	McCormick	3-0-0-4
Ben Longerbean	1-0-0-0	Province McCormick	1-9-0-12
R. S. Littlejohn	2-0-0-1	Charles & Saml	
George Lock	2-0-0-1	McCormick	1-7-4-13
Peter M. Lewis	0-3-1-2	Ben F. Mayhew	1-0-0-0
John W. Littleton	1-0-0-2	John N. Meade	1-2-1-9
Louisa Littleton	0-2-0-0	Isaac S. Manuel	1-0-0-3
		James Murphy	1-0-0-3
Peter McMurray	1-1-2-8	Sylvanus Moore	1-0-0-1
Saml McCormick	1-0-0-0	Revd. Wm Meade	1-0-0-1

Clarke County, Virginia Personal Property Tax Lists 1836-1853
1848

Stephen Marlow	1-0-0-1	Mrs. E. Nunn	0-0-0-0
Amishadai Moore	2-3-0-11	L. B. & B. T. Norris	1-5-0-10
Rebecca S. Meade	0-3-0-2	P. Nelson Jr.	1-1-1-6
Alexander Mason	1-0-0-0	John Nessmith	1-2-0-3
John G. McCauley	1-0-0-40		
Violett Mayers	0-0-0-2	Elizabeth Orear	0-8-1-8
D. H. McGuire	1-6-2-4	Enoch Orear	1-6-0-7
Alfred P. Moore	2-0-0-0	George Orear	1-3-0-7
George D. Moss	1-3-0-3	David Osbourn	1-0-0-1
Stephen R. Mount	1-1-1-1	Mason Olliver	1-0-0-1
Edmund W. Massey	2-3-1-2	George Osbourn	1-2-0-4
J. McCormick,		Hugh Orook	1-0-0-0
exr L. Glass	2-9-0-10	Elias Overall	1-2-0-2
Elijah Milton	1-0-0-1	James Orr	1-0-0-1
John Marple	1-0-1-0		
John McDonald	1-0-0-1	Matthew Pullium	1-0-0-0
George Marple	1-0-0-2	George Pultz	1-0-0-2
Province McCormick	1-2-0-3	John E. Page	1-13-2-19
Micale Moranghan	1-0-0-1	Mrs. E. M. Page	0-3-1-0
Seth Mason	1-3-4-9	John Page Jr.	1-7-3-12
Geo W. McCormick	1-0-0-2	Mann R. Page	2-9-3-17
Harrison McCormick	1-0-0-2	Isaac Pidgeon	1-0-0-2
John Maddox Senr.	1-0-0-2	Saml Pidgeon	1-0-0-4
Rich K. Meade	1-5-0-6	John Pierce Senr.	1-3-2-8
Moses Miley	1-0-0-5	Doct. R. Page	1-19-3-20
Saml Morgan	1-0-0-2	James M. Pine	See back of book
Susan McKee	1-0-0-0	Mary C. Page	1-6-0-9
Luther Martin	1-0-0-0	Joseph E. Peyton	2-0-0-4
		Paul Pierce	1-6-1-9
Doct. S. S. Neale	1-2-1-4	John W. Page	2-8-1-4
Wm Niswanger	2-0-0-6	D° as guardian for E. B. Page	
Hugh M. Nelson	1-12-0-12	John Pierce Jr.	2-2-0-8
Philip Nelson	1-13-3-10	James Puller	1-0-0-1
Thomas F. Nelson	2-12-2-13	Calvin Puller	1-0-0-2
James H. Neville	1-1-0-0	Peter Mc Pierce	1-4-0-6
Joseph Noble	1-0-0-0	Thornton P.	
Abby Nelson	0-3-0-0	Pendleton	2-18-3-27
Doct.Wm Nelson	1-2-2-4	Washington F.	
George R. Newman	3-1-0-2	Padgett	1-0-1-1

Clarke County, Virginia Personal Property Tax Lists 1836-1853
1848

Name	Values	Name	Values
Richd L. Page	0-3-0-1	Wm Riley	1-0-0-1
McFarland Puller	1-0-0-0	Michael Russell	1-0-0-1
John Patterson	1-0-0-2	Luster Riley	1-0-0-0
James Payne	1-0-0-1	James W. Relings [?]	
Barnett Prichett	1-0-0-1	Est.	2-3-0-4
Wm Pyle	1-0-0-0	Peter K. Royston	1-1-0-1
Conrad Pope	1-0-0-1	John Ramey	1-0-0-0
		Wm C. Ramey	1-0-0-1
Danl W. Rector	1-0-0-0	Thomas Reradan	1-0-0-1
Richd Ridgeway	2-2-0-5	Elisha Romine	1-0-0-1
Wm Reed	1-0-0-4	John M. Reed	1-0-1-0
Bennet Russell	3-8-2-11	Landon O. Reed	1-0-0-0
Miss E. Royster	0-1-1-0	Stephen Reed	1-0-0-1
Mat W. Royston	2-4-0-14		
Peter Royston	1-0-0-1	George Smith	1-0-0-1
John Roush	1-0-0-1	Joseph Stewart	1-0-0-0
Uriah B. Royston	1-0-0-4	Mrs. Susan Smith	0-1-0-0
John Reed	1-0-0-1	Edward L. Smith	1-7-0-11
Nancy Redmon	0-1-0-0	Wm D. Smith	1-21-2-20
Solomon Redmon	1-0-0-0	Joseph Smith	1-0-0-0
George Rutter	2-0-0-0	Wm Sowers	2-3-3-8
Danl B. Richards	2-0-1-2	Joseph Shepherd	1-7-1-10
Saml B. Redmon	1-0-0-1	Champ Shepherd	1-2-1-4
Addison Romine	1-3-0-6	Edward Shickles	1-0-0-2
James Ryan	2-1-0-0	Thomas Shumate	1-2-1-14
Joseph Ryan	1-0-0-4	John W. Sowers	1-4-3-12
Doct. R. C. Randolph	1-12-2-17	Wm G. Steele	1-0-0-0
John Russell	1-2-0-1	Danl W. Sowers	1-13-1-22
Jane Richardson	0-0-0-1	Saml Stipe	2-3-1-8
Wm Richardson	1-0-0-0	James Sowers	1-11-0-15
Joseph Richardson	1-0-0-0	Thomas Sprint	1-0-0-2
George Reno	1-0-0-1	Emanl Showers	4-1-1-1
Isaac Ramey	2-0-2-3	Barnett Smallwood	1-0-0-1
Mathew Rust	2-3-0-6	Fielding L. Sowers	1-4-1-9
Miss Betsy Roots	0-0-0-0	Wm B. Sowers	1-0-0-0
John Russell	1-0-0-1	P. D. Shepherd	2-4-1-9
James Russell	1-1-0-6	Doct. P. Smith	2-21-2-25
John Rowland	2-0-0-7	Col. T. Smith	1-16-1-19
Thompson Ritt	1-0-0-2	Kerfoot Sowers Est.	2-7-0-16

Clarke County, Virginia Personal Property Tax Lists 1836-1853
1848

John Stewart	3-2-1-8		Wm Turner	1-0-0-1
Elizabeth Strother	0-5-2-6		Abigail Tanquery	0-0-0-1
John Shafer	1-0-0-1		David Tristler	1-1-0-6
Jackson Shafer	1-0-0-1		Adam Towner	1-0-0-0
Burr Smallwood	1-0-0-1		Mrs. H. Taylor	1-9-0-8
Simon Stickles	1-0-0-1		Greenberry Thompson	3-0-0-3
George Smedley	1-0-0-1			
Danl H. Sowers	1-2-1-9		Harrison Thompson	1-0-0-1
Joseph Shipe	1-0-0-0		Doct. Saml Taylor	1-12-2-11
[Also in "L" list]			Ben Thompson Jr.	1-0-0-6
George Strother	1-2-0-5		Col. Joseph Tuley	1-22-7-22
James Shackelford	0-0-0-2		John Trussell	2-4-0-6
over for 1847			Charles H. Taylor	1-3-0-3
Mary E. Shirely	0-6-3-12		Wm Trinary	1-1-0-3
Henry Shepherd	1-0-1-1		Wm Tinsman	1-0-0-0
Henry Seevers	1-1-1-4		James Tansell	2-0-0-1
Abram Shipe	1-0-0-0		James W. Timberlake	1-6-1-9
Joseph Sprint	1-0-0-0			
John Shell	1-0-0-1		Adam Thompson	1-0-0-1
David Shaul	1-2-1-9		Mary Trinary	0-0-0-0
Jerry Shay	1-0-0-1		Robert Tapscott	1-0-1-0
Jonathan S. Smith	3-3-1-1		Montreval Tinsman	1-0-0-1
Wm L. Smith	1-0-0-0		Saml Tinsman Senr.	1-0-0-0
Erasmus Shackelford	1-0-0-0		A. S. Tidball	1-0-1-9
B. H. Sinnot	1-0-0-0		Wm Tomblin	1-0-0-0
Henry Stickles	1-0-0-0		George W. Taylor	1-0-0-1
Charles Showers	2-0-0-0		George W. Tinsman	1-0-0-1
Robert Seavur	1-0-0-0		Saml Tinsman Jr.	1-0-0-0
Saml Schooler	1-0-0-1		Enoch Triplett	1-0-0-0
James W. Smith	1-0-0-0		Warner A. Thompson	1-3-1-1
See back of book for slaves			Isaac Tally	1-0-0-1
Paul Smith	1-2-1-4		Howard F. Thornton	1-7-1-4
Philip Smith	1-0-0-0		Snowdon Tomblein	1-0-0-1
Sebastian Smith	1-0-0-0		Wm G. Taylor	1-3-0-1
Alexander Saunders	1-0-0-0		French Thompson	2-0-0-2
George Swarts	1-0-0-0		Moses B. Trussell	1-0-0-1
John B. Taylor	1-14-0-13		Peter Umbenhaur	1-0-0-0
Sarah Timberlake	2-8-0-12			

Clarke County, Virginia Personal Property Tax Lists 1836-1853
1848

Name	Values	Name	Values
Mason Tinsman	1-0-0-1	Henry R. Wilson	1-1-0-1
Calvin Thacker	1-0-0-0	N. B. Whiting	1-5-0-9
		Sydnor B. Windham	1-0-0-2
John Vanclief	2-1-0-6	Thomas E.	
Jacob Vanmeter	0-3-0-10	Woodward	1-0-0-2
Wm Violett	1-0-0-0	Thomas Woods	1-0-0-2
John Vincent	1-0-0-1	John Wilson	1-0-0-0
		Doct. H. Washington	1-1-0-1
Wm Willingham	1-0-0-1	Thomas C. Windham	1-0-0-0
Allen Williams	1-8-3-13	James E. Ware	1-0-0-0
Francis H. Whiting	1-3-0-8	James V. Wier	1-4-2-7
J. W. Ware &		Wm Willis See back of the book	
Mrs. Stribling	1-16-3-18	Revd. R. H. Wilmer	1-3-0-2
J. G. Wade &		Wm H. Whiting	1-6-1-8
Brothers	2-1-0-1	Alexander Wood	1-0-1-0
H. T. Wheat	3-3-0-3	James Wiley Jr.	1-0-0-1
Hezekiah Wiley	1-0-0-0	John Wiley	1-0-0-1
Saml Wiley	1-0-0-1	David Whittington	1-0-0-1
James Wiley	1-0-0-1	Jacob Welch	2-0-0-4
John Willingham	1-0-0-1	David H. Wilcox	1-0-0-0
Miss E. W.		Wm Wells Gone to Missouri	
Washington	0-0-0-0	Beverly Washington	1-0-0-0
Leroy P. Williams	4-8-1-9	Franklin Wilson	1-0-0-1
Wm P. Wigginton	1-2-0-3	James Wilson	1-0-0-0
Francis B. Whiting	2-20-3-14	Walter Watson	3-0-0-3
Wm W. Whiting	1-3-2-4		
Obed Willingham	1-0-0-0	Simeon Yowell	1-1-0-1
Bennet Wood	1-0-0-0	Wm Young	1-0-0-0

Clarke County, Virginia Personal Property Tax Lists 1836-1853
1848

Free Negroes Chargeable with state taxes

Columns: Blacks over 16, slaves, horses, common watches

Free Boy	1-0-0-0	Peter Coates	1-0-2-0
Bob Butler	1-0-0-0	Wat Howard	1-0-0-0
Thomas Gray	1-0-0-0	Frederick _____	1-0-0-0
Scimeon Parker	1-0-0-1	Lewis Clifton	1-0-0-0
John Clifton	1-0-0-0	Nick Voss	1-0-0-0
Jack Adam	1-0-0-0	Saml Ranson	1-0-0-0
Spencer Johnson	1-0-1-1	Lewis Toliver	1-0-0-0
Philip Martin	1-0-0-0	Bennet Taylor	1-0-0-0
Burwell Cook	1-0-0-0	Alfred _____	0-0-0-0
Mowen Harris	1-1-0-0	George Ranson	1-0-0-0
Wm Grayham	1-0-2-1	James Hatter	2-0-0-0
George Lee	1-0-0-0	Frederick Cooper	1-0-2-0
Nathan Johnson	1-0-0-0	Wm Davis	1-0-0-0
John Jackson	1-0-3-0	Bound Boy	1-0-0-0
George Davis	1-0-0-0		

[Additional information for white males]

Edward McCormick	1-12-0-12	James M. Pine	0-0-0-1
John Hay	1-1-1-0	James W. Smith	0-1-0-0
Wm Willis	1-0-1-0		

Clarke County, Virginia Personal Property Tax Lists 1836-1853

1849

Columns: 1) white males above 16 years, 2) slaves above 16 years, 3) slaves 12-16, 4) horses, mares, mules & colts.

Name	Values	Name	Values
Robert Ashby Senr.	1-0-0-1	Wm Alder	1-0-0-0
Mason Anderson	1-5-0-10		
David H. Allen	2-17-3-27	Nathaniel Burwell Jr.	1-8-3-14
John Alexander Senr.	1-18-2-20	Wm C. Benson	1-0-0-0
Wm C. Alexander	1-8-3-12	John Burchell	2-4-3-13
Augusta Athey	1-0-0-1	Archibald Bowen	1-4-0-8
Buckner Ashby	2-10-3-11	Hiram O. Bell	1-0-0-0
Joseph Anderson	1-2-0-5	Phinehas Bowen	1-3-1-9
Nancy Allen	2-1-1-9	Francis O. Byrd	1-10-2-9
A. S. Allen	2-9-1-11	Philip Berlin	2-4-2-5
John Ashby Senr.	1-0-0-0	George C. Blakemore	1-7-0-8
Robert Ashby Jr.	1-0-0-1	D° as guardian for Leonidas Enders	
Martin Ashby	1-0-0-1		
Thomas H. Alexander	2-1-0-2	Neille Barnett	1-3-2-6
Nimrod Ashby	1-0-0-1	D° as guardian for young Carters	1-0-0-0
David T. Armstrong	1-0-0-1		
Evan P. Anderson	1-1-0-1	Thomas Briggs Est.	0-4-0-8
Austin C. Ashby	1-0-0-4	Danl S. Bonham	1-4-2-7
Jeremiah Ashby	1-0-0-4	Fannie Brownley	1-8-2-13
James Allison	1-0-0-0	Wm Baker	1-2-0-4
Wm T. Allen	1-4-1-6	Isaac Berlin	3-0-1-1
Thomas Ashby	1-0-0-2	Strother Bell	1-0-0-0
John Anderson	1-0-0-0	Catharine Bales	0-0-0-0
George B. Ashby	1-0-0-0	Robert Burchell	1-4-1-5
John Allison	1-0-0-0	H. W. Brabham	1-0-0-0
Joel Alexander	1-0-0-0	Squire Bell	3-0-0-3
James Ash	1-0-0-0	Philip Burwells Est.	1-20-5-10
Dorcas Alexander	0-1-0-0	John W. Byrd	1-10-2-10
Washington Anderson	1-0-0-2	Thomas Briggs Senr.	7-6-1-20
		John Brumley	5-0-0-10
John W. Anderson	1-0-0-0	John D. Barr	1-0-0-0

Clarke County, Virginia Personal Property Tax Lists 1836-1853
1849

James W. Beck	3-0-0-2	Isaac Berlin Jr.	1-0-0-0
Mrs. Susan Burwell	0-8-3-2	Wm Berlin	3-2-1-6
John C. Bonham	1-6-1-10	Benjamin F. Boley	1-3-0-6
		Wm Bailey	1-0-0-0
Nathaniel Burwell		James S. Brown	1-1-0-0
Senr.	1-45-15-40	George H. Bell	1-0-0-1
Col. James Bell	1-9-3-11	Emily A. S. Berlin	0-0-0-0
Lewis Berlin	1-2-0-1		
Strother H. Bowen	2-1-1-1	Alfred Castleman	4-6-0-10
Ann C. Benn	1-1-0-2	Frederick Clopton	1-6-0-8
Wm Berry	3-14-1-11	George F. Calmese	1-6-1-8
George H. Burwell	3-38-5-39	Wm Carrington	1-1-0-1
George Bolen	1-0-0-0	Wm Carper	1-0-0-2
Doct. H. F. Barton	1-0-0-1	Ambrows Crawford	2-0-1-1
Saml Briarley	2-8-0-9	Robert A. Coltson	1-4-1-10
Christian Bowser	2-1-1-1	Wm H. Coltson	1-2-0-5
John Blue	2-2-0-8	Elizabeth K. Carter	2-1-0-6
Napoleon Baltrip	1-0-0-1	John Copenhaur	3-3-1-11
Abram Beevers	1-0-0-4	Miriam Catlett	1-6-0-12
James Bell	1-0-0-1	James H. Clarke	1-2-2-1
Adam Barr	1-0-0-0	Thomas H. Crow	2-4-1-4
Benjamin Barr	1-1-0-0	Wm. A. Castleman	1-3-2-9
Saml Bonham	2-13-1-20	John Cooper	1-0-0-2
Andrew Billmyre	1-0-0-1	Elizabeth Crampton's	
Jesse Butler	1-0-0-1	Est.	0-1-0-0
Juliet Boston	0-1-0-0	James Castleman	1-14-3-31
Nancy Boston	0-0-0-0	Thomas Carter	1-12-2-10
T. T. Byrd's Est.	0-1-0-1	Parkerson Corder	1-0-0-1
John R. Bell	1-3-0-5	John Carroll	1-0-0-1
Charles Blake	1-0-0-1	Lewis Carroll	1-0-0-1
Jacob Bowser	1-0-0-1	John Carpenter	1-1-0-0
James Brown	1-0-0-1	Dabney Cauthorn	1-0-0-0
John Brown	1-0-0-0	Elizabeth N. Carter	0-1-0-1
James Berlin	1-1-0-1	James Carter	2-0-0-0
Richard Billmyre	1-0-0-0	Thomas Cornwell	3-0-0-1
Jesse Bowen	2-2-0-2	David Coe	1-0-0-0
Henry W. Bayliss	1-0-0-0	Stephen Cauthorn	1-0-0-0
Lewis D. Ball	2-0-0-0	Aaron Chamblin	1-0-0-4
Jonas Berkheimr	1-0-0-0	Michael Copenhaur	1-1-0-1

Clarke County, Virginia Personal Property Tax Lists 1836-1853
1849

John G. Chapman	1-0-0-0	Wm Deakle	2-0-1-1
David L. Castleman	1-0-0-0	Saml Davis	1-0-0-0
Mrs. Ury Castleman	0-6-2-6	James Davis	1-0-0-0
Stephen D. Castleman	1-4-0-2	John Drish	2-0-0-2
John N. Collier	1-0-0-1	Michael Dermont	2-8-1-12
James Carper	1-3-2-9	Baalis Davis	1-2-1-1
Jacob Crim	1-0-0-1	Thomas Duke	1-0-0-1
Stephen B. Cook	2-0-0-5	James Doran	1-0-0-0
John B. Carter	1-4-0-4	Saml Dobbins	1-0-0-3
Peter Cain	3-0-0-6	George W. Diffenderfer	2-0-0-1
Wm H. Corbin	1-0-1-0		
Andrew Collins	1-0-0-0	Hugh Davis	1-0-0-0
Wm K. Carter	1-2-0-6	John Dow	1-2-1-5
Daniel Carroll	1-0-0-1	Aaron Duble	1-0-0-1
Miss Eloesa Castleman	0-0-0-0	John D. Davis	1-0-0-1
		Elijah Dulen	1-0-0-0
P. P. Cooke	1-0-0-2		
Edwin Cauthorn	1-0-0-0	Charles Eckhardt	1-0-0-0
John Carroll Jr.	1-0-0-0	Henry Edwards	1-0-0-1
Wm G. Carter	1-1-0-1	Wm G. Everheart	1-2-0-6
Doct. Chunn	1-3-0-1	John Eleyett	1-1-0-1
McClain Clingon	1-1-0-0	Henson Elliott	3-2-0-6
Charles M. Castleman	1-0-0-2	Alexander M. Earle	1-5-0-11
		Hiram P. Evans	2-1-1-0
Henry D. Castleman	1-0-0-2	Jacob Enders	1-5-0-9
John W. Carter	1-0-0-1	Jacob W. Everheart	1-0-0-1
James Carver	1-0-0-0	Edward Eno	2-3-0-5
John A. Carter	1-1-0-4	Nimrod T. Elgin	1-0-0-0
David Carper	1-2-0-7	Wm H. Edward	1-0-0-0
Creager & Duble	2-0-0-1	Saml Ellis	1-0-0-0
John Carper	1-3-1-5	Henry Evans	1-1-0-0
Michael Canty	1-0-0-1	Christopher Elliott	1-0-0-1
John Camell	1-0-0-0		
Edwell [?] Carter	1-0-0-1	Edward Franks	1-0-0-0
Henry Cohagen	1-0-0-0	Jesse Furr	0-0-0-2
Fenton Carpenter	1-0-0-1	Ephraim Furr	1-0-0-1
		Catharine S. Fyst	0-1-0-9
John Dermont	1-4-1-5	Doct. John Fauntleroy	1-3-1-3
Peter Dermont	1-2-0-0		

Clarke County, Virginia Personal Property Tax Lists 1836-1853
1849

Name	Values	Name	Values
Doct. Olliver Funston	1-10-0-15	James Gibs	1-0-0-0
Jane H. Forster	1-1-1-6	Lewis F. Glass	1-7-1-8
Moses Furr	2-1-0-4	Martin Gant	1-3-1-6
Thornton Farnsworth	1-0-0-2	Jemima Gant	0-2-0-1
Archibald Fleming	1-2-0-3	George Gardner	1-0-0-0
James Furr	1-0-0-1	Catharine Groves	0-0-0-0
Wm Fowler	1-0-0-5	Isabella Glass	0-1-1-0
Ben Franks	1-2-0-7	A. C. Grove	1-0-0-0
Washington Furgerson	1-4-0-4	John B. Gill	1-0-0-0
Martin Feltner	2-0-0-1	Joseph B. Gourley	1-0-0-2
Joseph Fleming	1-0-1-2	John Galloway	1-0-0-1
Thomas Fowler	1-0-0-2	Thornberry Grubs	2-0-0-0
Marcus R. Feehrer	1-2-0-1	John Gruber	2-0-0-6
John Fox	0-1-0-0	John Gardner	1-1-0-2
Josiah Furgerson	1-1-0-3	Joseph E. Gardner	1-0-0-2
Ben F. Fuller	1-0-0-1	George Gardner Senr.	1-0-0-0
Johnson Furr	1-0-1-9		
Matthew Frier	1-0-0-1	Joseph Hiett	1-0-0-6
Israel Fidler	1-0-0-0	Whiting Hamilton	1-1-0-2
Joshua Fellows	1-0-0-0	Henry D. Hooe	1-1-0-0
		John B. Hooe	1-0-0-0
Richard Green	1-0-0-0	Henry Horner	1-0-0-1
Thomas E. Gold	2-4-2-13	Edwin Hart	1-2-0-6
George Gordon	1-0-0-1	Abram Huyett	1-0-0-4
James Green	3-5-2-7	John Huyett	1-0-0-2
Stephen J. Gant	1-2-1-5	Saml Huyett	1-2-1-8
Thomas Grubs	1-0-0-0	James Harris	1-6-0-9
Joseph George	1-2-0-5	Levi Hiett	1-3-0-8
John S. Gordon	4-1-0-11	James M. Hite	1-0-0-2
Henry N. Grigsby	1-5-4-10	Wm Hummer	1-0-0-1
John Grant	1-2-0-3	Charles Hennis	1-1-0-1
Wm Gourley	2-0-1-5	Thomas Harris	1-3-1-4
Emanl Garmong	1-0-0-1	James H. Hooe	1-0-1-3
Saml Grubs	1-0-0-0	Saml Heflybour	1-3-2-10
Abram Grim	1-0-0-0	John Hay	See back of book
Richard N. Green	1-5-0-12	Jacob Heflybour	1-3-2-12
George W. Green	2-7-3-11	Wm Holtsclaw	1-0-0-1
John L. Grant	1-2-0-4	Blackwell Holtsclaw	1-0-0-1

Clarke County, Virginia Personal Property Tax Lists 1836-1853
1849

Mary Howard	0-3-0-0	Albert Johnson	1-0-0-1
Philip Hunsucker	2-0-0-3	Doct. J. J. Janey	1-2-1-3
George L. Harris	0-6-0-13	Thomas Jenkins	1-0-0-3
Wm B. Harris	1-6-2-8	Joseph M. Joliffe	2-0-0-5
Grafton Hillyard	1-0-0-0	Joseph Johnson	1-2-1-7
Cornelius Hoof	1-0-0-0	Alfred Jackson	1-3-0-5
John Hoof	1-0-0-0	Leonard Jones	1-0-0-1
Richard S. Hardesty	1-2-1-8	Wm H. Jones	3-2-0-6
Robert Haney	1-0-0-3	George W. Joy	1-0-0-0
Philip Host	1-0-0-0	James W. Johnson	1-0-0-1
John Hughes	1-0-0-1	Edward Jackson	1-2-0-2
Thomas Hughes	1-1-0-1	Elizabeth Iden	1-0-1-2
Armistead Hoof	1-1-1-0	Ransall Johnson	1-0-0-1
Wm G. Hardesty	1-3-1-8		
Thornton Hummer	1-0-0-0	George H. Isler	1-1-0-2
Sarah Hardesty	2-2-0-7		
John R. Hooper	1-0-0-1	Wm A. Jackson	1-5-0-7
Eliza Hay	0-13-0-15	George Janey	1-0-0-0
George Hunsucker	1-2-0-1		
Henry Huyett	1-1-0-4	James C. Kenan	1-0-0-0
Robert L. Horner	1-0-0-0	Doct. L. J. Kerfoot	1-11-0-13
Wm Hefflin	1-0-0-0	Revd. Thos Kennerly	1-21-2-19
Doct .B. Harrison	1-5-1-9	George Knight	2-7-0-12
Theobald B. Hiems	2-0-0-0	Wm C. Kerfoot	1-9-4-17
Wm H. Harrison	1-0-0-0	Ben M. Knight	1-1-0-1
Revd. John F. Hoof	1-1-0-1	George L. Kerfoot	1-10-5-17
John W. Hart	1-0-0-0	Ben Kent	1-0-0-0
Adrian D Hardesty	1-2-1-8	Doct. R. Kownslar	1-3-0-4
Giles C. Hamell	2-1-0-2	John Kable	2-1-0-1
Thomas B. Harvey	1-0-0-1	Wm F. Knight	1-0-0-1
		Nickolas Kriser	1-0-0-1
George Johnson	1-2-1-2	Mrs. Elizth Knight	0-0-0-0
Herod Jenkins	1-0-0-1	Geo & Wm C. Kerfoot	0-8-1-11
Solomon R. Jackson	1-0-0-0	Charles E. Kimble	1-4-1-7
Matthew Jones	3-1-0-7	Middleton Keeler	1-1-0-0
Reuben Jordan	1-3-0-2	Wm C. Kennerly	1-6-1-8
John Joliffe	1-8-0-11	Joseph Kline	1-0-0-1
Doct. R. R. Jordan	1-0-0-1	Saml G. Kneller	1-1-0-1
Jacob Isler	3-5-2-12	Doct. O. B.Knode	1-3-1-1

Clarke County, Virginia Personal Property Tax Lists 1836-1853
1849

John B. Kerfoot	1-0-0-2	Rice W. Levi	1-0-0-0
James M. Kiger	1-3-1-5	David Loyd	1-0-0-0
Edward V. Kercheval	2-0-0-0	James Larue's heirs	0-1-0-1
Isaac Kiger	2-0-0-2	Squire Lee	2-0-0-1
John Kelly	1-0-0-0	Alfred Lyons	1-0-0-1
Ben T. Kercheval	2-0-0-1	George Lanham	1-0-0-2
Henry Kenneford	1-0-0-0	James Lanham	1-0-0-0
		R. S. Littlejohn	2-0-0-1
Wm Lee	1-0-0-0	George Lock	2-0-0-0
Doct. J. M. Lindsay	1-0-0-0	Wm Lock	0-0-0-3
Franklin & Wm		in possession of George	
Littleton	2-1-0-4	D° for 1848	0-0-0-3
Henry Lloyd	1-0-0-2	Mrs. E. M. Lewis	0-3-1-2
John Lock	1-0-0-2	John W. Littleton	1-0-0-2
James W. Larue	1-4-1-6	Charles M. Littleton	1-0-0-0
Wm Longerbeam	1-0-0-1	John Longerbeam	1-0-0-0
Washington Lee	2-0-0-2	Ben Longerbeam	1-0-0-2
Charles Littleton	1-1-0-1	James Loyd Jr.	1-0-0-2
Doct. R. H. Little	1-5-3-6	John W. Luke	1-9-0-7
John Louthan	4-2-0-1	Charles Leech Jr.	1-0-0-1
Lorenzo Lewis Est.	1-22-5-21		
Saml Larue	1-14-2-13	Peter McMurray	2-1-2-8
Col. John Larue	2-13-3-28	Saml McCormick	1-9-1-10
John Lloyd	1-0-0-1	John J. Monroe	1-3-1-5
George Longerbeam	1-0-0-1	John Maddex Jr.	3-0-1-5
James Lloyd Senr.	2-0-0-1	James Michell	1-1-0-6
Saml Loyd	1-0-0-1	Doct. Wm D.	
Edgar Lanham	1-0-0-0	McGuire	1-9-2-10
Saml Lanham	1-0-0-2	Otway McCormick	2-6-2-8
Abram Longerbeam	1-0-0-0	Francis B. Meade	1-5-0-13
Elizabeth Lanham	0-0-0-1	Mrs. L. W. Meade	0-2-1-1
A. L. P. Larue	1-0-0-1	Philip N. Meade	1-6-3-9
Wm D. Littleton	2-2-0-6	Wm Meade Jr.	1-3-0-6
Harrison Loyd	1-0-0-1	Miss Mary Meade	0-2-1-0
Alfred Lee	1-0-0-0	Thomas McCormick	1-9-1-7
Richard Lanham	0-0-0-1	John Marts Senr.	1-0-0-1
John T. Lindsay	1-1-1-3	Doct. & Saml	
Minor Lanham	1-0-0-1	McCormick	3-14-4-20
Ben Lock	1-0-0-4	Levi Marquess	2-0-0-4

Clarke County, Virginia Personal Property Tax Lists 1836-1853
1849

Jesse P. Mercer	2-0-0-1	Saml Morgan	2-0-0-0
John & James		Jacob Missmore	0-1-0-0
Michum	2-0-0-3	D° for 1848	0-1-0-0
Col. B. Morgan	2-20-5-28	John Mohaney	1-0-0-0
Col. Francis		Edward McCormick	1-11-0-16
McCormick	1-20-5-21	Harrison Mcatee	1-0-0-1
Susan Marshall	0-3-0-6		
John Marshall	1-1-1-4	Doct. S. S. Neille	1-3-0-4
Alexander Marshall	1-1-0-1	Wm Niswanger	4-0-0-8
John McPhillin	5-3-3-12	Hugh M. Nelson	1-14-0-13
Wm Mason	1-0-0-1	Philip Nelson Senr.	1-13-2-13
John Morgan	1-8-1-10	Thomas F. Nelson	2-12-3-13
James McCormick	2-1-0-5	James H. Nevill	1-1-0-0
Saml McCormick	1-0-0-0	Joseph Noble	1-0-1-0
Ben F. Mayhew	1-0-0-0	Miss Abby Nelson	0-3-1-0
John N. Meade	1-3-1-9	Doct. Wm Nelson	1-2-2-5
Isaac S. Manuel	1-0-0-3	George R. Newman	3-1-1-3
James Murphy	2-1-0-2	John Nessmith	1-1-0-1
Revd. Wm Meade	1-0-0-1	Philip Nelson Jr.	1-1-1-8
Stephen Marlow	1-0-0-1	James Nugent	4-0-0-3
Amishadai Moore	2-4-0-10	John B Norris	0-1-1-3
Rebecca S. Meade	0-3-1-2	Mary N Nicklin	0-1-0-0
John G. McCauley	1-0-0-1	Wm Nicklin	1-0-0-0
Violett Mayers	1-0-0-2		
David H. McGuire	1-7-1-4	Elizabeth Orear	0-9-1-7
Alfred P. Moore	2-0-0-1	George Orear	1-3-0-9
George D. Moss	1-1-0-3	David Osbourn	1-0-0-2
Stephen R. Mount	1-2-0-1	Mason Olliver	2-0-0-1
Edmund W. Massey	2-5-1-8	George Osbourn	1-1-1-4
Isaac McCormick	1-1-0-1	Hugh Orork	1-0-0-0
John Marple	1-1-0-0	Elias Overall	1-2-1-2
John McDonald	1-0-0-1	James Ore [sic]	1-0-0-1
P. McCormick Senr.	1-9-0-17		
Seth Mason	1-5-1-9	John Pierce Jr.	2-2-0-10
Geo W. McCormick	1-0-0-3	Matthew Pullium	2-1-0-0
Harrison McCormick	1-0-0-3	George Pultz	1-0-0-2
John Maddox Senr.	1-0-0-0	John E. Page	1-14-1-21
R. K. Meade	1-7-1-9	Mrs. E. M. Page	0-3-1-0
Moses G. Miley	1-1-0-4	John Page Jr.	1-9-2-11

Clarke County, Virginia Personal Property Tax Lists 1836-1853
1849

Mann R. Page	2-9-2-17		John Reed	1-0-0-1
Isaac Pidgeon	1-0-0-2		Nancy Redmon	0-1-0-0
Saml Pidgeon	1-0-0-5		Solomon Redmon	1-0-0-0
Doct. R. P. Page	1-19-3-20		George Rutter	2-0-0-0
James M. Pine	1-0-0-0		Danl B. Richards	2-0-0-1
Mary C. Page	2-8-2-10		Saml B. Redmon	1-0-0-1
Joseph E. Peyton	1-0-0-6		Addison Romine	1-4-0-6
Paul Pierce	1-5-2-9		James Ryan	2-1-0-0
John W. Page	2-5-0-5		Joseph Ryan	1-0-0-4
D° as guardian			John Russell	1-0-0-1
for C. B. Page			Jane Richardson	0-0-0-1
John Pierce Senr.	1-4-1-8		George Reno	1-0-0-1
James Puller	2-0-0-1		Isaac Ramey	2-2-0-5
Peter MC Pierce	1-4-0-8		Mathew Rust	2-3-0-6
Pendleton &			James Russell	1-1-0-5
Richardson	2-20-2-22		John Rowland	3-0-0-6
Washington F.			Thompson Ritt	1-0-0-2
Padgett	1-0-0-1		Doct. R. C. Randolph	1-12-3-19
Richd L. Page	0-3-1-1		Wm Riley	1-0-0-1
McFarland Puller	1-0-0-0		Luster Riley	1-0-0-0
John Patterson	1-1-0-2		Joseph Richardson	1-0-0-0
James Payne	1-0-0-2		James W. Rileys Est.	1-3-0-6
Barnett Prichett	1-0-0-1		Peter K. Royston	1-1-0-2
Uriah Petit	1-0-0-0		John Ramey	1-0-0-0
Wm Pyle	1-0-0-0		Wm C. Ramey	1-0-0-3
Alfred Prescott	1-0-0-10		Thomas Reradan	1-0-0-1
Conrad & Michael			Elisha Romine	1-0-0-0
Pope	2-0-0-2		Landon O. Reed	1-0-0-0
Richard Parker	1-0-0-1		Stephen Reed	1-0-0-0
Mrs. Elizth H. Parker	0-5-0-2		John Richardson	1-0-0-2
			Thomas Russell	1-0-0-1
Richd Ridgeway	2-2-0-5		John W. Russell	1-0-0-1
Wm Reed	1-0-1-3			
Thomas W. Raynolds	2-6-2-1		George Smith	1-0-0-1
Bennet Russell	2-9-2-9		Joseph Stewart	1-0-0-0
Miss E. Royster	0-1-1-0		Susan Smith	0-1-0-0
M. W. Royston	1-5-0-12		Edward J. Smith	1-0-0-0
Peter Royston	1-0-0-0		Wm D. Smith	1-27-4-29
Uriah B. Royston	1-0-0-4		Joseph Smith	1-0-0-0

Clarke County, Virginia Personal Property Tax Lists 1836-1853
1849

Name	Values	Name	Values
Wm Sowers	2-2-2-8	Erasmus Shackelford	1-0-0-1
Joseph Shepherd	1-7-0-11	Henry Stickles	1-0-0-0
Champ Shepherd	1-1-2-3	Charles Showers	1-0-0-0
Edward Shickles	1-0-0-2	Saml Schooler	1-0-0-0
Thomas Shumate	1-2-1-10	James W. Smith	1-0-0-0
John W. Sowers	1-6-2-12	Paul Smith	1-3-1-6
Wm G. Steele	1-0-0-0	Philip Smith	1-0-0-0
Danl W. Sowers	1-13-0-22	Elisha Smallwood	1-0-0-1
Saml Shipe	1-4-0-7	Alexander Saunders	1-0-0-0
James Sowers	1-10-0-10	George Swarts	1-0-0-0
Thomas Sprint	2-0-0-1	Jonathan S. Smith	2-3-0-2
Emanl Showers	3-1-0-1	James H. Swain	1-0-0-0
Barnett Smallwood	2-0-0-1	Thomas L. Skinker	1-5-1-6
Fielding L. Sowers	1-5-1-8		
P. D. Shepherd	3-5-1-9	Sarah Timberlake	1-7-0-9
Doct. Philip Smith	2-23-1-23	Wm Turner	1-0-0-1
Col. T. Smith	1-15-1-20	Abigail Tanquery	1-0-0-1
Kerfoot Sowers Est.	1-5-0-15	David Tristler	1-1-0-5
John Stewart	3-3-1-7	Adam Towner	1-0-0-0
John Shell Jr.	1-0-0-1	Mrs. Hannah Taylor	1-1-0-12
Elizabeth Strother	0-8-1-6	Greenberry	
John Shafer	1-0-0-1	Thompson	3-0-0-2
Jackson Shafer	1-0-0-0	Doct. Saml Taylor	1-12-2-10
Alfred Smallwood	1-0-0-0	Ben Thompson Jr.	2-0-0-6
Burr Smallwood	1-0-0-1	Col. Joseph Tuley	1-23-5-22
Simon Stickles	1-0-0-1	John Trussell	2-4-1-6
George Smedley	1-0-0-1	Charles H. Taylor	1-3-1-5
Danl H. Sowers	1-2-0-10	Wm Trinary	1-1-0-0
Joseph Shipe	1-0-0-1	Wm Tinsman	1-0-0-0
George Strother	1-2-1-4	James W.	
Mary E. Shirely	0-9-2-9	Timberlake	1-7-0-6
Henry Shepherd	1-1-1-1	Adam Thompson	1-0-0-2
Henry Seevers	2-2-0-3	Mary Trinary	0-0-0-0
Abram Shipe	1-0-0-1	Robert Tapscott	1-1-0-0
Joseph Sprint	1-0-0-0	Saml Tinsman	1-0-0-0
Wm B. Sowers	1-0-0-1	A. S. Tidball	1-7-2-13
John Shell Senr.	1-0-0-1	Wm Tomblin	1-0-0-0
Jerry Shay	1-1-0-1	George W. Tinsman	1-0-0-4
Wm L. Smith	1-0-0-0	Enoch Triplett	1-0-0-0

Clarke County, Virginia Personal Property Tax Lists 1836-1853
1849

Name	Values	Name	Values
Howard F. Thornton	1-5-0-7	Wm W. Whiting	1-5-2-6
Snowdon Tomblin	1-0-0-1	Obed Willingham	1-0-0-0
French Thompson	3-0-0-3	Bennet Wood	1-0-0-0
Addison Timberlake	1-0-0-1	Henry R. Wilson	1-1-0-2
Moses B. Trussell	1-0-0-2	Nathaniel B. Whiting	1-6-0-10
Mason Tinsman	1-0-0-1	Sydnor B. Windham	2-0-1-3
Calvin Thacker	1-0-0-0	John Wilson	1-0-0-0
		Doct. H. Washington	1-1-0-1
Thomas Russell	1-0-0-0	Thomas C. Windham	1-0-0-0
		James E. Ware	1-0-0-0
Mrs. Mary Taylor	2-13-1-12	James V. Wier	1-4-1-6
James Tracy	1-0-0-1	Wm Willis	1-0-0-0
		Revd. R. H. Wilmer	1-3-0-1
Peter Umpenhaur	1-0-0-0	Jeremiah Wilson	1-0-0-0
		Wm H. Whiting	1-6-1-10
John Vanclief	1-0-0-5	Alexander Wood	1-1-0-0
Jacob Vanmeter	0-4-0-10	James Wiley Jr.	1-0-0-0
		John Wiley	1-0-0-1
Wm Willingham	2-0-0-1	David Whittington	1-0-0-0
Allen Williams	3-10-0-12	Jacob Welch	2-0-0-6
Francis H. Whiting	2-2-0-5	David H. Wilcox	1-0-0-0
John Ware &		Franklin Wilson	1-0-0-1
Mrs. Stribling	1-15-3-12	James Wilson	1-0-0-0
J. G. Wade		Lewis Weaver	1-0-0-0
& Brothers	2-2-0-1	Walter Watson	3-0-0-2
H. T. Wheat	3-3-1-3	James Whittington	1-0-0-0
Hezekiah Wiley	1-0-0-0	Charles P. Woods	1-0-0-0
Saml Wiley	1-0-0-0	Wm Wolf	1-0-0-0
James Wiley	1-0-0-1	Jesse Wright	1-0-0-3
John Willingham	1-0-0-1	Robert Whittington	1-0-0-0
Miss E. W.		Harriet Wilson	0-0-0-1
Washington	0-0-0-0		
Leroy P. Williams	2-7-1-8	Simeon Yowell	1-1-0-2
Wm P. Wigginton	2-2-0-3	Wm Young	1-0-0-0
Francis B. Whiting	2-17-3-15		

Clarke County, Virginia Personal Property Tax Lists 1836-1853
1849

Free Negroes chargeable with state tax

Columns: 1) males, 2) slaves above 16, 3) slaves above 12, 4) horses, mules, etc.

John Clifton	0-0-0-0	Spencer Johnson	0-0-0-1
Mowen Harris	0-1-0-0	Frederick Cooper	0-0-0-1
John Jackson	0-0-0-2	Peter Coates	0-0-0-2

[Additional names added after recapitulation]

John Hay	1-1-1-0	Eben T. Hancock	1-0-0-1

Clarke County, Virginia Personal Property Tax Lists 1836-1853

1850

Columns: 1) white males above 16 years, 2) slaves above 16 years, 3) slaves 12-16, 4) horses, mares, mules & colts.

Name	Values	Name	Values
Robert Ashby Senr.	1-0-0-1	Augustin Athey	1-0-0-1
Mason Anderson	1-7-0-8	Wm Ashby & Lewis	
David H. Allen	2-16-3-20	Edmunds	0-3-0-0
John Alexander	1-18-4-17	Levi Athey	1-0-0-0
Wm C. Alexander	1-11-1-16	Susan Burwell	0-9-0-2
Buckner Ashby	2-11-5-19	John C. Bonham	1-4-2-10
Joseph Anderson	1-2-0-8	Nathaniel Burwell Jr.	1-8-4-16
Nancy Allen	1-2-0-6	Wm C. Benson	1-0-0-0
James M. Allen	1-0-0-0	John Burchell	2-6-2-12
A. S. Allen	2-10-1-11	Archibald Bowen	1-4-0-9
John Ashby Senr.	1-0-0-0	Hiram O. Bell	1-0-0-0
Robert Ashby Jr.	1-0-0-1	Phinehas Bowen	1-5-0-10
Martin Ashby	1-0-0-1	Francis O. Byrd	1-10-2-9
Thomas H.		Philip Berlin	2-6-1-5
Alexander	2-1-0-2	George C. Blakemore	1-7-0-9
Nimrod Ashby	1-0-0-1	D° as guardian for	
David T. Armstrong	1-0-0-0	L. Enders	
Evan P. Anderson	1-1-0-1	Neille Barnett	1-3-2-7
Austin C. Ashby	1-0-0-4	D° as guardian for	
Jeremiah Ashby	1-0-0-2	young Carters	1-0-0-0
James Allison	1-0-0-0	Thomas Briggs Est.	1-4-1-6
Wm T. Allen	1-5-2-9	Daniel S. Bonham	2-4-0-8
Thomas Ashby	2-0-0-1	Fanny Brownley	0-9-1-12
John Anderson	1-0-0-0	Wm Baker	1-5-1-4
George B. Ashby	1-0-0-1	Isaac Berlin	2-0-0-1
John Allison	1-0-0-0	Strother Bell	1-0-0-0
James Ash	1-0-0-0	Catharine Bales	0-0-0-0
Joel Alexander	1-0-0-0	Robert Burchell	1-4-2-7
Washington		H. W. Brabham	1-0-0-0
Anderson	1-0-0-2	Squire Bell	2-0-0-4
Wm Alder	1-0-0-0	P. Burwells Est.	0-19-2-11
Richard Adams	1-0-0-1	John W. Byrd	1-10-2-10

Clarke County, Virginia Personal Property Tax Lists 1836-1853
1850

Thomas Briggs	7-6-1-18	Richard S. Briarley	1-3-0-4
John Brumley	4-0-0-14	Stephen Barr	1-1-0-0
John D. Barr	1-0-0-0	George H. Bell	1-1-1-1
Doct. James W. Beck	4-0-0-1	Henry W. Bayliss	1-0-0-0
Col. James Bell	1-8-3-14		
Lewis Berlin	1-3-0-1	Alfred Castleman	3-6-1-9
Col. Strother H.		Frederick Clopton	1-5-0-8
Bowen	5-3-0-3	George F. Calmese	2-6-1-10
Ann C. Benn	0-1-1-2	Wm Carrington	1-1-0-1
Wm Berry	3-10-2-13	Wm Carper	1-0-0-2
George H. Burwell	2-44-7-43	Robert A. Coltson	1-4-1-9
George Bolen	1-0-0-0	Elizabeth K. Carter	2-2-1-7
Doct. H. F. Barton	1-0-0-2	John Copenhaur	3-2-2-11
Saml Briarley	1-8-0-7	Miriam Catlett	1-5-0-12
Christian Bowser	2-0-1-1	James H. Clarke	2-3-2-0
John Blue	2-1-0-8	Thomas H. Crow	1-4-0-5
Napoleon Balthrope	1-0-0-1	Wm. A. Castleman	1-3-2-10
Abram Beevers	2-0-0-2	John Cooper	1-0-0-3
James Bell	2-0-0-1	Ben Crampton	0-1-0-0-
Adam Barr	1-0-0-0	James Castleman	1-19-0-29
Ben Barr	1-1-0-0	Thomas Carter	1-5-0-7
Saml Bonham	2-13-1-22	Park Corder	1-0-0-1
Andrew Billmyre	1-0-0-1	John Carroll	1-0-0-1
Jesse Butler	1-0-0-0	Lewis Carroll	1-0-0-1
Juliet Boston	0-1-0-0	Dabney Cauthorn	1-0-0-0
Nancy Boston	0-0-0-0	Elizabeth N. Carter	0-1-0-1
T. T. Byrd's Est.	0-1-0-2	James Carter	2-0-0-0
John R. Bell	1-3-1-6	Thomas Cornwell	2-0-0-1
James Boown [sic]	2-0-0-1	Stephen Cauthorn	1-0-0-0
Richard Billmyre	1-0-0-0	Aaron Chamblin	2-0-0-5
Jesse Bowen	1-1-1-2	Michael Copenhaur	2-0-1-1
Henry Ballmain	1-0-0-1	John N. Collier	1-0-0-1
Lewis D. Ball	1-0-0-0	Martin Creager	1-0-0-1
Jonas Berkheimer	1-0-0-0	Ury Castleman	0-7-1-6
Isaac Berlin Jr.	1-0-0-0	Stephen D.	
Wm Berlin	1-3-1-3	Castleman	1-4-1-2
Ben F. Boley	1-2-1-5	James Carper	1-4-2-8
Elizabeth Burwell	0-31-9-32	Jacob Crim	1-0-0-1
George W. Berlin	1-0-0-1	Stephen B. Cook	2-0-0-6

Clarke County, Virginia Personal Property Tax Lists 1836-1853
1850

John B. Carter	1-4-0-5	James Davis	1-0-0-0
Peter Cain	3-0-0-8	John Drish	1-0-0-1
Wm. H. Corbin	1-0-1-0	Michael Dermont	2-8-2-16
Andrew Collins	1-0-0-0	Baalis Davis	1-2-1-1
Wm K. Carter	1-2-1-5	Thomas Duke	1-0-0-1
Daniel Carroll	1-0-0-1	James Doran	1-0-0-1
Samuel Camell	1-0-0-0	Saml Dobbins	1-0-0-2
Eloesa M. Castleman	0-0-0-0	George W. Diffenderfer	2-0-0-0
Edwin Cauthorn	1-0-0-0	Hugh Davis	1-0-0-0
John Carroll Jr.	1-0-0-0	John Dow	1-1-1-7
Wm G. Carter	1-1-0-1	John D. Davis	1-0-0-1
Mclain Clingon	2-0-0-1	Elijah Dulen	1-0-0-0
Henry D. Castleman	1-0-0-1	John W. Davis	1-0-0-0
John W. Carter	1-0-0-1	Henry Edwards	1-0-0-1
James Carver	1-0-0-0	Wm G. Everheart	2-2-0-5
John A. Carter	1-2-0-4	John Eleyett	1-1-0-1
David Carper	2-1-2-5	Henson Elliott	3-1-1-7
John Carper	1-3-1-6	Alexander M. Earle	1-5-1-12
Michael Canty	1-0-0-1	Hiram P. Evans	2-1-1-1
John Camell	1-0-0-0	Jacob Enders	1-7-0-10
Fenton Carpenter & J. R. Bell	2-2-0-4	Jacob W. Everheart	1-0-0-1
Ann B. Cook	0-2-0-1	Edward Eno	1-4-0-4
George W. Cooper	1-0-0-0	Wm H. Edwards	2-0-0-0
James N. Carpenter	1-0-0-0	Henry Evans	1-1-1-1
Elisha Carver	1-0-0-0	John Evans	1-0-0-1
Elizabeth Carver	0-0-0-0	John W. Everheart	1-0-0-0
John P. Carrigan	1-0-0-0	Jackson Elliott	1-0-0-0
James Clevinger	1-0-0-0	Albert Elsy	1-0-0-1
David L. Castleman	1-0-0-0		
George Cooper	1-0-0-0	Edward Franks	1-0-0-0
Michael Crim	1-0-0-1	Jesse Furr	0-0-0-1
Charles M. Chamblin	1-0-0-0	Ephraim Furr	1-0-0-0
		Catharine S. Fyst	0-1-0-8
Aaron Duble	0-0-0-1	Doct. J. Fauntleroy	1-2-1-3
John Dermont	1-5-1-3	Doct. O. Funston	1-7-3-15
Peter Dermont	1-2-0-0	Jane H. Foster	1-1-1-5
Wm Deakle	1-0-1-1	Moses Furr	1-1-0-5
Saml Davis	1-0-0-0	Thornton Farnsworth	1-0-0-1

Clarke County, Virginia Personal Property Tax Lists 1836-1853
1850

Archibald Fleming	1-2-0-3		John L. Grant	1-2-0-6
James Furr	1-0-0-1		James Gibs	1-0-0-0
Wm Fowler	1-0-0-4		Lewis F. Glass	1-8-1-9
Washington			Martin Gant	1-4-0-6
Furgerson	1-1-0-4		Jemima Gant	0-2-0-1
Martin Feltner	1-0-0-2		George Gardner	1-0-1-0
Joseph Fleming	1-0-0-3		Catharine Groves	0-0-1-0
Thomas Fowler	1-0-0-3		Isabella Glass	0-1-1-0
Marcus P. Feehrer	1-1-0-2		A. C. Grove	1-0-0-0
John Fox	0-1-0-0		Joseph B. Gourley	1-0-0-2
Josiah Furgerson	1-0-1-2		John Galloway	1-0-0-0
Ben F. Fuller	1-0-0-1		Thornberry Grubs	2-0-0-0
Johnson Furr	1-2-0-6		John Gruber	2-1-0-6
Matthew Frier	2-0-0-2		John Gardner	1-0-0-1
Ebin Frost	1-0-0-2		Joseph E. Gardner	1-0-0-0
Israel Fidler	1-0-0-0		John J. Gordon	1-0-0-3
Joshua Fellows	1-0-1-0		George W. Grubs	1-0-0-0
John W. Feltner	1-0-0-0		E. C. Gruber	0-2-0-0
Daniel Furr	1-0-0-0		Adam Greenwall	0-0-0-1
Enoch Furr	1-0-0-1		Whiting Hamilton	1-0-0-2
Kemp B. Furr	1-0-0-2		James H. Hooe	1-0-0-4
Wm M. Furgerson	1-0-0-2		Henry Horner	1-0-0-1
			Edwin Hart	1-2-0-0
Edward Gorman	1-0-0-1		Abram Huyett	1-0-0-5
Richard Green	1-0-0-0		John Huyett	1-0-0-1
Thomas E. Gold	2-5-2-14		Saml Huyett	1-4-0-8
George Gordon	1-1-0-0		Levi Hiett	1-4-0-8
James Green	2-4-2-8		James M. Hite	1-0-0-3
Stephen J. Gant	1-2-2-5		Wm Hummer	1-0-0-1
Thomas Grubs	1-0-0-0		Charles Hennis	1-0-0-1
Joseph George	1-2-1-6		Thomas Harris	1-2-0-7
John S. Gordon	3-1-0-9		Henry D. Hooe	1-1-0-0
Henry N. Grigsby	1-6-2-9		Saml Heflybour	2-4-4-9
Wm Gourley	2-0-1-5		Jacob Heflybour	1-4-1-11
Emanl Garmong	1-0-0-1		Wm Holtsclaw	1-0-0-1
Saml Grubs	1-0-0-0		Blackwell Holtsclaw	1-0-0-1
Richard N. Green	1-4-0-10		Mary Howard	0-3-0-0
Abram Grim	1-0-0-0		Philip Hunsucker	2-0-0-2
George W. Green	2-8-2-12		George L. Harris	0-4-0-10

Clarke County, Virginia Personal Property Tax Lists 1836-1853
1850

Wm B. Harris	1-6-1-10	Jacob Isler	3-8-1-15
Grafton Hillyard	1-0-0-0	Albert Johnson	1-0-0-1
Cornelius Hoof	1-0-0-0	Doct. J. J. Janey	1-2-1-6
Richard S. Hardesty	1-3-0-8	Thomas Jenkins	1-0-0-5
Philip Host	1-0-0-0	Joseph M. Joliffe	2-0-0-5
John Hughs	1-0-0-1	John Johnson Jr.	1-0-0-1
Thomas Hughs	1-1-0-0	Joseph Johnson	1-1-1-6
Armistead Hoof	1-2-0-1	Alfred Jackson	1-2-0-5
Harrison Hoof	1-0-0-0	Wm H. Jones	3-3-0-10
Wm G. Hardesty	1-4-1-9	George W. Joy	1-0-0-0
Thornton Hummer	1-0-0-1	James W. Johnson	1-0-0-1
Sarah Hardesty	2-3-0-9	Edward Jackson	1-2-0-2
Eliza Hay	1-8-0-15	Elizabeth Iden	2-0-0-2
George Hunsucker	2-0-0-1	George H. Isler,	
Henry Huyett	1-1-0-5	charge to Jacob Isler	
Robert L. Horner	1-0-0-1	Wm A. Jackson	1-4-1-7
Wm Heflin	1-0-0-0	Amelia A. Jordan	0-1-0-2
Doct. Ben Harrison	1-5-1-12	Ransall Johnson	1-0-0-1
Theobald B. Hiems	4-2-0-0	Rev. Wm Johnston	not a citizen
Revd. John F. Hoof	1-4-0-1		
Adrian D. Hardesty	1-2-0-5	James C. Kenan	1-0-0-0
Giles C. Hamell	2-1-0-2	Doct. F. J. Kerfoot	1-12-0-12
Thomas B. Harvey	1-0-0-0	Revd. Thomas	
John Hodge	1-0-0-0	Kennerly	3-2-2-16
Enoch Haney	1-0-0-0	George Knight	1-8-1-10
Elijah Haney	1-0-0-0	Wm C. Kerfoot	1-11-2-16
Thomas L. Humphrey	1-0-0-1	Ben M. Knight	0-1-0-0
Wm H. Harrison	1-0-0-0	George L. Kerfoot	1-9-6-18
Abram Hess	1-0-0-0	Doct. R. Kownslar	1-4-2-4
Abram Heskit	1-0-0-0	John Kable	2-1-0-1
Doct. James A.		Wm F. Knight	1-0-0-1
Haynes	1-3-0-2	Nickolas Kriser	1-0-0-1
		Elizabeth Knight	0-0-0-0
George Johnson	1-2-0-2	Geo & Wm C. Kerfoot	0-6-1-10
Herod Jenkins	1-0-0-0	Charles E. Kimball	1-4-1-7
Solomon R. Jackson	1-0-0-0	Middleton Keeler	1-0-1-0
Matthew Jones	3-1-0-6	Wm C. Kennerly	1-5-2-6
John Joliffe	1-6-0-8	Joseph Kline	1-0-0-1
Doct. R. R. Jordan	1-0-0-1	Saml G. Kneller	1-1-0-1

Clarke County, Virginia Personal Property Tax Lists 1836-1853
1850

Name	Values	Name	Values
Doct. O. B. Knode	1-1-1-1	Ben Lock	2-0-0-4
John B. Kerfoot	1-0-0-2	Rice W. Levi	1-0-0-0
James M. Kiger	1-3-1-4	David Loyd	1-0-0-0
Edward V. Kercheval	2-0-0-1	James Larues heirs	0-1-0-1
Isaac Kiger	2-0-0-2	Squire Lee	3-0-0-1
Jacob Kriser	2-0-0-1	George Lanham	1-0-0-1
John Kelly	1-0-0-0	James Lanham	1-0-0-0
Ben T. Kercheval	2-1-1-1	R. S. Littlejohn	1-0-0-0
Henry Kenneford	1-0-0-0	George Lock	2-0-0-4
James L. Kercheval	2-0-0-0	Mrs. E. M. Lewis	0-3-3-2
Elias Kline	1-0-0-0	John W. Littleton	1-0-0-2
James H. Kenan	1-0-0-0	John Longerbeam	1-0-0-0
Catharine Kenneford	1-0-0-0	Ben Longerbeam	1-0-0-2
		James Loyd Jr.	1-1-0-2
Wm Lee	1-0-0-0	John W. Luke	1-8-1-8
Doct. J. M. Lindsay	1-0-0-0	Charles Leech Jr.	1-0-0-1
Wm Littleton	1-1-1-2	Wm H. Levi	1-0-0-0
Henry Lloyd	2-0-0-4	Charles M. Littleton	1-0-0-0
John Lock	2-0-1-7	P. O. Littlejohn	0-0-0-1
James W. Larue	1-4-2-6	James W. Lewis	1-0-0-0
Wm Longerbeam	1-0-0-0		
Washington Lee	2-0-0-2	Peter McMurray	2-2-1-8
Doct. R. H. Little	1-5-2-6	Saml McCormick	1-0-0-0
John Louthan	4-4-0-1	John J. Monroe	1-3-1-6
Lorenzo Lewis' Est.	1-29-5-23	John Maddex	2-1-1-6
Saml Larue	1-14-2-13	James Michell	1-3-0-6
Col J. B. Larue	2-13-3-21	Doct. Wm D.	
John Lloyd	1-0-0-2	McGuire	1-9-1-10
James Lloyd Senr.	0-0-1-2	Otway McCormick	2-7-1-5
Saml Loyd	1-0-0-0	Francis B. Meade	1-7-1-10
Edgar Lanham	1-0-0-0	Philip N. Meade	1-5-3-11
Abram Longerbeam	1-0-0-0	Wm Meade Jr.	1-5-1-10
Elizabeth Lanham	0-0-0-1	Thomas McCormick	1-10-2-8
A. L. P. Larue	1-0-0-1	John Marts Senr.	1-0-0-0
Wm D. Littleton	2-2-0-7	Doct. & Saml	
Harrison Loyd	1-0-0-2	McCormick	2-20-3-27
Alfred Lee	1-0-0-0	Levi Marquiss	1-0-0-2
John T. Lindsay	1-2-0-2	Jesse P. Mercer	1-0-0-1
Minor Lanham	1-0-0-1		

Clarke County, Virginia Personal Property Tax Lists 1836-1853
1850

John & James Michum	2-0-0-3	Henry Mason	1-0-0-0
Col F. McCormick	1-11-3-15	James Marcus	1-0-0-0
Susan Marshall	0-4-1-6	Louisa W. Meade	0-3-0-1
John Marshall	2-1-1-3	Col. B. Morgan	1-21-6-22
Alexander Marshall	1-1-0-1	Mary Meade	0-2-1-0
John McPhillin	4-3-3-10	Doct. S. S. Neale	1-3-1-4
John Morgan	2-9-1-11	Wm Niswanger	3-0-0-9
James McCormick	1-1-0-5	Hugh M. Nelson	1-11-0-9
Ben F. Mayhew	1-3-2-6	Philip Nelson Senr.	1-16-3-16
John N. Meade	1-3-2-6	Thomas F. Nelson	2-11-2-15
Horace Mayers	1-0-0-0	James H. Neville	2-1-0-0
Isaac S. Manuel	1-0-0-3	Joseph Noble	1-0-1-0
James Murphy	2-1-0-2	Abby Nelson	0-3-0-0
Revd. Wm Meade	1-0-0-1	Doct. Wm Nelson	1-2-1-4
Stephen Marlow	1-0-0-1	George R. Newman	3-2-1-2
Amishadai Moore	3-3-1-8	John Nessmith	1-1-0-1
John G. McCauley	1-0-0-1	Philip Nelson Jr.	1-2-1-7
Violett Mayers	0-0-0-1	John B. Norris	0-4-1-3
David H. McGuire	1-7-0-4	Wm Nicklin	1-0-0-0
Alfred P. Moore	1-0-0-1	Philip C. Nicholas	1-0-0-0
A. R. Milton	1-3-1-3	Elizabeth Orear	0-10-1-11
Edmund W. Massey	1-5-3-7	George Orear	1-4-0-6
John Marple	1-0-0-0	David Osbourn	1-0-0-2
John McDonald	1-0-0-1	Mason Olliver	2-0-0-1
P. McCormick Senr.	1-8-1-15	George Osbourn	1-2-0-6
Seth Mason	1-5-1-8	Hugh Orook	1-0-0-0
Harrison McCormick	1-0-0-3	Elias Overall	1-0-0-1
Richard K. Meade	1-5-0-9	Ben F. Orear	1-4-0-5
Moses G. Miley	2-2-0-4	Susan Orear	0-0-0-2
Wm McCormick	1-7-0-8	Wm OConnell	1-0-0-0
Saml Morgan	1-0-0-0		
Jacob Mesmore	0-1-0-0	John Pierce Jr.	2-3-1-13
Edward McCormick	2-11-2-15	Matthew Pullium	2-1-0-0
Harrison Mcatee	1-0-0-1	George Pultz	1-0-0-2
George Marple	1-0-0-0	John E. Page	1-14-1-21
John Martin	2-0-0-1	Eliza M. Page	0-3-1-0
Wm Morris	1-0-0-0	John Page Jr.	1-9-2-10
P. McCormick Jr.	2-1-0-3	Mann R. Page	2-11-4-15

Clarke County, Virginia Personal Property Tax Lists 1836-1853
1850

Saml L. Pidgeon	1-0-0-8		John Reed	1-0-0-1
Susan R. Page	0-17-3-20		Nancy Redmon	0-1-0-0
James M. Pine	1-0-0-0		George Rutter	1-0-0-0
Mary C. Page	0-6-0-4		Danl B. Richards	2-0-0-1
Joseph E. Peyton	2-0-0-5		Saml B. Redmon	1-0-0-1
Paul Pierce	1-5-2-8		Addison Romine	2-2-0-6
John W. Page	2-4-0-5		James Ryan	2-1-0-0
D° as guardian for			Joseph Ryan	1-0-0-4
C. B. Page			John Russell	1-0-0-1
John Pierce Senr.	1-4-1-8		George Reno	1-0-0-1
James Puller	1-0-0-0		Isaac Ramey	2-2-0-5
Peter Mc Pierce	1-3-0-7		Mathew Rust	2-4-0-6
Pendleton &			James Russell	1-1-1-3
Richardson	2-19-4-28		Thomson Ritt	1-0-0-1
Washington F.			Doct. R. C. Randolph	2-13-2-21
Padgett	1-0-0-0		Wm Riley	1-0-0-1
Leuit. R. L. Page	0-4-0-4		Michael Russell	1-0-0-1
Conrad Pope	1-0-0-1		Joseph Richardson	1-0-0-0
McFarland Puller	1-0-0-0		Alexander Riley	1-3-0-5
John Patterson	1-0-0-1		Peter K. Royston	1-0-0-2
James Payne	1-0-0-3		John Ramey	1-0-1-2
Barnett Prichett	1-0-0-0		Thomas Reradan	2-0-0-1
Uriah Petit	1-1-0-0		Betsy Romine	0-0-1-0
Wm Pyle	1-0-0-0		Stephen Reed	1-0-0-1
Alfred Prescott	1-0-0-0		Thomas Russell	1-0-0-2
Michael Pope	2-0-0-1		John W. Russell	1-1-0-2
Richd E. Parker	1-0-0-1		John Russell	1-0-0-5
Elizabeth H. Parker	0-5-0-2		Henrietta C.	
Archibald C. Page	1-1-0-8		Randolph	0-0-0-0
P. H. Powers	1-0-0-0		Children of R. C.	
Revd. Joshua			Randolph	0-0-0-0
Peterkin	1-2-1-2		Beverly Randolph	1-7-2-10
Richard Ridgeway	1-2-0-5		Perry G. Rice	3-0-0-2
Thomas W. Raynolds	1-1-0-1		R. S. Robinson	1-0-0-1
Bennet Russell	1-7-2-9			
Miss E. Royster	0-1-1-0		Samuel Showers	1-0-0-1
Matthew W. Royston	1-2-1-7		Vincent T. Settle	1-0-0-0
Peter Royston	1-0-0-0		Elisha Smallwood	1-0-0-1
Uriah B. Royston	1-0-0-5		George Smith	1-0-0-0

Clarke County, Virginia Personal Property Tax Lists 1836-1853
1850

Joseph Stewart	1-0-0-0		John Shell Senr.	1-0-0-1
Susan Smith	0-2-0-0		Jerry Shay	1-0-0-2
Wm D. Smith	1-23-3-26		Wm L. Smith	1-0-0-1
Wm Sowers	3-6-1-15		Erasmus Shackelford	2-0-0-1
D° Omitted by			Henry Stickles	1-0-0-0
agent 1849	0-4-0-7		Saml Schooler	1-0-0-0
Joseph Shepherd	1-7-0-7		James W. Smith	1-0-0-0
Champ Shepherd	1-3-2-3		Paul Smith	1-3-2-11
Thomas Shumate	1-3-0-10		John R. Stewart	3-1-0-3
John W. Sowers	1-6-2-14		Doct. Taliaferro	
Danl W. Sowers	1-12-1-23		Stribling	1-3-1-3
Saml Stipe	2-4-0-7		Alexander Sanders	1-0-0-0
James Sowers Est.	0-6-0-9		George Swarts	1-0-0-0
Thomas Sprint	1-0-0-1		Jonathan S. Smith	2-3-0-2
Emanl Showers	2-1-0-0		Charles Showers	2-1-0-2
Barnett Smallwood	2-0-0-2		Thomas J. Skinker	1-5-1-8
Fielding L. Sowers	1-3-2-8		Wm H. Spicknell	2-1-0-0
P. D. Shepherd	2-6-1-9		James S. Steel	1-0-0-0
Doct. P. Smith	2-19-3-21		Margaret Swann	0-0-1-0
Elizabeth Sowers	0-3-0-1		George Strother	0-0-0-0
Col. T. Smith	1-15-3-18		Gdn of Lewis	
Kerfoot Sowers Est.	1-4-0-14		Strother	0-0-0-0
John Stewart	1-1-0-3		D° for Sarah A.	
Elizabeth Strother	0-7-1-5		Reed	0-0-0-0
John Shafer	1-0-0-0		D° for James W.	
Jackson Shafer	1-0-0-0		Strother	0-0-0-0
Alfred Smallwood	1-0-0-0		Ben Stonestreet	1-0-0-0
Burr Smallwood	1-0-0-1		Thomas Smallwood	1-0-0-0
Wm & John Stewart	2-0-0-5			
Simon Stickles	1-0-0-1		Sarah Timberlake	1-5-0-11
George Smedley	1-0-0-1		Abigail Tanquerry	0-0-0-1
Danl H. Sowers	1-2-1-0		James W. Tanquerry	1-0-0-0
Joseph Shipe	1-0-0-0		David Tristler	1-1-0-5
George Strother	2-0-0-4		Adam Towner	1-0-0-0
Mary E. Shirely	0-9-2-10		Wm Taylor	1-15-0-16
Henry Shepherd	2-7-1-3		Greenberry Thomson	4-0-0-4
Henry Seevers	2-2-0-3		Doct. Saml Taylor	1-11-2-9
Joseph Sprint	1-0-0-0		Ben Thomson Jr.	2-0-0-5
Wm B. Sowers	1-0-0-0		Col. Joseph Tuley	1-19-7-20

Clarke County, Virginia Personal Property Tax Lists 1836-1853
1850

Name	Values	Name	Values
John Trussell	3-4-0-7	Wm W. Whiting	1-5-0-5
Charles H. Taylor	2-3-0-4	Henry R. Wilson	1-0-0-1
Wm Trinary	1-1-1-3	Nathaniel B. Whiting	1-5-1-8
Wm Tinsman	1-0-0-0	Sydnor B. Windham	1-0-1-2
Adam F. Thomson	1-0-0-2	John Wilson	2-0-0-1
Robert Tapscott	1-1-1-0	Doct. H. Washington	
Saml Tinsman	1-0-0-0	back of book	
A. S. Tidball	1-7-0-7	Thomas C. Windham	1-0-0-0
Wm Tomblin	1-0-0-0	James W. Ware	1-0-0-0
Enoch Triplett	1-0-0-0	James V. Wier	1-4-2-7
Howard F. Thornton	1-7-1-6	Wm Willis	1-1-0-0
Snowden Tomblin	1-0-0-1	Jeremiah Wilson	1-0-0-0
French Thomson	3-0-0-5	Wm H. Whiting	1-6-1-11
Moses B. Trussell	1-0-1-2	James Wiley Jr.	1-0-0-1
Mason Tinsman	1-0-0-0	John Wiley	1-0-0-0
Calvin Thacker	1-0-0-0	David Whittington	1-0-0-1
Mary Taylor	2-9-1-10	Jacob Welch	1-0-0-4
James Tracy	2-0-0-0	David H. Wilcox	1-0-0-0
John Turner	1-0-0-0	Franklin Wilson	1-0-0-0
Thomas Turner	1-0-0-0	James Wilson	1-0-0-0
		Lewis Weaver	1-0-0-0
Peter Umpenhaur	1-0-0-0	Walter Watson	2-0-0-2
		Wm Wolfe	1-0-0-0
John Vanclief	1-0-0-5	Jesse Wright	1-0-0-3
Jacob Vanmeter	0-3-0-5	Robert Whittington	1-0-0-0
George West	1-0-0-0	Lucinda Washington	0-3-0-1
Wm Willingham	2-0-0-2	John Welch	1-0-0-0
Allen Williams	2-10-1-15	George F. Woodward	1-0-0-1
Francis H. Whiting	1-3-0-6	George W. Watkins	1-0-0-0
J. W. Ware &		Richard B. Welch	2-1-0-1
Mrs. Stribling	2-16-5-15	Charles L. Wright	1-2-1-2
D. Wade & Co.	2-1-0-1	Thornton O.	
H. T. Wheat	4-3-1-5	Windham	1-0-0-0
Hezekiah Wiley	1-0-0-0	Bennet Wood	1-0-0-0
Saml Wiley	1-0-0-0	Charles P. Woods	0-0-0-0
James Wiley	1-0-0-0	West & Neill	3-0-0-2
John Willingham	1-0-0-1		
Leroy P. Williams	3-8-2-8	Simeon Yowell	1-0-0-2
Francis B. Whiting	2-17-3-14	Wm Young	1-0-0-0

Clarke County, Virginia Personal Property Tax Lists 1836-1853
1850

Free Blacks

"I am compelled to charge the free negroes in 2 lines so as to assignate [sic] the ages according to Law."

Columns: 1) over 55 years, 2) above 16 years, 3) those bound out, 4) horses, mules, etc.

Name	Values	Name	Values
Nicodemas _____	1-0-0-0	John Howard	0-1-0-0
Alfred _____	0-0-1-0	David Collins	0-1-0-0
Frederick Cooper	1-0-0-1	Edmund Brown	0-1-0-0
George Davis	0-1-0-0	Scimeon Parker	0-1-0-0
George Lee	0-1-0-0	John Robertson	1-0-0-0
Wm Toler	0-1-0-0	John Clifton	1-0-0-0
Wm Parker	0-1-0-0	Spencer Johnston	0-1-0-1
John McCoy	0-0-1-0	Philip Martin	1-0-0-0
Frank Stephens	0-1-0-0	Burwell Cook	0-1-0-0
Levi _____	0-1-0-0	Mowen Harris	0-1-*-0
Wm H. Thornton	0-1-0-0	*1 slave above 16	
James Thornton	0-1-0-0	Jacob Johnson	0-1-0-0
Thomas Ransom	0-1-0-0	John Jackson	0-1-0-0
Richard Lee	0-1-1-0	Peter Coates	0-1-0-4
Washington Newman	0-0-*-0	Wat Howard	1-0-0-0
*1 slave above 16		Charles Strange	0-0-1-0
Henry Johnston	0-1-0-0		

Clarke County, Virginia Personal Property Tax Lists 1836-1853

1851

Columns: 1) White males above 16 years, 2) Slaves above 16 years, 3) Slaves above 12 years, 4) Horses, mules, etc.
For "back of book" see page 161

Buckner Ashby	3-9-3-15	Levi Athey	1-0-0-0
James M. Allen	1-2-0-8	James Athey	1-0-0-0
Mason Anderson	2-6-1-8	Joel Alexander	1-0-0-0
David H. Allen	2-16-5-17		
John Alexander	1-20-2-21	Nathaniel Burwell	1-10-5-21
Susan C. Alexander	1-8-0-7	Wm C. Benson	1-0-0-0
Augustine Athey	1-0-0-1	John Burchell	2-6-2-15
Robert Ashby	1-0-0-2	Archibald Bowen	1-4-0-7
Joseph Anderson	1-1-0-8	Hiram O. Bell	1-0-0-0
Nancy & Wm Allen	1-3-0-8	Phinehas Bowen	1-4-0-8
Algernon S. Allen	2-9-1-10	Francis O. Byrd	1-10-2-9
John Ashby Senr.	1-0-0-0	Philip Berlin	2-6-2-7
Robert Ashby Jr.	1-0-0-0	George C. Blakemore	1-7-0-10
Martin Ashby	1-0-0-2	D° guardian for	
Thomas H.		L. Enders	
Alexander	1-0-0-3	Niell Barnett	1-5-0-7
Nimrod Ashby	1-0-0-0	D° guardian for	
David T. Armstrong	1-0-0-0	Carters	
Evan P. Anderson	1-1-0-1	Thomas Briggs Est.	0-1-1-5
Nimrod F. Anderson	1-0-0-1	Daniel S. Bonham	2-3-0-11
Austin C. Ashby	1-0-0-2	Fanny Brownley	0-8-3-9
Jeremiah Ashby	1-0-0-0	Isaac Berlin Senr.	2-0-1-1
James Allison	1-0-0-0	Strother Bell	1-0-0-0
Wm T. Allen	1-3-3-9	Catharine Bales	0-0-0-0
John Anderson	1-0-0-0	Robert Burchell	1-4-2-7
George B. Ashby	1-0-0-0	H. W. Brabham	1-0-0-0
John Allison	1-0-0-0	Squire Bell	2-0-0-2
James Ash	1-0-0-0	Philip Burwells Est.	0-18-1-11
Washington		John W. Byrd	1-10-3-10
Anderson	1-0-0-2	Thomas Briggs	7-7-0-14
Richard Adams	1-0-0-1	John Brumley	6-0-0-14
William Alder	1-0-0-0	John D. Barr	1-0-0-0

Clarke County, Virginia Personal Property Tax Lists 1836-1853
1851

James W. Beck	1-0-0-1	Ben F. Boley	1-3-0-5
Oscar L. Beck	1-0-0-0	George H. Bell	1-1-0-2
Susan R. Burwell	0-8-0-2	Peter Bennet	1-0-0-0
John C. Bonham	1-5-2-9	George W. Berlin	2-0-0-0
Col. James Bell	1-8-3-14	Henry M. Bowen	1-0-0-1
Lewis Berlin	1-4-0-1	Saml Booker	1-0-0-0
Col. Strother H.		Robert Bull	2-0-0-0
Bowen	9-1-1-4	Miranda Bowen	1-0-2-0
Ann C. Ben	0-1-1-2	Joseph C. Bartlet	2-3-0-7
Charles Ben	1-0-0-0	Thomas Bar	1-0-0-0
William Berry	3-10-2-14	Stephen Barr	1-1-0-0
George H. Burwell	2-44-7-43	Thomas W. Belt	1-0-0-0
George Bolen	1-0-0-0	John H. Beatley	1-0-0-0
Doct. H. F. Barton	1-0-0-1		
Richard E. Byrd	0-1-0-0	Alfred Castleman	3-8-0-8
Richard S. Briarly	1-8-0-9	Frederick Clopton	1-5-0-8
Christian Bowser	1-0-0-0	George F. Calmese	2-5-3-9
James Bogs	1-0-0-0	William G.	
Napoleon Balthrope	1-0-0-2	Carrington	1-0-0-1
Abram Beevers	1-0-0-4	William Carper	1-0-0-2
James Bell	2-0-0-1	Robert A. Coltson	1-5-1-9
Adam Barr	1-0-0-0	Elizabeth K. Carter	2-2-1-5
Ben Barr	1-0-0-0	John Copenhaur	2-3-1-13
Saml Bonham	2-13-2-21	Miriam Catlett	1-5-1-11
Andrew Billmyre	1-0-0-1	James H. Clarke	2-3-2-1
Jesse Butler	1-0-0-1	Thomas H. Crow	1-4-0-8
Juliet Boston	0-1-0-0	Wm. A. Castleman	1-4-0-9
Nancy Boston	0-0-0-0	John Cooper	1-0-0-1
T. T. Byrd's Est.	0-1-0-2	George D. Cooper	1-0-0-2
John R. Bell	1-1-1-4	James Castleman	2-21-1-27
James Brown	2-0-0-1	Thomas Carter	1-7-1-10
Richard Billmyre	1-0-0-0	Parkerson Corder	1-0-0-1
Jesse Bowen	1-1-1-3	John Carroll	1-0-0-1
Henry W. Bayliss	1-0-0-0	Dabney Cauthorn	1-0-0-0
Lewis D. Ball	1-0-0-0	Elizabeth N. Carter	0-1-0-1
Jonas Berkheimer	1-0-0-0	James Carter	2-0-0-0
Isaac Berlin Jr.	2-0-0-1	Thomas Cornwell	2-0-0-1
William Berlin	2-3-2-3	Stephen Cauthorn	1-0-0-0
Henry Bellmain	1-0-0-1	Aaron Chamblin	2-0-0-5

Clarke County, Virginia Personal Property Tax Lists 1836-1853
1851

Michael Copenhaur	1-0-1-1	Benjamin Crampton	0-0-0-0
Martin Creager	1-0-0-1		
Ury Castleman	1-8-1-12	John Dermont	1-4-1-3
Stephen D.		Peter Dermont	1-2-0-0
Castleman	3-5-2-2	Wm Deahle	2-0-1-1
John N. Collier	1-0-0-2	Saml Davis	2-0-0-0
James Carper	2-3-1-9	John Davis	1-0-0-0
Jacob Crim	1-0-0-0	James Davis	1-0-0-0
Stephen B. Cook	2-0-0-6	John Drish	1-5-1-9
John B. Carter	1-5-0-6	Thomas J. Dow	1-0-0-0
Peter Cain	3-0-0-8	Baalis Davis	1-2-1-1
Wm. H. Corbin	1-0-1-0	Thomas Duke	1-0-0-2
Andrew Collins	1-0-0-0	James Doran	2-0-0-1
Wm. K. Carter	1-2-1-5	Saml Dobbins	1-0-0-3
Daniel Carroll	1-0-0-1	George W.	
Samuel Camell	1-0-0-0	Diffenderfer	2-0-0-1
Eloesa M.		Hugh Davis	1-0-0-0
Castleman	0-0-0-0	John Dow	1-2-0-7
Edwin Cauthorn	1-0-0-0	Elijah Dulen	1-0-0-0
John Carroll Jr.	1-0-0-0	Aaron Duble	1-0-0-0
Wm G. Carter	1-0-0-1	Joseph Detter	1-0-0-1
M^clain Clingon	1-0-0-0	Washington	
Henry W. [?]		Dermont	1-1-2-9
Castleman	1-0-0-1	David A. Dick	1-0-1-2
John W. Carter	1-0-0-1	Matthew Dent	1-0-0-0
John A. Carter	1-2-0-5	Thomas Duke Jr.	1-0-0-0
David Carper	1-1-2-9	Thomas Dwier	1-0-0-0
James N. Carpenter	1-0-0-1		
John Carper	1-5-1-6	Henry Edwards	2-0-0-1
Michael Canty	1-0-0-1	William G. Everheart	2-1-0-4
Fenton Carpenter &		John Eleyett	1-1-0-1
J. R. Bell	2-2-0-6	Henson Elliott	3-3-0-8
Ann B. Cook	0-14-1-15	Alexander M. Earle	1-4-1-12
Henry Cook	1-0-0-0	Hiram P. Evans	2-2-1-1
Elisha Carver	1-0-0-0	Jacob Enders	2-7-0-10
James Clinger	1-0-0-0	Jacob W. Everheart	1-0-0-1
Jacob Clink	2-1-2-7	Edward Eno	2-4-0-2
Jacob Cutwalt	1-0-0-0	John Kelly included	
Mary S. Chunn	0-1-0-0	William H. Edwards	1-0-0-1

Clarke County, Virginia Personal Property Tax Lists 1836-1853
1851

Henry Evans	1-1-1-1		Thomas G. Flag	1-0-0-0
Christopher Elliott	1-0-0-1			
John R. Evans	1-0-0-0		Edward Gormon	1-0-0-1
Albert Ellsy	2-1-0-1		Thomas E. Gold	2-4-3-14
Newton Ellsy	1-0-0-1		George Gordon	1-0-0-0
			Mary Green	2-5-2-8
Edward Franks	1-0-0-0		Stephen J. Gant	1-3-0-5
Jesse Furr	0-0-0-1		Thomas Grubs	1-0-0-0
Ephraim Furr	1-0-0-2		Joseph George	1-2-1-5
Daniel Furr	1-0-0-0		John S. Gordon	2-2-0-9
Doct. John			Henry N. Grigsby	1-6-0-10
Fauntleroy	1-4-1-2		William Gourley	1-0-2-5
Doct. O. Funston	Back of Book		Emanuel Garmong	1-0-0-1
James A. Foster	1-1-1-5		Samuel Grubs	1-0-0-0
Moses Furr	1-0-0-0		Abram Grim	1-0-0-0
Thornton Farnsworth	1-0-0-3		Richard N. Green	1-6-0-9
Archibald Fleming	1-2-0-3		George W. Green	2-8-0-11
James Furr	1-0-0-1		John L. Grant	1-2-0-5
Wm Fowler	1-0-0-4		James Gibs	1-0-0-0
Washington			Lewis F. Glass	1-9-0-9
Furgerson	1-1-2-2		Martin Gant	1-4-0-6
Martin Feltner	1-0-0-2		Jemima Gant	0-2-0-1
John W. Feltner	1-0-0-0		John Greenwall	0-0-0-0
Joseph Fleming	1-0-0-4		George Gardner	1-0-0-0
Thomas Fowler	1-0-0-2		Isabella Glass	0-1-0-0
Marcus P. Feehrer	1-1-0-2		Andrew C. Grove	1-0-0-0
Josiah Furgerson	1-0-1-2		Joseph B. Gourley	1-0-0-1
Ben F. Fuller	1-0-0-1		John Galloway	1-0-0-0
Johnson Furr	1-1-1-5		Thornberry Grubs	1-0-0-0
Matthew Frier	2-0-0-3		John W. Gill	1-0-0-0
Ebin Frost	1-0-0-1		John J. Gordon	2-1-0-6
Israel Fidler	1-0-0-0		Elizabeth C. Gruber	1-0-0-1
Joshua Fellows	1-0-0-0		Adam Greenwall	0-0-0-1
William M.			Harrison Gordon	1-0-0-0
Furgerson	1-1-1-2		John Green	2-1-0-5
Jeremiah Fehy	1-0-0-2		Elias M. Green	1-0-0-0
Henry Franks	2-0-0-0		James W. Galloway	1-0-0-0
John A. Finnell	1-1-0-0		James W. Grim	1-0-0-0
John Fox	0-2-0-0			

Clarke County, Virginia Personal Property Tax Lists 1836-1853
1851

Name	Values	Name	Values
Whiting Hamilton	1-0-0-3	Doct. B. Harrison	1-5-1-12
James H. Hooe	1-0-0-4	Theobald B. Heims	3-1-2-0
Abram Huyett	2-0-1-5	Abram Hess	1-0-0-1
John Huyett	1-0-0-0	Revd. J. F. Hoof	1-4-0-1
Saml Huyett	Back of book	Adrian D. Hardesty	1-1-2-6
Levi Hiett	1-3-2-8	Giles C. Hamell	3-1-0-2
Doctr. James A. Haynes	1-3-0-2	Thomas B. Harvey	1-0-0-0
		John Hodge	1-0-0-0
James M. Hite	1-0-0-4	Nancy Henry	1-0-0-0
William Hummer	1-0-0-1	Abram Heskitt	1-0-0-0
Charles Hennis	1-0-0-1	Harrison Hoof	1-0-0-0
Thomas Harris	1-0-0-6	Elijah Haney	1-0-0-0
Henry D. Hooe	2-1-0-0	James M. Howard	1-0-0-0
Saml Heflybour	1-5-1-10	William Hanrey	1-0-0-1
John Hay	Back of book	Edward E. Hall	1-6-1-8
Jacob Heflybour	1-4-1-11	Nelson E. Hall	1-0-0-0
William Holtsclaw	1-0-0-0	Nimrod Henry	1-0-0-0
William Holtsclaw Jr.	1-0-0-1	John W. Hall	1-0-1-0
Blackwell Holtsclaw	1-0-0-0		
Mary Howard	0-3-0-0	Wm Johnson	2-0-0-1
Philip Hansucker	1-0-1-1	George Jenkins	1-0-0-0
George L. Harris	0-5-0-14	Elizabeth Jackson	0-1-0-0
William B. Harris	1-6-1-9	Sidnor B. Johnson	1-0-0-0
Grafton Hillyard	1-0-0-0	George Johnson	1-1-1-1
Cornelius Hoof	1-0-0-0	Herod Jenkins	1-0-0-0
John Hoof	1-0-0-0	Solomon R. Jackson	1-0-0-0
Richard S. Hardesty	1-2-0-8	Matthew Jones	3-2-0-5
Philip Host	1-0-0-0	John Joliffe	1-6-1-8
John Hughs	1-0-0-1	Doct. R. R. Jordan	1-0-0-1
Thomas Hughs	1-0-0-1	Col. Jacob Isler	4-9-1-15
Armistead Hoof	1-1-0-0	Albert Johnson	1-0-0-1
Wm G. Hardesty	1-2-2-9	Doctr. J. J. Janey	1-3-1-4
Thomas L. Humphrey	1-0-1-1	Thomas Jenkins	2-0-0-4
Sarah Hardesty	2-2-0-9	Joseph N. Joliffe	2-0-0-5
Eliza Hay	1-9-1-13	Wm F. Ingle	1-0-0-0
George Hansucker	2-0-1-1	John Johnson	1-0-0-0
Henry Huyett	1-1-0-5	Joseph Johnson	1-4-1-9
Robert L. Horner	1-0-0-0	Alfred Jackson	1-3-1-7
William Heflin	1-0-0-0	Wm H. Jones	1-5-0-7

Clarke County, Virginia Personal Property Tax Lists 1836-1853
1851

George W. Joy	1-0-0-0		Edward V. Kercheral	1-0-0-0
James W. Johnson	1-0-0-1			
Edward Jackson	1-0-0-0		Wm Lee	1-0-0-0
Elizabeth Iden	2-0-0-2		Doct. J. M. Lindsay	1-0-0-0
Ransall Johnson	1-0-0-2		William Littleton	1-1-0-4
William A. Jackson	1-5-0-9		Henry Loyd	2-0-0-3
Amelia Jordan	0-2-0-2		John Lock	2-0-0-8
			James W. Larue	1-4-2-6
James C. Kenan	2-0-0-0		Wm Longerbeam	1-0-0-1
Doct. F. J. Kerfoot	1-10-0-15		Doct. R. H. Little	1-5-2-6
Revd Thomas			John Louthan	4-5-0-7
Kennerly	4-19-4-14		Lorenzo Lewis Est.	Back of book
George Knight	Back of book		Col. John B. Larue	2-13-0-19
Charged to Wm F. Knight			John Loyd	1-0-0-1
William C. Kerfoot	2-13-1-14		James Loyd Senr.	1-0-0-0
George L. Kerfoot	2-10-3-18		Saml Loyd	1-0-0-0
Doct. R. Kownslar	1-4-1-4		Edgar Lanham	1-0-0-0
John Kable	3-1-0-1		Abram Longerbeam	1-0-0-0
William F. Knight	Back of Book		Elizabeth Lanhams	
Nickolas Kriser	1-0-0-1		Est.	0-0-0-2
Elizabeth Knight	Back of Book		A. L. P. Larue	1-3-1-6
Geo & Wm C.			Wm D. Littleton	2-2-0-7
Kerfoot	0-9-0-11		Harrison Loyd	1-0-0-2
Charles E. Kimball	1-4-1-9		John T. Lindsay	2-5-1-4
Middleton Keeler	1-0-0-0		Minor Lanham	1-0-0-2
Wm C. Kennerly	1-5-1-6		Rice W. Levi	1-1-0-1
Joseph Kline	1-0-0-1		David Loyd	1-0-0-0
Saml G. Kneller	1-1-0-1		James Larues heirs	0-1-0-1
John B. Kerfoot	1-0-0-3		Squire Lee	3-0-0-2
James M. Kiger	1-3-0-4		George Lanham	2-0-0-2
Jacob Kriser	2-0-0-1		James Lanham	1-0-0-0
Ben T. Kercheval	2-0-1-2		R. S. Littlejohn	0-0-0-0
Henry Kenneford	1-0-0-0		George Lock	2-0-0-5
James L. Kercheval	1-0-1-0		Easther M. Lewis	Back of book
Elias Kline	1-0-0-0		John W. Littleton	1-0-0-2
Franklin Kenneford	1-0-0-0		John Longerbeam	1-0-0-0
Jeremiah Kane	1-0-0-0		Ben Longerbeam	2-0-0-3
John N. Kemmill			James Loyd Jr.	1-0-0-2
& Co.	3-0-0-0		John W. Luke	0-5-0-0

Clarke County, Virginia Personal Property Tax Lists 1836-1853
1851

Charles Leech Jr.	1-0-0-0	John N. Meade	1-4-0-6
William H. Levi	1-0-0-0	James Murphy	2-1-0-2
Josiah Lock	1-0-0-3	Revd. Wm Meade	Back of Book
John Landers	1-0-0-0	Stephen Marlow	1-0-0-1
John D. Larue	1-5-1-6	Amishadai Moore	1-3-2-8
James W. Lewis	1-0-0-0	John G. McCauley	1-0-0-1
		David H. McGuire	1-8-0-8
Peter McMurray	2-1-2-7	Alfred P. Moore	1-0-0-1
Saml McCormick	2-0-0-1	William B. Moore	1-0-0-0
John J. Munroe	1-3-1-5	Andrew R. Milton	1-4-0-3
John Maddex	3-2-1-9	Catharine Michell	0-1-0-0
James Michell	1-2-1-3	Edmund W. Massey	1-5-0-7
Doct. Wm D.		John Marple	1-2-0-0
McGuire	1-10-2-11	John McDonald	1-0-0-1
Otway McCormick	2-6-1-4	Province McCormick	2-1-0-4
Francis B. Meade	1-6-0-11	Seth Mason	1-3-2-11
Louisa W. Meade	0-3-0-1	Harrison McCormick	2-1-0-4
Philip N. Meade	Back of book	Richard K. Meade	1-4-1-10
Wm Meade Jr.	1-5-1-10	Moses G. Miley	2-0-0-6
Mary Meade	Back of book	Wm McCormick	1-6-0-7
Thomas McCormick	1-8-3-9	Henry Mason	1-0-0-0
John Marts Senr.	1-0-0-1	Sidnor Miley	1-0-0-1
Saml T. Marts	1-0-0-0	Edward McCormick	2-12-2-16
Doct. C. & Saml		John Martin	1-0-0-3
McCormick	2-20-3-27	George Marple	1-0-0-1
Levi Marquiss	1-0-0-1	Province McCormick	1-7-0-9
James Marquess	1-0-0-0	Nathaniel B. Meade	1-5-0-6
Jesse P. Mercer	2-0-0-2	Christian Moyer	4-0-0-4
James Michum	1-0-0-2	James McCaury	2-0-0-1
Thomas Murphy	1-0-0-0	Milton H. Moore	1-5-0-8
Col. Benj Morgan	1-24-4-27	Daniel G. Mallory	1-0-0-1
Col. Frank			
McCormick	1-10-1-11	Doct. S. S. Neill	1-5-1-6
Susan Marshal	0-4-1-5	Wm Niswanger	1-0-0-3
John Marshal	2-1-1-3	Hugh M. Nelson	1-11-1-12
Alexander Marshal	1-1-0-0	Philip Nelson Senr.	1-16-3-11
John McPhillin	2-3-1-7	Thomas F. Nelson	2-11-3-16
John Morgan	1-9-3-8	James H. Neville	2-1-0-0
James McCormick	1-1-0-7	Joseph Noble	1-0-1-0

Clarke County, Virginia Personal Property Tax Lists 1836-1853
1851

Abby Nelson	0-3-1-0	Richard L. Page	0-3-1-4
Doctr. Wm Nelson	1-3-0-3	Conrad Pope	1-0-0-1
John Nessmith	2-2-0-2	McFarland Puller	1-0-0-0
Philip Nelson Jr.	1-2-1-6	John Patterson	1-0-0-2
John B. Norris	0-4-0-4	James Payne	1-0-0-2
Philip C. Nicholas	1-0-0-0	Barnett Prichett	1-0-0-0
Lewis Neill	1-0-0-0	Uriah Petit	1-0-0-1
Lucy Newman	0-1-0-0	Calvin Puller	1-0-0-0
William Oconnel	1-0-0-0	William Pyle	1-0-0-0
Elizabeth Orear	0-9-1-10	Alfred Prescott	1-0-0-1
George Orear	1-3-0-7	Richard Parker	Back of Book
David Osbourn	1-0-0-3	Elizabeth H. Parker	0-2-0-0
Mason Olliver	2-0-0-1	Archibald C. Page	1-2-0-8
George Osbourn	1-1-0-5	Michael Pope	2-0-0-1
Hugh Orook	1-0-0-0	Susan R. Page	0-17-3-10
Elias Overall	1-2-1-2	D° at Saratoga	0-15-3-13
Benjamin F. Orear	1-4-0-4	John Pigott	1-0-0-0
Susan Orear	1-0-0-1	Alfred Parkins	0-1-0-0
		Benjamin Perry	1-0-0-0
John Pierce Jr.	2-4-1-10		
Matthew Pullum	3-1-0-0	Thomas W. Ridings	Back of book
George Pultz	1-0-0-1	John Rowland	Back of book
John E. Page	1-14-1-21	Richard Ridgeway	2-2-0-6
Eliza M. A. Page	0-4-1-0	Thomas W. Reynolds	1-0-0-0
John Page Jr.	1-9-2-10	Bennet Russell	2-8-1-9
Mann R. Page	3-12-3-17	Elizabeth W. Royster	0-2-0-0
Saml L. Pidgeon	2-0-0-7	Matthew W. Royston	2-3-2-11
Revd. Joshua Peterkin	1-3-0-2	Peter Royston	1-0-0-0
James M. Pine	1-0-0-0	Uriah B. Royston	1-0-0-4
Mary C. Page	0-4-1-4	John Reid	1-0-0-1
Paul Pierce	2-6-2-9	Nancy Redmon	0-0-1-0
John Pierce Senr.	1-4-1-8	George Rutter	1-0-0-0
James Puller	1-0-0-0	Danl B. Richards	2-0-0-1
Peter Mc Pierce	Back of Book	Saml B. Redmon	1-0-0-1
Pendleton & Richardson	2-21-4-29	Addison Romine	1-2-0-7
Washington F. Padgett	1-0-0-0	James Ryan	2-1-0-0
		Joseph Ross	0-0-0-0
		Joseph Ryan	1-0-0-4
		John Russell	2-0-0-2

Clarke County, Virginia Personal Property Tax Lists 1836-1853
1851

George Reno	1-0-0-1	Danl W. Sowers	1-11-1-20
Marcus Reed	1-0-0-2	Saml Stipe	2-5-0-7
Isaac Ramey	2-2-0-6	Thomas Sprint	2-0-0-1
Mathew Rust	2-3-2-8	Emanl Showers	2-1-0-0
James Russell	1-3-1-4	Barnett Smallwood	2-0-0-1
Beverly Randolph	1-15-4-18	Fielding L. Sowers	1-4-2-8
Thomson Ritt	1-0-0-0	Parkerson D. Shepherd	2-5-2-9
Doct. R. C. Randolph	2-13-2-20	Col. T. Smith	2-17-3-21
D° for Charles Lucius		Kerfoot Sowers Est.	1-3-2-16
William Riley	1-0-0-1	John Stewart	1-0-0-4
Michael Russell	1-0-0-2	Elizabeth Strother	0-7-1-5
Joseph Richardson	1-0-0-0	John Shafer	1-0-0-0
Alexander Riely	1-3-0-7	Jackson Shafer	1-0-0-0
John Riely	1-1-0-2	Alfred Smallwood	1-0-0-0
Peter K. Royston	1-2-0-3	Burr Smallwood	1-0-0-1
John Ramey	1-0-0-2	Simon Stickles	1-0-0-1
Thomas Roradan	2-0-0-1	George Smedley	1-0-0-1
Stephen Reed	1-0-0-0	Danl H. Sowers	1-4-3-11
Thomas W. Russell	1-0-1-2	Mary E. Shirely	0-7-2-10
John W. Russell	3-1-0-3	Henry Shepherd	2-6-1-3
Conrad Rinyman	0-0-0-0	Joseph Sprint	1-0-0-0
Perry G. Rice	3-0-0-3	John Shell	1-0-0-1
Peter G. Ringer	1-0-0-0	Wm L. Smith	1-0-0-0
Charles W. Rivers	1-0-0-0	Erasmus Shackelford	2-0-0-1
Bushrod C. Reynolds	1-0-0-1	Charles Showers	2-0-0-1
		Saml Schooler	1-0-0-0
Mary Stribling	0-4-0-2	James W. Smith	1-0-1-0
Samuel Showers	1-0-0-0	Paul Smith	3-3-2-11
Avery Stipe	1-1-1-4	Shedrick Shrout	0-0-0-1
Daniel A. Sowers	1-1-0-0	John R. Stewart	2-1-0-2
Elizabeth Sowers	0-4-0-3	Alexander Sanders	1-0-0-0
William Stewart	2-0-0-5	Sanders & Ridings	1-0-0-1
George R. Smith	1-0-0-0	Jonathan S. Smith	2-4-0-0
William D. Smith	2-24-5-31	Thomas J. Skinker	1-7-1-9
William Sowers	1-5-1-16	George Strother	2-0-0-3
Joseph Shepherd	1-6-0-7	D° as Guardian for	
Champ Shepherd	1-3-2-5	J. W. Strother	
Thomas Shumate	1-3-0-10	D° for Sarah A. Reed	
John W. Sowers	2-4-4-17	D° for Lewis Strother	

Clarke County, Virginia Personal Property Tax Lists 1836-1853
1851

Name	Values	Name	Values
Wm H. Spicknell	2-0-0-1	Andrew J. Tinsman	1-0-0-0
Robert N. Stumb	1-0-0-0	Calvin Thacker	1-0-0-0
Margaret Swann	0-1-0-0	Mary Taylor	1-8-1-10
Richard Swift	1-0-0-0	James Tracy	2-0-0-0
Ben Stonestreet	1-0-0-0	John Turner	1-0-0-0
Joseph Stewart	1-0-0-0	Thomas Turner	1-0-0-0
Elisha Smallwood	1-0-0-0	William Timberlake	1-2-0-5
Braxton D. Smith	1-0-0-0	James Tansell	1-0-0-0
Daniel Snyder	3-0-0-5	Ludwell Tinsman	1-0-0-0
John W. Steel	1-0-0-1	Bailiss Thomson	1-0-0-4
Isaac Starkey	1-0-0-0	Charles H. Taylor	Back of book
Reuben Sims	1-0-0-0		
Wm R. Stewart	2-1-0-2	John R. [illegible]	1-0-0-0
John W. Sprint	1-0-0-0	John Vanclief	1-0-0-5
James L. Showers	1-0-0-1	Jacob Vanmeter	0-4-0-0
		Oliver H. Von	1-0-0-1
Sarah Timberlake	0-4-0-9		
James W. Tanquerry	1-0-0-1	Wm Willingham	2-0-0-2
David Tristler	1-1-0-4	Allen Williams	2-9-1-15
Adam Towner	1-0-0-0	Francis H. Whiting	1-3-0-6
William Taylor	2-12-4-19	J. W. Ware &	
Greenberry Thomson	4-0-0-4	Mrs. Stribling	1-14-5-16
Doct. Saml Taylor	1-7-1-2	D. Wade & Co.	3-1-0-1
Benjamin		Horatio T. Wheat	4-4-0-5
Thomson Jr.	2-0-0-6	Benjamin F. Wilson	1-0-0-0
Col. Joseph Tuley	1-16-7-20	Hezekiah Wiley	1-0-0-0
John Trussell	2-4-1-6	Saml Wiley	1-0-0-1
William Trinary	1-2-1-3	James Wiley Senr.	1-0-0-1
Wm Tinsman	1-0-0-0	John Willingham	1-0-0-0
Adam F. Thomson	1-0-0-2	Leroy P. Williams	1-8-1-7
Robert Tapscott	1-2-0-0	Francis B. Whiting	2-22-3-13
William Tomblin	1-0-0-0	Wm W. Whiting	1-4-1-5
Enoch Triplett	1-0-0-0	Bennet Wood	Back of book
Howard F. Thornton	1-7-0-13	Nathaniel B. Whiting	1-5-1-9
Snowdon Tomblin	1-0-0-1	Sydnor B. Windham	1-0-1-1
John Tally	1-0-0-0	John Wilson	2-0-0-0
French Thomson	3-0-0-4	Doct. H. Washington	1-0-0-0
Maria Thomson	1-0-0-0	Thomas C. Windham	1-0-0-0
Moses B. Trussell	1-0-1-2	James W. Ware	1-0-0-0

Clarke County, Virginia Personal Property Tax Lists 1836-1853
1851

James V. Wier	1-4-2-7	P. N. Meade	1-7-0-10
William Willis	1-1-0-0	Revd. Wm Meade	1-0-0-1
Jeremiah Wilson	1-0-0-0	Mary Meade	0-2-1-0
William H. Whiting	1-7-1-12		
James Wiley Jr.	1-0-0-0	Scimeon Yowell	2-1-0-2
John Wiley	1-0-0-0	Wm Young	1-0-1-0
David Whittington	1-0-0-1		
Jacob Welch	1-1-0-4	[Back of the book]	
David H. Wilcox	1-0-0-0		
James Woods	1-0-0-0	John Rowland	4-0-0-8
James Wilson	1-0-0-0	R. S. Littlejohn	1-0-0-0
Andrew Willingham	1-0-0-0	Richard Parker	1-0-0-1
James Willingham	1-0-0-0	Saml Huyett	1-3-0-8
George W. Wiley	1-0-0-0	Wm B. C. Sowers	1-1-3-0
Wm Wolfe	2-0-0-0	Wm Stolle	1-0-0-0
Jesse Wright	1-0-0-3	John A. Snyder	1-0-0-0
Robert Whittington	1-0-0-0	Crow & Snyder	1-0-0-0
George B. West	1-0-0-1	Charles H. Taylor	1-0-1-3
George F. Woodward	1-0-0-1	Wm. F. Knight	2-7-1-11
Horace A. West	2-0-0-0	George Knight Included	
Richard B. Welch	1-1-0-0	Elizabeth Knight	0-0-0-0
Charles L. Wright	1-0-0-1	Oliver R. Funston	1-10-3-15
Benjamin Wharton	5-0-1-3	Peter McPierce	1-4-1-9
Thornton O. Windham	1-0-0-1	Bennet Wood	1-0-0-0
		Thomas W. Ridings	1-0-0-0
James S. Welch	2-6-0-3	Easther M. Lewis	0-3-2-2
Doctr. Edward L. Wager	1-0-0-1	Loving Lewis Est.	1-29-5-22
		Mary C. Randolph Request Tax from N. Burwell	
Joseph Wood	2-1-0-4		
James H. Willis	1-0-0-0		
John W. Weidman	1-0-0-1	Susan R. Page Request Tax from N. Burwell	
Lucinda Washington	0-3-0-1		
		Thomas Carter	1-4-0-6

Clarke County, Virginia Personal Property Tax Lists 1836-1853
1851

Labourers [Free Negroes]
over 35 years, many with ages unknown

John Clifton	54 years
Scimeon Parker	
George Ranson	0-1-0-0 Labourer over 55 years
Winny [Ranson]	
Hannah	
Julia	
Lydia	
Richard	
Frances	
Spencer Johnson	0-0-0-1 carpenter
Robert Diggs	twenty two shoe maker
Philip Martin	1 free negro labourer
Jenny	
Lucy	fourteen years old
Seneora	twelve years
Burwell Cook	labourer
Mowen Harris	forty one years old, stone mason
Jacob Johnson	forty four labourer
John Jackson	over 55 years labourer
Maria Jackson	
Samuel Jackson	fourteen years labourer
Nathaniel Johnson	twenty three
Peter Coates	Back of Book
George Lee	twenty one or two years, labourer
Wat Howard	sixty three, blacksmith
Wm H. Allen	twenty three
Lydia A. Allen	twenty three
Daniel Gracen	forty six, cooper
Jemima [Gracen]	forty four
Richard Lee	labourer, age unknown
Ann M. Michell	twenty three
Billy Butler	1 free negro over fifty five, labourer
Wm Toler	twenty two years old, labourer
Wm Parker	labourer
Alfred Mason	1 free negro, twenty two years, labourer
Scimeon Parker	labourer
Jess Jackson	forty years old, labourer
Levinia Broomsick	twelve years old
Joseph Jackson	1 free negro, seventeen years old, labourer
Jane Lee	sixty years old
George Broomsick	sixty or seventy years old, labourer

Clarke County, Virginia Personal Property Tax Lists 1836-1853
1851

Lewis Ransom	fourteen years old, labourer	Jane	twenty one
		Sally Young	sixty eight
Thomas Ranson	1 free negro over 16	Lewis Toliver	1 free negro over 16
Ellen Gray	fifty years old	James Hatter	1 free negro,
James	thirteen years	sixty or seventy	
Lewis Clifton	twenty one	Lewis	unknown
Ralph Grey	unknown	Levi Proctor	1 slave over 12
Sandy Carter	thirty years old	about 53, labourer	
Levinia Menifee	twenty five year	Hannah Proctor	fifty
		Eliza J.	fourteen years
James Gumby	1 free negro, twenty years old	Ellen Smith	forty
		Victoria Smith	thirteen
Polly Gumby	fifty six years	Alice Collins	sixty six
Lucy Gumby	twenty two	Ann Clifton	forty five
Alfred Thomson	twenty eight	Wm Michell	thirty five labourer
Henson Toliver	thirty five		
Nancy Robinson	sixty five	John Gordon	twenty eight or thirty labourer
John McCoy	twenty one		
John L. Howard	twenty nine		

[After recapitulation]

John Hay   1-0-3-1   E. T. Hancock   2-0-0-1

Clarke County, Virginia Personal Property Tax Lists 1836-1853

1852

Columns: 1) Free males above 16 years of age [not yet 21] 2) slaves above 16 years of age, 3) White males of 21 years of age, 4) Males free negroes between the ages of 21 and 55 years, 5) Slaves who have attained the age of 12 years and upwards slaves above 12, 6) Horses, mules, etc.

Buckner Ashby	1-9-1-0-3-12
James M. Allen	0-3-1-0-1-7
Mason Anderson	1-7-1-0-0-11
John Alexander	0-23-1-0-1-22
Susan C. Alexander [inkblot]	0-6-1-0-0-8
Augustin Athey	0-0-1-0-0-2
John Anderson	0-0-1-0-0-0
John H. Anderson	0-1-1-0-0-0
Robert Ashby Senr.	0-0-1-0-0-2
Joseph Anderson	0-2-2-0-0-10
Geo Wm Allen	0-3-1-0-1-7
Algernon S. Allen	0-9-1-0-1-13
John Ashby Senr.	0-0-1-0-0-0
Robert Ashby Jr.	0-0-1-0-0-0
Nancy Allen	0-0-0-0-0-0
Martin Ashby	0-0-1-0-0-1
Thos H. Alexander	0-1-1-0-0-1
Nimrod Ashby	0-0-1-0-0-0
David T. Armstrong	0-0-1-0-0-1
Evan P. Anderson	0-2-1-0-0-2
Nimrod F. Anderson	0-0-0-0-0-0
Austin C. Ashby	0-0-1-0-0-2
Jeremiah Ashby	0-0-1-0-0-1
James Allison	0-0-1-0-0-0
Wm T. Allen	0-6-1-0-3-8
John W. Anderson	0-0-1-0-0-0
Capt. Geo B. Ashby	0-0-1-0-0-0
John Allison	0-0-1-0-0-0
James Ash	0-0-1-0-0-0
Wm Asberry	1-0-1-0-0-0
Geo W. Anderson	0-0-1-0-0-2
Richard Adams	0-0-1-0-0-1
Joel Alexander	0-0-1-0-0-0
Levi Athey	0-0-1-0-0-0
James Athey	0-0-1-0-0-1
Jacob Anderson	1-0-1-0-0-1
George F. Anderson	0-0-1-0-0-2
Nathaniel Burwell	0-10-1-0-4-16
John D. Barr	0-0-1-0-0-0
Brown & Stoll	2-1-1-0-0-3
Wm C. Benson	0-0-1-0-0-0
John Burchell	0-6-1-0-0-12
Archibald Bowen	0-1-4-0-0-7-73
Hiram O. Bell	0-2-1-0-2-3
Phinehas Bowen	0-2-1-0-1-8
Francis O. Byrd	0-14-1-0-0-10
Philip Berlin	0-7-2-0-0-8
George C. Blakemore	0-8-1-0-0-11
D° as guardian for L. Enders	0-0-0-0-0-0

Clarke County, Virginia Personal Property Tax Lists 1836-1853
1852

Niell Barnett	0-5-2-0-1-8	Saml Bonham	2-11-1-0-3
Jackson Berlin	0-0-1-0-0-0	Andrew Billmyre	0-0-2-0-0-0
Thomas Briggs Est.	02-0-0-0-5	Jesse Butler	0-0-1-0-0-1
		Richard E. Byrd	0-1-0-0-0-0
Daniel S. Bonham	1-4-1-0-0-10	Juliet Boston	0-1-0-0-0-0
John R. Bell	0-2-1-0-1-5	Nancy Boston	0-0-0-0-0-0
Strother Bell	1-0-1-0-0-4	T. T. Byrd's Est.	0-1-0-0-0-1
Robert Burchell	0-6-1-0-2-7	John R. Bell	0-1-1-0-0-3
H. W. Bratham	0-0-1-0-0-0-0	James Brown	0-0-1-0-0-0
Squire Bell	0-0-1-0-1-0	Richard Billmyre	0-0-1-0-0-0
Philip Burwells Est.	0-19-0-0-11	Jesse Bowen	0-1-1-0-1-2
		John H. Barr	0-0-1-0-0-0
John W. Byrd	0-10-1-3-9	James Board	1-0-1-0-0-0
Thomas Briggs	1-7-5-0-2-15	Jonas Berkheimer	0-0-1-0-0-0
John S. Briggs	0-0-1-0-0-0-0	Isaac Berlin Est.	0-0-0-0-0-1
John Brumley	1-0-1-0-0-8	Wm Butin	1-2-1-0-0-0
Susan R. Burwell	0-7-0-0-2-2	Benjamin F. Boley	0-2-1-0-0-0
John C. Bonham	2-4-1-0-0-7	Geo H. Bell	0-2-1-0-1-4
Lewis Berlin	0-3-1-0-1-1	Geo W. Berlin	1-1-1-0-0-1
Strother H. Bowen	0-1-1-0-1-1	Geo W. Bradfield	1-2-1-0-0-0
		Henry M. Bowen	0-3-1-0-1-2
Ann C. Ben	0-0-0-0-0-2	James Berlin	0-0-1-0-0-0
Wm Berry	0-11-3-0-0-15	Robert Bull	1-1-1-0-0-1
Hector Bell	0-0-10-0-0-2	Emily Bell	0-0-0-0-0-1
Geo H. Burwell	0-41-2-0-10-46	Joseph C. Bartlett	1-4-1-0-0-7
Geo S. Bacon	0-0-1-0-0-0	Nancy Beck	1-0-1-0-0-0
John Bursey	0-0-1-0-0-0	John F. Burchell	0-1-1-0-0-4
George Bolen	0-0-1-0-0-0	Peter Bennett	0-0-1-0-0-0
Alfred Bishop	0-0-1-0-0-0		
Doct. H. F. Barton	0-0-1-0-0-2	Alfred Castleman	2-5-2-0-2-14
Richard S. Briarly	0-7-1-0-1-10	Fredk Clopton	0-4-1-0-2-8
Saml Booker	0-0-1-0-0-0	George F. Calmese	1-5-1-0-3-10
Christian Bowser	0-0-1-0-0-0		
John Blue	1-1-1-0-0-7	Wm Carper	0-0-1-0-0-2
Napoleon Balthrope	1-0-1-0-0-2	Robert A. Colston	0-4-1-0-0-9
		Elizabeth K. Carter	0-2-2-0-1-5
Abram Beevers	0-0-1-0-0-3		
James Bell	1-0-1-0-0-1	John Copenhaur	1-3-1-0-1-13
Adam Barr	0-0-1-0-1-0	Miriam Catlett	0-5-1-0-1-7

Clarke County, Virginia Personal Property Tax Lists 1836-1853
1852

James H. Clarke	0-4-1-0-0-1	M^clain Clingon	Back of Book
Thomas H. Crow	1-4-1-0-2-9	Elizabeth Clink	0-0-0-0-1-0
George W. Cooper	0-0-1-0-0-0	James Carver	0-0-1-0-0-0
		John A. Carter	0-1-1-0-0-4
Wm A. Castleman	0-4-1-0-0-9	David Carper	0-4-1-0-2-0
Parkerson Corder	0-0-1-0-0-1	James N. Carpenter	0-0-1-0-0-1
Thomas Carter	1-10-1-0-2-14	John Carper	0-4-2-0-2-7
John Carroll	0-0-1-0-0-1	James P. Carrigan	0-0-1-0-0-0
Dabney Cauthorn	0-0-1-0-0-0	Wm Chapman	0-0-1-0-0-0
Elizabeth N. Carter	0-0-0-0-0-1	Ann B. Cook	0-16-0-0-3-12
		Elisha Carver	1-0-1-0-0-0
James & John W. Carter	1-0-2-0-0-2	Jacob Clink	0-2-1-0-2-8
		George D. Cooper	0-0-1-0-0-0
Thomas Cornwell	1-0-1-0-0-1	Saml Coleman	0-0-1-0-0-0
Stephen Cauthorn	0-0-1-0-0-0	Creager & Wharton	0-1-2-0-0-2
Aaron Chamblin	0-0-1-0-0-6	James W. Conrad	0-1-1-0-0-6
Michael Copenhaur	0-0-1-0-1-1	James Castleman	0-18-2-0-1-17
Ury Castleman	0-4-0-0-1-1		
Stephen D. Castleman	0-4-4-0-1-2	John Dermont	0-4-1-0-2-2
		Peter Dermont	0-2-1-0-0-1
John N. Collier	0-1-1-0-0-2	Wm Deahle	1-1-1-0-0-1
Charles D. Castleman	1-3-0-0-0-5	Saml Davis	0-0-1-0-0-0
		John W. Davis	0-0-1-0-0-0
Jacob Crim	0-0-1-0-0-0	Moses T. Davis	1-0-0-0-0-0
Stephen B. Cook	1-0-1-0-0-5	George H. Davis	1-0-0-0-0-0
John B. & J. W. Carter	0-6-2-0-0-6	John Drish	0-0-1-0-0-1
		Michael Dermont	0-6-1-0-2-11
Peter Cain	0-0-2-0-1-7	Washington Dermont	0-0-1-0-0-3
Wm. H. Corbin	0-0-1-0-1-0		
Wm. K. Carter	0-1-1-0-1-5	Baalis Davis	0-1-1-0-1-1
Danl Carroll	0-0-1-0-0-1	Thomas Duke	0-0-1-0-0-2
Saml Camell	0-0-1-0-0-0	James Doran	1-0-1-0-0-1
Eloesa M. Castleman	0-0-0-0-1-0	Saml Dobbins	0-0-1-0-0-3
Edwin Cauthorn	0-0-1-0-0-0	George W. Diffenderfer	0-0-1-0-0-1
Wm G. Carter	0-1-1-0-0-2		

Clarke County, Virginia Personal Property Tax Lists 1836-1853
1852

Hugh Davis	0-0-1-0-0-0		
John Dow	0-3-1-0-1-7	Edward Franks	0-0-1-0-0-0
James Davis	0-0-1-0-0-0	Ephraim Furr	0-0-1-0-0-1
Elijah Dulen	0-0-1-0-0-0	Danl Furr	0-0-1-0-0-0
Aaron Dubal	0-0-2-0-0-0	Doct. John	
Joseph Detter	0-0-1-0-0-1	Fauntleroy	0-4-1-0-1-3
Thomas Dwier	0-0-1-0-0-0	Doct. O. R.	
Thomas Duke	0-0-1-0-0-0	Funston	0-10-1-0-0-16
Margaret Drish	1-0-0-0-0-0	James A. Foster	0-2-1-0-0-5
Jefferson Dove	0-0-1-0-0-0	Moses Furr	0-0-1-0-0-1
James Duke	0-0-1-0-0-0	Ann Farnsworth	2-0-0-0-0-2
Charles Dulaney	0-0-1-0-0-0	Elizabeth Fleming	0-2-0-0-0-4
David Dicks	0-2-1-0-1-3	James Furr	0-0-1-0-0-0
Joseph W. Dills	0-0-1-0-0-0	Wm Fowler	0-0-1-0-0-4
Robert N. Duke	0-3-2-0-0-5	Washing [sic]	
Michael Dillwood	0-0-1-0-0-0	Furgerson	0-2-1-0-1-2
Lewis Dick	0-0-1-0-0-0	Martin Feltner	1-0-1-0-0-2
		Joseph Fleming	0-0-1-0-0-3
Henry Edwards	1-0-1-0-0-2	Thomas Fowler	0-0-1-0-0-2
Wm G. Everheart	2-1-1-0-0-5	Marcus R.	
John Eleyett	0-1-1-0-0-2	Feehrer	0-1-1-0-3-4
Henson Elliott	0-1-3-0-1-7	John Fox	0-2-0-0-0-0
Alexander M.		A. Williams agent	
Earle	0-4-1-0-1-11	Josiah Furgerson	0-0-1-0-1-2
Hiram P. Evans	0-2-1-0-0-1	Johnson Furr	0-0-1-0-2-6
Jacob Enders	1-7-1-0-0-10	John W. Feltner	0-0-1-0-0-0
Jacob W.		Matthew Frier	0-0-1-0-0-1
Everheart	0-0-1-0-0-1	Ebin Frost	0-0-1-0-0-1
Edward Eno	0-4-1-0-0-1	Joshua Fellows	0-0-1-0-0-0
William H. Edwards	0-0-1-0-0-1	Wm M. Furgerson	0-1-1-0-0-2
Henry Evans	0-1-1-0-1-0	Jeremiah Fehy	0-0-1-0-0-3
Christopher		Henry Franks	1-0-1-0-0-0
Elliott	0-0-1-0-0-1	Thomas J. Flagg	0-0-1-0-0-0
John R. Evans	0-0-1-0-0-0	John A. Finnell	0-1-1-0-0-0
Albert Ellsy	0-1-1-0-0-1		
Newton Ellsy	0-0-1-0-0-0	Perry Goddell	0-0-1-0-0-0
Jackson Elliott	0-0-1-0-0-0	Emanl Garmong	1-0-1-0-0-1
Frederick Eckholt	0-0-1-0-0-0	James W.	
Elliott & Parker	0-0-0-0-0-0	Galloway	0-0-1-0-0-0

Clarke County, Virginia Personal Property Tax Lists 1836-1853
1852

James W. Grim	0-0-1-0-0-0	Doct. James A.	
Edward Gormon	1-0-0-1	Haynes	0-3-1-0-1-4
Thomas E. Gold	0-6-2-0-1-14	James M. Hite	0-0-1-0-0-3
D° as guardian		Wm Hummer	0-0-1-0-0-3
for B. Crampton		Charles Hennis	0-0-1-0-0-1
George Gordon	0-0-1-0-0-0	Henry D. Hooe	1-1-1-0-0-0
Mary Green	0-5-0-0-2-6	Eliza Hay	1-10-0-0-1-12
James F. Green	0-0-1-0-0-2	Jacob Heflybour	0-5-1-0-2-12
Stephen J. Gant	0-4-1-0-0-5	Adam Hubbard	0-0-1-0-0-
Joseph George	0-2-1-0-0-5	Wm Holtsclaw	
John S. Gordon	0-2-1-0-0-6	Senr.	0-0-1-0-0-0
George Gordon	0-0-1-0-0-1	Wm Holtsclaw Jr.	0-0-1-0-0-1
Henry N. Grigsby	0-7-1-0-0-10	Blackwell	
Wm Gourley	0-0-1-0-2-6	Holtsclaw	0-0-1-0-0-0
Saml Grubs	0-0-1-0-0-0	Mary Howard	0-4-0-0-0-0
Abram Grim	0-0-1-0-0-0	Philip Hansucker	1-0-1-0-1-1
Richard N. Green	0-6-1-0-0-7	George L. Harris	1-5-0-0-1-15
Chloe E. Gruber	0-0-0-0-0-1	Elizabeth C. Hay	0-2-0-0-0-0
George W. Green	0-6-2-0-2-11	Cornelius Hoof	0-0-1-0-0-0
John L. Grant	1-1-1-0-0-5	Richard S.	
Lewis F. Glass	0-7-1-0-0-9	Hardesty	0-0-1-0-0-7
Martin Gant	0-3-1-0-2-6	Philip Host [?]	0-0-1-0-0-0
Jemima Gant	0-1-0-0-0-1	John Hughs	0-0-1-0-0-1
Mason Green	0-0-1-0-0-0	Thomas Hughs	0-0-1-0-0-1
George Gardner	0-0-1-0-0-0	Armistead Hoof	0-1-1-0-0-0
Isabella Glass	0-1-0-0-0-0	Wm G. Hardesty	0-2-1-0-1-11
Andrew C. Grove	0-0-1-0-0-0	Sarah Hardesty	1-2-0-0-0-9
Thornbury Grubs	1-0-1-0-0-0	Wm G. Harris	0-5-1-0-4-0
John J. Gordon	0-1-2-0-1-6	George	
John Gruber	0-1-1-0-0-4	Hansucker	0-0-1-0-0-2
John S. Green	0-2-1-0-0-7	Henry Huyett	0-1-1-0-0-6
		Robert L. Horner	0-0-1-0-0-1
Whiting Hamilton	1-0-1-0-0-2	Wm Heflin	0-0-1-0-0-0
James H. Hooe	0-0-1-0-0-4	Doct. B. Harrison	0-5-1-0-0-14
Abram Huyett	0-0-1-0-0-2	Theobold B.	
John Huyett	0-0-0-0-0-0	Haines	0-2-4-0-0-0
Saml Huyett	0-2-1-0-0-10	Abram Hess	0-0-1-0-0-0
Henry H. Hibbard	0-0-1-0-0-0	Revd. John F.	
		Hoof	0-2-1-0-1-1

Clarke County, Virginia Personal Property Tax Lists 1836-1853
1852

Adrian D. Hardesty	0-3-1-0-1-5	Leonard Jones	0-1-1-0-0-3
John Hodge	0-0-1-0-0-0	Alfred Jackson	0-3-1-0-0-7
Wm Heskit	0-0-1-0-0-0	James C. Kenan	1-0-1-0-0-0-2
Abraham Heskit	0-0-1-0-0-0	Doct. F. J. Kerfoot	1-8-1-0-0-12
Harrison Hoof	0-0-1-0-0-0	Revd. Thomas Kennerly	0-17-2-0-4-16
James M. Howard	0-0-1-0-0-0	George Knight	0-8-2-0-0-13
David Hays	0-0-1-0-0-0	Wm C. Kerfoot	1-11-1-0-5-15
John Hoof	0-0-1-0-0-0	Geo L. Kerfoot	1-13-1-0-2-14
Nelson E. Hall	0-0-1-0-0-1	Doct. R. Kownslar	0-4-1-0-2-3
Thomas L. Humphrey	0-1-1-0-0-1	John Kable	0-2-2-0-0-1
Francis W. Heskit	0-0-1-0-0-3	Elizabeth Knight	0-0-0-0-0-0
Edward E. Hall	0-8-1-0-0-8	Geo & Wm C. Kerfoot	0-8-0-0-0-11
John W. Hall	0-0-1-0-0-0	Charles E. Kimball	0-5-1-0-0-11
George Johnson	0-1-1-0-0-2	Middleton Keeler	0-0-1-0-0-0
Herod Jenkins	0-0-1-0-0-0	Wm C. Kennerly	0-6-1-0-1-5
Capt. Solomon R. Jackson	0-0-1-0-0-0	Joseph Kline	0-0-1-0-0-1
Matthew Jones	1-2-1-0-0-5	Saml G. Kneller	0-5-1-0-0-7
John Joliffe	0-6-1-0-2-9	John B. Kerfoot	0-0-1-0-0-4
Col. Jacob Isler	0-5-4-0-3-13	James M. Kiger	0-3-1-0-0-5
Doct. J. J. Janey	0-2-1-0-1-5	Jacob Kriser	0-0-2-0-0-1
Thomas Jenkins	0-0-1-0-0-5	Henry Kenneford	0-0-1-0-0-0
Joseph N. Joliffe	1-0-1-0-0-6	Jeremiah Kane	0-0-1-0-0-0
George Janey	0-0-1-0-0-0	John N. Kimmell	0-0-1-0-0-0
Wm H. Jones	0-4-1-0-1-9	James H. Kenan	0-0-1-0-0-0
Geo W. Joy	0-0-1-0-0-0	John Kelly	0-0-1-0-0-0
James W. Johnson	0-0-1-0-0-1	Wm G. Kendall	0-0-1-0-0-0
Edward Jackson	0-0-1-0-0-0	Edward V. Kercheral	0-0-2-0-0-0
Ransall Johnson	0-0-1-0-1-2	Charles Kitchen	1-1-0-0-1-4
Wm A. Jackson	0-5-1-0-0-8		
Amet: a [sic] Jordan	0-1-0-0-0-2	Wm D. Lee	0-0-1-0-0-0
Wm Johnson	0-0-1-0-0-0	Doct. J. M. Lindsay	0-0-1-0-0-0
George Jenkins	0-0-1-0-0-0	Eli Littleton	0-2-1-0-0-0
Thomas Jones	0-3-1-0-0-5	Henry Loyd	1-0-1-0-0-3
		John Lock	0-0-2-0-1-5

Clarke County, Virginia Personal Property Tax Lists 1836-1853
1852

James W. Larue	0-6-1-0-1-5	John M. Lupton	0-1-1-0-1-0
Sally Longerbeam	0-0-0-0-0-0	Franklin Littleton	0-0-1-0-0-0
Doct. R. H. Little	0-5-1-0-1-5	John McPhillin	0-4-2-0-1-6
John Louthan	0-5-3-0-1-8	Saml McCormick	1-0-1-0-0-1
Lorenzo Lewis Est.	0-19-0-0-4-23	Wm B. Moore	0-0-1-0-0-0
		Wm Miles	0-0-1-0-0-0
Col. John B. Larue	1-13-2-0-2-18	Miss L. R. Mason	0-0-0-0-0-0
John Loyd	0-0-1-0-0-0	Peter McMurray	1-3-1-0-0-6
James Lloyd	0-0-1-0-0-0	John Maddex	2-1-1-0-0-9
Edgar Lanham	0-0-1-0-0-0	James Michell	0-0-1-0-0-3
Abram Longerbeam	0-0-1-0-0-0	Doct. Wm D. McGuire	0-10-0-2-11
A. L. P. Larue	0-4-1-0-0-8	Otway McCormick	1-7-1-0-0-6
Wm Littleton	0-1-1-0-1-4	Francis B. Meade	0-6-1-0-1-8
Harrison Loyd	0-0-1-0-0-0	Philip N. Meade	0-8-2-0-1-8
John T. Lindsay	0-3-1-0-2-3	Wm W. Meade	0-6-1-0-2-10
Rice W. Levi	0-0-1-0-1-2	Thomas McCormick	0-9-1-0-0-9
David Loyd	0-0-1-0-0-0	Geo W. McCormick	0-0-1-0-0-0
James Larues heirs	0-1-0-0-0-1	John Marts	0-0-1-0-0-1
Squire Lee	2-0-2-0-0-3	Doct. C. & Saml McCormick	0-23-2-0-0-30
James Lanham	0-0-1-0-0-0	C. C. McIntyre	0-3-1-0-2-6
Mrs. E. M. Lewis	0-4-0-0-1-2	James S. Maddex	0-0-1-0-0-1
Mrs. E. P. Lewis	0-1-0-0-0-0	Lorenzo D. Maddex	0-0-1-0-0-1
John W. Littleton	0-0-1-0-0-2	Levi Marquess	0-0-1-0-0-1
John Longerbeam	0-0-1-0-0-0	Jesse P. Mercer	0-0-1-0-0-1
Ben Longerbeam	0-0-1-0-0-3	Thomas Murphy	0-0-1-0-0-0
John W. Luke	0-1-1-0-1-1	Col. Benjamin Morgan	1-23-1-0-4-30
Charles Leech Jr.	0-0-1-0-0-0	D° as guardian for Miss Alexander	
Wm H. Levi	0-1-1-0-0-0		
Josiah Lock	0-0-1-0-0-4	Jacob May – Exempt	
George Lanham	1-0-1-0-0-2	Col. Frank McCormick	0-20-1-0-2-18
Wm D. Littleton	0-0-1-0-0-4		
Minor Lanham	0-0-1-0-0-1		
George W. Lewis	0-0-1-0-0-0		
John D. Larue	0-3-1-0-1-6		
James L. Loyd	0-0-1-0-0-0		
James Loyd Jr.	0-0-1-0-0-2		
Henry W. Light	1-0-1-0-0-0	N. B. Meade	0-7-1-0-0-7

Clarke County, Virginia Personal Property Tax Lists 1836-1853
1852

Name	Values	Name	Values
Susan Marshall	0-5-0-0-0-5	James W. Miller	0-0-1-0-0-0
John Marshall	0-2-1-0-1-3	P. McCormick	0-6-1-0-1-8
Alexander Marshall	0-0-1-0-0-0	Milton H. Moore	0-6-1-0-1-8
John Morgan	1-8-1-0-2-10	James McClaury	2-0-1-0-0-2
D° as guardian for children		James Marquess	0-0-1-0-0-0
		Christian Moyer	1-0-1-0-0-3
James McCormick	0-1-1-0-0-9	Albert A. Morris	1-0-0-0-0-0
		Wm G. Morris	0-0-1-0-0-0
John N. Meade	0-6-1-0-1-6	N. B. Meade	0-3-1-0-1-7
James Murphy	1-0-1-0-0-4	Hugh M. Nelson	0-11-1-0-3-12
Stephen Marlow	1-0-1-0-0-1	Thomas F. Nelson	0-11-1-0-3-15
Amishadai Moore	0-4-1-0-2-8	John Newcom [sic]	0-0-1-0-0-3
John G. McCauley	0-0-1-0-1-1	James H. Neville	1-1-1-0-0-0
		Joseph Noble	0-0-1-0-1-0
David H. McGuire	0-8-1-0-1-9	Abby & A. R. Nelson	0-2-0-0-1-0
D° as trustee to children		John Nessmith	1-1-2-0-0-2
		Philip Nelson Jr.	0-2-1-0-0-6
Alfred P. Moore	0-0-1-0-0-1	John B. Norris – Exempt	0-4-0-0-0-4
A. R. Milton	0-5-1-0-0-5	Lewis Neill	0-0-1-0-0-1
George Marple	0-0-1-0-0-1	John R. Nunn	0-3-1-0-1-4
Edmund W. Massey	1-5-1-0-0-9	Wm M. Nelson	0-0-1-0-0-1
John Marple	0-1-1-0-0-1	Archie Nelson	0-0-1-0-0-7
Province McCormick Jr.	1-0-1-0-0-3	Sarah Nelson	0-17-0-0-7-4
Seth Mason	0-5-1-0-1-10	George Osbourn	0-1-1-0-0-5
Harrison McCormick	0-0-1-0-0-4	Overseers of the Poor	0-2-0-0-0-4
Richard K. Meade	0-4-1-0-1-11	Elizabeth Orear	0-9-0-0-0-10
Moses G. Miley	1-0-1-0-0-6	George Orear	0-4-1-0-0-9
Wm McCormick	0-0-1-0-0-2	David Osbourn	0-0-1-0-0-3
Revd. D. G. Mallory	0-2-1-0-0-0	Mason Olliver	1-0-1-0-0-1
		Hugh Orook	0-0-1-0-0-0
Henry Mason	1-0-1-0-0-0	Elias Overall	0-2-1-0-1-2
Edward McCormick	0-13-1-0-2-16	Ben F. Orear	0-4-1-0-0-4
		Susan Orear	1-0-0-0-0-0

Clarke County, Virginia Personal Property Tax Lists 1836-1853
1852

Susan R. Page, Admx. of E. Burwell Legacy to T. Nelson	0-0-0-0-0-0
	0-0-0-0-0-0
	0-0-0-0-0-0
D° To Mildred Nelson	
D° to Jurdon [?]H. Pendleton	
D° to R. C. Randolph	
D° N. B. Cook	
D° M. C. Page	
Susan R. Page	0-13-0-0-2-14
D° at Saratoga Farm	0-15-0-0-3-10
John Pierce Jr.	0-4-2-0-1-14
Matthew W. Pullum	1-1-1-0-0-1
George Pultz	0-0-1-0-0-1
John E. Page	0-13-1-0-5-22
Eliza M. N. Page	0-4-0-0-1-0
John Page Jr.	0-9-1-0-3-11
Mann R. Page	0-11-2-0-2-17
D° as Guardian H. M. Neuin [sic]	
Saml L. Pidgeon	0-0-2-0-0-6
Revd. Joshua Peterkin	0-4-1-0-0-2
James M. Pine	0-0-1-0-0-0
Mary C. Page	0-4-0-0-1-2
Paul Pierce	1-6-1-0-3-9
John Pierce Senr.	0-4-1-0-1-7
James Puller	0-0-1-0-0-0
Peter McPierce	0-3-1-0-1-9
Pendleton & Richardson	0-18-2-0-3-36
Washington F. Padgett	0-0-1-0-0-0
Benjamin Perry	0-0-1-0-0-0
Richard L. Page, U. S. Navy	0-4-0-0-0-4
McFarland Puller	0-0-1-0-0-0
John Patterson	0-0-1-0-0-2
James S. Payne	0-0-1-0-0-1
Barnett Prickett	0-0-1-0-0-0
Uriah Petit	0-0-1-0-0-0
Wm Pyle	0-0-1-0-0-0
Archibald C. Page	0-2-1-0-0-12
Richard E. Parkers Est.	0-0-1-0-0-0
Conrad Pope	0-0-1-0-0-1
Richard Parker	0-0-1-0-0-3
Michael P. Pierce	0-4-1-0-1-10
John Rowland	2-0-2-0-0-9
Thomas W. Raynolds	0-0-1-0-0-0
Bennet Russell	0-9-1-0-3-11
Elizabeth W. Royster	0-0-1-0-0-0
Matthew W. Royston	0-3-1-0-0-10
Peter Royston	0-0-1-0-0-0
Uriah B. Royston	0-0-1-0-0-3
John Reid	0-0-1-0-0-0
~~Nancy Redmon~~	0-0-1-0-0-0
George Rutter	0-0-1-0-0-0
Danl B. Richards	0-1-1-0-0-0
Saml B. Redmon	0-0-1-0-0-1
Addison Romine	0-2-1-0-0-5
James Ryan	0-0-1-0-0-0
James W. Ryan	0-0-1-0-0-0
Capt. Joseph Ryan	0-0-1-0-1-3
John Russell	0-1-1-0-0-3
George Reno	0-0-1-0-0-0
Mary Richardson D° as Guardian for young Kirby	0-0-0-0-0-0

Clarke County, Virginia Personal Property Tax Lists 1836-1853
1852

Name	Values	Name	Values
Isaac Ramey	0-1-2-0-0-5	Wm D. & E. J. Smith	0-26-2-0-5-30
Mathew Rust	0-3-2-0-1-9	Wm Stoll	0-1-1-0-0-0
James Russell	0-4-1-0-0-6	Wm Sowers	1-7-1-0-1-13
Beverly Randolph	0-15-1-0-8-20	Joseph Shepherd	0-6-1-0-1-7
Thomson Ritt	0-0-1-0-0-0	Champ Shepherd	0-3-1-0-0-7
Doct. R. C. Randolph	1-14-1-0-2-22	D° as guardian for J Shepherd Jr.	
D° Est. of P Burwell		Thomas Shumate	0-3-1-0-1-10
F. B. Meade Legacy		John W. Sowers	0-8-1-0-1-16
R. P. Burwell D°		Danl W. Sowers	0-15-1-0-2-21
L. G. Burwell D°		James A. Steel	1-0-3-0-0-0
Mary C. Roots	0-0-0-0-0-0	Thomas Sprint	0-0-1-0-0-1
Richards & Wharton	0-0-2-0-0-0	Saml Showers	0-1-2-0-0-1
Wm Riely	0-0-1-0-0-1	Barnett Smallwood	2-0-1-0-0-3
Michael Russell	0-0-1-0-0-2	Fielding L. Sowers	0-3-1-0-1-8
Joseph Richardson	0-0-1-0-0-0	P. D. Shepherd	1-7-1-0-0-9
Wm A. Riely	0-4-1-0-0-6	Doct. Philip Smith	0-19-2-0-0-19
John J. Riely	1-2-0-0-0-4	Col. T. Smith	0-15-2-0-5-19
Peter K. Royston	0-2-1-0-0-5	Kerfoot Sowers Est.	1-5-0-0-0-13
Wm C. Ramey	0-0-2-0-0-3	James Sowers	0-1-1-0-0-4
Thomas Roradan	0-0-2-0-0-1	John Stewart	0-0-1-0-0-4
Stephen Reed	0-0-1-0-0-0	Elizabeth Strother	0-7-0-0-2-5
Thomas W. Ridings	0-0-1-0-1-0	John Shafer	0-0-1-0-0-0
Conrad Rinyman – Exempt	0-0-0-0-0-0	Jackson Shafer	0-0-1-0-0-0
Bushrod C. Raynolds	0-0-1-0-0-1	Burr Smallwood	0-0-1-0-0-1
James Rose	0-0-1-0-0-0	Simon Stickles	0-0-1-0-0-2
Marcus Reed	0-0-1-0-0-0	George Smedley	0-0-1-0-0-0
Joseph Ross	0-0-1-0-0-1	Danl H. Sowers	0-3-1-0-2-11
John Russell	0-0-1-0-0-1	D° as guardian for E. Strothers heirs	
Theoerick [sic] Russell	0-0-1-0-0-1	Wm Strother	0-0-1-0-0-1
James M. Reed	0-0-1-0-0-0	Mary E. Shirely	0-5-0-0-1-3
		Henry Shepherd	0-6-2-0-1-1
		Joseph Sprint	0-0-1-0-0-0
		John Sprint	0-0-1-0-0-0
		Wm L. Smith	0-0-1-0-0-0

Clarke County, Virginia Personal Property Tax Lists 1836-1853
1852

Erasmus Shackelford	1-0-1-0-0-1	Eliza Taylor	0-0-0-0-0-1
Charles Showers	0-0-2-0-0-1	Doct. Saml Taylor	0-6-1-0-2-2
Susan T. Smith	0-1-0-0-0-0	Benjamin Thomson Jr.	1-0-1-0-0-8
Alexander Sanders	0-0-1-0-1-0	Col. Joseph Tuley	0-29-1-0-5-22
Paul Smith	1-2-1-0-11-75	George Thomson	0-0-1-0-0-0
George R. Smith	0-0-1-0-0-0	John Trussell	1-4-1-0-1-7
John R. Stewart	1-0-1-0-0-1	Charles H. Taylor	0-0-1-0-0-0
Sanders & Ridings	1-0-0-0-0-1	Wm Trenary	0-2-1-0-1-4
Jonathan S. Smith	0-3-1-0-0-1	Adam Thomson	0-0-1-0-0-2
Thomas J. Skinker	0-6-1-0-1-13	Robert Tapscott	0-2-1-0-0-0
John H. P. Stone	0-0-1-0-0-0	Wm Tomblin	0-0-1-0-0-0
Wm D. Stewart	1-0-0-0-0-0	Enoch Triplett	0-0-1-0-0-0
Robert N. Stump	0-0-1-0-0-0	French Thomson	2-0-1-0-0-6
Margaret Swann	0-3-0-0-0-2	Howard F. Thornton	0-6-1-0-1-13
Danl Snyder	1-0-1-0-0-6	Moses B. Trussell	0-1-1-0-0-2
Joseph Stewart	0-0-1-0-0-0	Andrew J. Tinsman	0-0-1-0-0-0
Braxton D. Smith	0-0-1-0-0-1	Calvin Thacker	0-0-1-0-0-0
Stephen Shell	0-0-1-0-0-1	Mary Taylor or P. McCormick	0-11-1-0-5-14
Isaac Starkey	0-0-1-0-0-1	Wm D. Timberlake	0-2-1-0-0-4
Mary Stribling	0-4-0-0-1-1	Ludwell Tinsman	0-0-1-0-0-1
John H. Spots	0-1-1-0-0-0	Baalis Thomson	0-0-1-0-0-3
Geo W. Shultz	0-0-1-0-0-1	Saml Tinsman	1-0-0-0-0-0
John W. Shell	0-0-1-0-0-0		
Dennis Sheheen	0-0-2-0-0-1	John R. Utter	0-0-1-0-0-0
Wm B. C. Sowers	0-0-1-0-0-6		
Reuben Sims	0-0-1-0-0-0	John Vanclief	0-0-1-0-0-4
Edward Smith	0-0-1-0-0-0	Jacob Vanmeter	0-5-0-0-0-6
		James E. Vincent	0-0-1-0-0-0
Sarah Timberlake	0-4-1-0-0-8		
David Tristler	0-0-1-0-0-2	Geo B. West	0-0-1-0-0-1
Adam Towner	0-0-1-0-0-0	Wm Willingham	0-0-2-0-0-3
Greenberry Thomson	1-0-1-0-0-3	Allen Williams	1-10-1-0-1-13
James F. Thomson	0-0-1-0-0-2	Francis H. Whiting	0-2-1-0-0-7
Wm Taylor	1-15-1-0-3-19		

Clarke County, Virginia Personal Property Tax Lists 1836-1853
1852

J. W. Ware & Mrs. Stribling	1-17-1-0-6-20	Robert Whittington	0-0-1-0-0-0
Danl Wade & Brother	0-1-2-0-0-1	Wm Walters	0-0-1-0-0-0
H. T. Wheat	1-5-1-0-0-5	Benjamin Wharton	2-1-2-0-0-2
Hezekiah Wiley	0-0-1-0-0-0	Thornton O. Windham	0-0-1-0-0-1
Saml Wiley	0-0-1-0-0-1	James S. Welch	0-6-2-0-0-3
John Willingham	0-0-1-0-0-1	Joseph Wood	0-1-1-0-0-5
Sidnor B. Willingham	0-0-1-0-0-1	James H. Willis	0-0-1-0-0-1
John Wilson	0-0-1-0-0-1	Benjamin F. Wilson	0-0-1-0-0-0
Leroy P. Williams	1-8-1-0-1-8	Wm Webster	0-0-1-0-0-0
Francis B. Whiting	0-20-1-0-3-15	Greenberry W. Weaver	0-0-1-0-0-2
Wm W. Whiting	0-4-1-0-4-5	Lucinda Washington	0-0-4-0-0-0
N. B. Whiting	0-7-1-0-0-9	P. H. Woodward	0-0-1-0-0-0
Doct. H. Washington	0-1-1-0-0-0	Col. James W. Walker	0-8-1-0-1-8
Thomas C. Windham	0-0-1-0-0-0		
James V. Wier	0-2-1-0-0-2	Wm H. Young	0-1-1-0-0-1
Wm H. Whiting	0-7-1-0-1-12		
James Wiley	0-0-1-0-0-1	Mary Meade	0-3-0-0-0-0
John Wiley	0-0-1-0-0-0	Revd Wm Meade	0-0-1-0-0-0
Jacob Welch	1-0-1-0-0-4	Louisa W. Meade	0-3-0-0-1-1
David H. Wilcox	0-0-1-0-0-0	David H. Allen	0-15-2-0-3-17
Obidiah Willingham	0-0-1-0-0-0	Thomas J. Bragg	0-2-1-0-0-2
George W. Wiley	0-0-1-0-0-0	Mclain Clingon	0-0-1-0-0-0
Wm Wolfe	1-1-1-0-0-0		
Jesse Wright	0-0-1-0-0-2		

Clarke County, Virginia Personal Property Tax Lists 1836-1853
1852

List of Free Negroes

Columns: 1) free males above 16 years, 2) over 21 & under 55, 3) over 55 years

John Clifton	0-0-1		Wat Howard	0-0-1
George Jones	1-0-0		Jacob Johnson	1-0-0
Philip Martin	0-1-0		George Vernon	0-0-1
James Gumby	0-1-0		Wm H. Thornton	0-1-0
John Gordon	0-1-0		Newman Thomson	0-1-0
Philip Askins	0-1-0		Peter Coates	0-1-0
Frederick Cooper	0-0-1		3 horses	
2 horses, 7 cattle			Nathan Johnson	0-1-0
Ralph Bray	0-1-0		Billy Butler	0-0-1
Lewis Clifton	0-1-0		Burwell Cook	0-1-0
Spencer Johnson	0-1-0			
1 horse				

Clarke County, Virginia Personal Property Tax Lists 1836-1853

1853

Columns: 1) free male persons above 16 years, 2) slaves who have attained the age of 16 years, 3) white male inhabitants who have attained the age of 21 years, except those exempted from taxation on account of bodily infirmity, 4) male free negroes between the ages of 21 and 55 years, 5) Slaves who have attained the age of 12 years, 6) Horses, mules, asses & jennets

Name	Values	Name	Values
Buckner Ashby	1-9-2-0-1-13	Thos. H. Alexander	0-1-1-0-0-5
James M. Allen	0-4-1-0-1-8	Joel Alexander	0-0-1-0-0-0
Mason Anderson	1-4-1-0-0-9	Nimrod Ashby	0-0-1-0-0-0
John H. Anderson	1-4-1-0-0-0	____ Austin	0-0-1-0-0-0
David H. Allen	0-13-3-0-0-20	John Ashby	0-0-1-0-0-1
Jesse Allen	0-0-1-0-0-1	Wm Asbury	1-1-1-0-0-1
Evan P. Anderson	0-1-1-0-0-1	Jos E. Anderson	0-0-1-0-0-1
John Alexander	?-12-1-0-0-23	Jno & Nimrod	
John Anderson	0-0-1-0-0-0	Anderson	0-2-2-0-0-10
D. T. Armstrong	0-0-1-0-0-0	John Amick	0-0-1-0-0-0
Augustine Athey	0-0-1-0-0-1		
Robt Ashby Senr.	0-0-1-0-0-2	Nathl Burwell	0-10-1-0-4-19
Robt Ashby Junr.	0-0-1-0-0-0	Hector Bell	0-0-1-0-0-1-1
Jos Anderson	0-0-1-0-0-0	Wm C. Benson	0-0-1-0-0-0
Geo W. Allen	0-4-1-0-0-10	John Burchell	0-8-1-0-0-12
Algernon S. Allen	0-8-1-0-2-16	Archibald Bowen	1-4-1-0-1-10
Austine C. Ashby	0-0-1-0-0-1	Hiram O. Bell	0-3-1-0-1-4
Jeremiah Ashby	0-0-1-0-0-0	Francis O. Byrd	0-13-1-0-0-9
James Allison	0-0-1-0-0-0	Philip Berlin	0-6-2-0-0-7
Wm T. Allen	0-3-1-0-1-11	Andrew J. Berlin	0-6-2-0-0-7
Geo W. Ashby	0-1-1-0-0-1	Wm Brown	0-0-1-0-0-0
John Anderson	0-0-1-0-0-0	Geo C. Blakemore	0-7-1-0-1-11
George B. Ashby	0-0-1-0-0-0	D° as guardian for	
John Allison	0-0-1-0-0-0	Leonidas Enders	
James Ash	0-0-1-0-0-0	Niell Barnett	0-5-2-0-1-8
Washington		Maranda Bowen	0-1-1-0-0-2
Anderson	0-0-1-0-0-2	Thos Briggs Est.	0-3-0-0-1-6
Richard Adams	0-0-1-0-0-1	Danl S. Bonham	1-2-2-0-1-8
Levi Athey	0-0-1-0-0-0	Strother H. Bell	2-0-1-0-0-5

Clarke County, Virginia Personal Property Tax Lists 1836-1853
1853

Robt Burchell	0-6-1-0-2-7		Juliet Boston	0-1-0-0-0-0
H. W. Brabham	1-0-1-0-0-0		Nancy Boston	0-0-0-0-0-0
Squire Bell	0-0-1-0-0-0		T. T. Byrd's Est.	0-1-0-0-0-0
			Richard E. Byrd	0-1-0-0-0-0
Armstd M. Johnson	0-1-1-0-0-4		Arthur Briggs	0-0-0-0-0-2
			John R. Bell	1-2-1-0-0-3
John W. Byrd	0-12-1-0-2-10		James Brown	0-0-1-0-0-0
John S. Briggs	0-0-1-0-0-0		Richd Billmire	0-0-1-0-0-0
John Brumley	0-0-1-0-0-8		Jesse Bowen	0-2-1-0-0-3
Susan R. Burwell	0-9-0-0-0-2		James I. Board	1-0-1-0-0-0
John C. Bonham	2-1-1-0-0-5		James Bales	0-0-1-0-0-0
Ralph Bray [FN]	0-0-0-1-0-0		Jonas Berkheimer	0-0-1-0-0-1
Thomas Briggs	0-6-5-2-2-10		Wm Berlin	0-2-1-0-2-1
Wm Brentten	0-0-1-0-0-1		Benjn F. Boley	0-2-1-0-2-1
Lewis Berlin	0-3-1-0-0-1		Geo W. Berlin	0-1-1-0-0-0
Strother H. Bowen	0-1-1-1-1-0		Geo W. Bradfield	1-2-1-0-0-0
Bowen & Eberhart	4-1-2-0-0-7		Henry M. Bowen	1-1-2-0-1-10
Ann C. Benn	0-0-0-0-0-2		Bushrod & Buckley	0-0-1-0-0-0
John H. Barr	0-0-1-0-0-0		James Berlin	0-0-1-0-0-0
Wm Berry	0-8-3-0-2-14		Robt Bull	1-1-1-0-0-0
Geo H. Bell	0-0-10-0-0-0		Emily Bell	0-0-0-0-0-1
John Bursey	0-0-1-0-0-0		Jos C. Bartlett	1-3-1-0-1-9
Geo H. Burwell	0-49-2-0-7		John F. Burchell	0-0-1-0-0-4
Geo Bolen	0-0-1-0-0-0		Robt & James	
Cornelius Bursey	0-0-1-0-0-0		Briggs	0-5-2-0-1-4
H. T. Barton	0-0-1-0-0-3		George Board	0-0-1-0-0-0
Saml Booker	0-0-1-0-0-0		James W. Boarde	0-0-1-0-0-2
Richard Bryarly	0-7-1-0-1-11		Thomas Brown	0-1-1-0-0-0
C. Bowser	0-0-1-0-0-0		James Bales	0-0-1-0-0-0
John Blue	1-2-1-0-0-7		Geo W. Brumly	0-0-1-0-0-4
N. B. Balthrope	2-0-1-0-0-3			
Abram Beevers	0-0-1-0-0-3		Alfred Castleman	1-5-4-0-3-14
James Bell	0-0-1-0-0-1		Frederick Clopton	0-5-1-0-3-8
Peter Bennett	0-0-1-0-0-0		Geo F. Calmese	1-6-1-0-1-9
Adam Barr	0-1-1-0-0-0		Wm Carper	0-0-1-0-0-2
Thomas Barr	0-0-1-0-0-0		Robt A. Colston	0-4-1-0-0-9
Saml Bonham	1-10-1-0-4-21		Elizabeth K. Carter	0-2-3-0-1-6
Andrew J. Billmire	0-0-0-0-0-0		John Copenhaur	1-4-1-0-1-12
Jesse Butler	0-0-1-0-0-1		Burwell Cooke [FN]	0-0-0-1-0-0

Clarke County, Virginia Personal Property Tax Lists 1836-1853
1853

Miriam Catlett	0-4-1-0-1-9		Saml Camell	0-0-1-0-0-0
James H. Clark	0-4-1-0-0-1		Eloesa Castleman	0-0-0-0-0-0
Thomas H. Crow	1-4-1-0-0-9		Saml Tinsman Jr.	0-0-1-0-0-0
R. T. Colston	0-5-0-0-0-7		Edward Couthon	0-0-1-0-0-0
Geo W. Cooper	0-0-1-0-0-0		Wm G. Carter	0-1-1-0-0-2
Parkison Corder	0-0-1-0-0-1			
James Castleman	0-17-2-0-0-28		McLane McLingen	0-0-1-0-1-0
Wm A. Castleman	0-4-1-0-0-8			
John Cooper	0-0-1-0-0-2		Elizabeth Clink	0-0-1-0-0-0
Thomas Carter	0-6-1-0-1-9		John A. Carter	0-2-1-0-0-5
John Carroll	1-0-1-0-0-0		David Carper	0-4-1-0-0-8
Dabney Cauthorn	0-0-1-0-0-0		Ann B. Cooke	0-14-0-0-3-15
Peter Cooley	0-0-1-0-0-0		Michael Crim	0-0-1-0-0-0
Elizabeth N. Carter	0-0-0-0-0-1		Elisha Carver	1-0-1-0-0-1
James Carter	0-0-2-0-0-2-		Jacob Clink	0-1-1-0-2-6
Thos Cornwell	1-0-1-0-0-1		Jeremiah Cain	0-0-1-0-0-0
Stephen Cauthorn	0-0-1-0-0-1		Creager &	
Aaron Chamblin	0-0-1-0-0-1		Wharton	1-1-2-0-0-2
H. Chamblin	0-0-1-0-0-0		James W. Conrad	0-2-1-0-2-7
Michael			Andrew Cornwell	0-1-1-0-0-0
Copenhaver	0-0-1-0-1-1		John Carper Senr.	0-6-2-0-0-9
Ury Castleman	0-3-0-0-2-1		James Clevenger	0-0-1-0-0-0
Stephen D.			Isaac Cornwell	0-0-1-0-0-0
Castleman	0-3-3-0-1-2		John P. Caragan	0-0-1-0-0-0
John N. Collier	0-0-1-0-0-2		Henry W.	
Charles D.			Castleman	0-3-1-0-1-10
Castleman	0-2-2-0-0-8		Wm Chapman	0-0-1-0-0-0
Henry C. Carr	0-0-1-0-0-0			
Jacob Crim	0-0-1-0-0-0		Moses T. Davis	0-0-1-0-0-0
Stephen B. Cook	0-0-2-0-0-7		Peter Dearmont	0-5-2-0-2-3
Jno B. Carter &			Wm Deahle	2-1-1-0-0-1
Brother	0-3-2-0-1-6		Saml Davis	1-0-1-0-0-0
Peter Cain	1-0-1-0-1-6		John Drish	0-0-1-0-0-1
Augustine Cain	0-0-1-0-0-0			
Wm H. Corbin	0-0-1-0-1-0		John Clifton	0-0-0-1-0-0
David Collins	0-0-0-1-0-0			
Wm. K. Carter	0-1-1-0-1-6		Michael Dearmont	1-5-1-0-3-11
Danl Carroll	0-0-1-0-0-0		Wash Dearmont	0-0-1-0-0-2
Elias Cline	0-0-1-0-0-0		Baalis Davis	0-1-1-0-1-1

Clarke County, Virginia Personal Property Tax Lists 1836-1853
1853

Name	Values	Name	Values
Thomas Duke Senr.	1-0-1-0-0-2	Isaac N. Elsey	0-0-1-0-0-0
James Doran	1-0-1-0-0-1	Elliott & Parker	0-0-0-0-0-0
James Duke	0-0-1-0-0-0	Edward Franks	0-0-1-0-0-0
Saml Dobbins	0-0-1-0-0-1	Ephraim Furr	0-0-1-0-0-1
Geo W. Diffenderfer	0-0-2-0-1-1	J. F. Fauntleroy	0-4-1-0-1-4
		O. R. Funsten	0-9-1-0-1-16
Hugh Davis	0-0-1-0-0-0	Henry G. Flagg	0-0-1-0-0-5
John Dow	0-3-1-0-0-5	James A. Foster	0-2-1-0-0-5
Wm Doherty	0-0-1-0-0-0	Moses Furr	0-0-1-0-0-0
John D. Davis	0-0-1-0-0-0	Israel Fiddler	0-0-1-0-0-0
James Davis	0-0-1-0-0-0	Ann Farnsworth	2-0-0-0-0-2
Aaron Dubal	0-0-2-0-0-1	Elizabeth Fleming	0-2-0-0-0-3
Joseph Detter	0-0-1-0-0-1	James Furr	0-0-1-0-0-1
Thomas Duke Junr.	0-0-1-0-0-0	Joseph Fleming Senr.	0-0-1-0-0-0
Jefferson Dove	0-0-1-0-0-0		
Charles Dulaney	0-0-1-0-0-1	Washington Ferguson	0-1-1-0-0-4
David Dick	0-1-1-0-0-4	Enoch Furr	0-0-1-0-0-0
Joseph W. Dills [?]	0-0-1-0-0-0	Martin Feltner	1-0-1-0-0-3
Robt N. Duke	0-4-1-0-1-7	Jos Fleming Junr.	1-0-1-0-0-3
Edward Dorsey	0-0-1-0-0-0	Wm Fowler	0-0-1-0-0-1
Lewis Dick	0-0-1-0-1-0	Thomas Fowler	0-0-1-0-0-2
		Marcus R. Feehrer	0-1-1-0-2-4
Henry Edwards	1-0-1-0-0-2	John Fox, or A. Williams	0-1-0-0-1-0
Wm G. Everhart	2-1-1-0-0-5	John Frasier	0-2-0-0-0-0
John Elleyett	0-1-1-0-0-2	John Finch	0-0-0-1-0-1
Henson Elliott	0-3-3-0-0-8	Josiah Fergurson	0-1-1-0-0-4
Wm Elliott	0-0-1-0-0-0	Johnson Furr	0-1-1-0-1-5
A. M. Earle	0-4-1-0-1-11	John A. Finnell	0-1-1-0-0-1
H. P. Evans	0-3-1-0-0-1	Ebin Frost	0-0-1-0-0-1
Jacob Enders	0-7-1-0-0-9	Joshua Fellows	0-0-1-0-0-0
John Eberhart	0-1-1-0-0-0	Wm M. Furgerson	0-1-1-0-1-2
Jacob W. Everhart	0-0-1-0-0-1	Jeremiah Falvey	0-0-3-0-0-5
Edwd Eno	0-4-2-0-1-2	Henry Franks	1-0-1-0-0-0
Wm H. Edwards	0-0-1-0-0-2	Thomas G. Flagg	0-0-1-0-0-0
Henry Evans	0-1-1-0-0-1	Jesse Furr	0-0-1-0-0-0
Christopher Elleyett	0-0-1-0-0-0	Dennis Fenton	0-0-1-0-0-0
John R. Evans	0-0-1-0-0-0		
Albert Elsey	0-1-1-0-0-4		

Clarke County, Virginia Personal Property Tax Lists 1836-1853
1853

Perry Goddell	0-0-1-0-0-0	Abram Huyett	0-0-1-0-0-2
Emanuel Gormong	1-0-1-0-0-2	John Huyett	0-0-0-0-0-0
James W. Galloway	0-0-1-0-0-0	Saml Huyett	0-3-1-0-0-10
James F. Green	0-0-1-0-0-2	Henry A. Hibbard	1-0-1-0-0-0
Thomas E. Gold	0-5-2-0-2-15	James A. Haynes	0-5-1-0-0-4
D° as guardian for		James M. Hite	0-1-1-0-0-3
Ben Crampton		Wm Hanvey	1-0-1-0-0-0
Geo F. Gordon	0-0-1-0-0-0	Wm Hummer	0-0-1-0-0-1
Mary Green	0-6-0-0-1-5	Charles Hennis	0-0-1-0-0-1
Stephen J. Gant	0-4-1-0-0-4	Wm Heflin	0-0-1-0-0-0
Geo W. Gordon	0-0-1-0-0-1	Henry D. Hooe	2-1-1-0-0-0
John S. Gordon	0-2-1-0-0-7	Saml Heflebower	0-3-1-0-2-9
Henry N. Grigsby	0-5-1-0-3-7	Charles W.	
Wm Gourley	0-2-1-0-0-4	Hardesty	0-0-1-0-0-1
Saml Grubs	0-0-1-0-0-0	John E. Hibbert	0-0-1-0-0-0
Geo W. Green	0-5-1-0-1-9	Jacob Heflebower	0-6-1-0-0-9
Richd N. Green	0-5-1-0-0-6	Adam Hubbard	0-0-1-0-0-0
John L. Grant	1-0-1-0-0-4	Wm Holtsclaw	
Lewis F. Glass	0-6-1-0-0-9	Senr.	0-0-1-0-0-1
Martin Gant	0-5-1-0-1-6	Wm Holtsclaw	
Jemima Gant	0-1-0-0-0-1	Junr.	0-0-1-0-0-0
James Gumby	0-0-0-1-0-0	Blackwell	
Isabella Glass	0-0-0-0-0-0	Holtsclaw	0-0-1-0-0-0
Thornbury Grubb	0-0-1-0-0-0	Mary Howard	0-4-0-0-0-0
Wm Grubb	0-0-1-0-0-0	Philip Hansucker	1-0-1-0-1-1
John J. Gordon	0-2-2-0-1-8	Geo L. Harris	0-6-1-0-1-12
John Gruber	0-2-2-0-1-8	Cornelius Hoff	0-0-1-0-0-0
John Green	0-2-1-0-0-6	Richd S. Hardesty	0-1-1-0-0-6
Geo W. Grubb	0-0-1-0-0-0	John Hughs	0-0-1-0-0-1
Wm B. Grubb	0-0-1-0-0-1	Thos Hughs	0-0-1-0-0-1
Geo Gardiner	0-0-1-0-0-0	Edwd E. Hall	0-7-1-0-0-0
Elias M. Green	0-0-1-0-0-0	Armstead Hoff	0-0-1-0-0-0
Jefferson Grubb	0-0-1-0-0-0	Wm G. Hardesty	0-2-1-0-1-11
Nathan Grubb	0-0-1-0-0-0	Mrs. Sarah	
Andrew Greenwald	0-0-1-0-0-0	Hardesty	1-3-0-0-2-9
Zebedee Gray	1-0-1-0-0-1	Wm B. Harris	0-6-1-0-1-9
		George Hansucker	0-0-1-0-0-2
Whiting Hamilton	1-0-1-0-0-2	Henry Huyett	0-1-1-0-1-7
James H. Hooe	0-0-1-0-0-2	Robt L. Horner	0-0-1-0-0-0

Clarke County, Virginia Personal Property Tax Lists 1836-1853
1853

Name	Values	Name	Values
James Hamilton	0-0-1-0-0-0	Thomas Jones	0-3-1-0-0-5
Benjn Harrison	0-5-1-0-0-14	Leonard Jones	0-2-1-0-0-5
T. B. Heims	0-3-3-0-0-0	Jacob Jackson	0-0-0-1-0-0
Rev. J. F. Hoff	0-5-1-0-0-1	Franklin Ingle	0-0-1-0-0-0
Adrian D. Hardesty	0-2-1-0-0-5	Thomas D. Johnson	0-0-1-0-0-0
John Hodge	0-0-1-0-0-0		
Wm Heskitt	0-0-1-0-0-0	Frank J. Kerfoot	0-8-1-0-0-10
Wm Heflin	0-0-1-0-0-0	Thos Kennerly Est.	0-14-1-0-3-13
Harrison Hoff	0-0-1-0-0-0	Dr. C. F. Knight	0-0-1-0-0-1
James M. Howard	1-0-1-0-0-0	Wm C. Kerfoot	0-10-1-0-3-15
John Hoff	0-0-1-0-0-0		
Nelson E. Hall	0-0-1-0-0-0	Spence Johnson	0-0-0-1-0-1
Eliza Hay	0-10-0-0-1-12		
Thomas L. Humphrey	0-1-1-0-0-1	Geo L. Kerfoot	0-12-1-2-2-13
		Wm F. Knight	0-6-2-0-1-13
Henry Huntsbery	0-0-1-0-1-2	John Kable	0-3-1-0-1-1
James M. Hardesty	0-0-1-0-0-5	Randolph Kownslar	0-5-1-0-1-3
Wm Howard	0-0-0-1-0-0	Geo & Wm C. Kerfoot	0-8-0-0-0-10
Mowen Harris	0-0-0-2-0-0		
John Henry	0-0-1-0-0-0	Charles E. Kimball	0-5-1-0-0-10
		Middleton Keeler	0-0-1-0-0-0
George Johnson	0-1-1-0-0-1-2	Wm C. Kennerly	0-5-1-0-1-4
Herod Jenkins	0-0-1-0-0-0	Jos Kline	0-0-1-0-0-1
S. R. Jackson	0-0-1-0-0-0	Saml G. Kneller	0-5-1-0-0-8
Mathew Jones	1-3-1-0-1-6	John B. Kerfoot	0-0-1-0-0-4
John Joliffe	0-6-1-0-0--9	James M. Kiger	0-3-1-0-0-6
Jacob Isler	0-5-3-0-1-13	Jacob Kriser	0-0-1-0-0-2
Joseph Janey	1-2-1-0-1-4	Henry Kenneford	0-0-1-0-0-0
Thomas Jenkins	0-0-1-0-0-6	John N. Keimmell	0-0-1-0-0-0
John Johnson Junr.	0-0-1-0-0-1	James H. Kennan	0-0-1-0-0-0
Alfred Jackson	0-3-1-0-1-8	John Kelly	0-0-1-0-0-0
Wm H. Jones	0-4-1-0-?-11	Wm B. Kennan	0-0-1-0-0-0
Geo W. Joy	0-0-1-0-0-0	Edwd V. Kercheral	0-0-1-0-0-0
James W. Johnson	0-0-1-0-0-1	Franklin Kenneford	0-0-1-0-0-0
Ransel Johnson	0-0-1-0-1-2	Charles Kitchen	0-2-1-0-0-5
Wm A. Jackson	0-5-1-0-0-10		
Amelia Jordan	0-0-0-0-0-2	Geo Lanham	1-0-1-0-0-2
Wm Johnson	0-0-1-0-0-0	John D. Larue	0-2-2-0-0-8
George Jenkins	0-0-1-0-0-0	Wm D. Lee	0-0-1-0-0-0

Clarke County, Virginia Personal Property Tax Lists 1836-1853
1853

James M. Lindsey	0-0-1-0-0-0	Josiah Lock	0-0-1-1-0-4
Eli Littleton	0-2-1-0-0-0	James L. Loyd	0-0-1-0-0-1
Henry Loyd	0-0-1-0-0-3	James Loyd Junr.	1-0-1-0-0-2
John Lock	0-1-2-0-1-7	Geo Langley	0-0-1-0-0-0
James W. Larue	0-4-1-0-1-7	John M. Lupton	0-2-2-0-0-0
Wm D. Littleton	0-0-1-0-0-4		
Sally Longerbeam	0-0-0-0-0-0	Francis B. Meade	0-6-1-0-0-10
Geo Longbeam	0-0-1-0-0-0	Saml McCormick	1-0-1-0-0-0
James T. Louthan	0-0-1-0-0-0	at A. S. Allen	
R. H. Little	0-5-1-0-0-5	Wm Miles	0-0-1-0-0-0
John Louthan	1-6-1-0-1-7	Peter McMurray	1-3-1-0-0-7
Charles Leach	0-0-1-0-0-0	John Maddex	1-1-2-0-2-9
John Lee	0-0-1-0-0-0	James Mitchell	0-0-1-0-0-4
Lorenzo Lewis Est.	0-24-1-0-8-17	Wm D. McGuire	0-9-1-0-2-13
John B. Larue	0-11-2-0-3-19	H. H. McGuire	0-0-0-0-0-2
Moses Lewin	0-0-1-0-0-0	Otway McCormick	1-7-1-0-0-5
John Loyd	0-0-1-0-0-3	L. W. Meade	1-3-0-0-0-1
James Loyd	0-0-1-0-0-0	Philip N. Meade	1-7-1-0-0-5
Edgar Lanham	0-0-1-0-0-1	Wm W. Meade	0-5-1-0-2-10
Wm Loyd	0-0-1-0-0-2	Miss Mary Meade	0-3-0-0-0-0
Minor Lanham	0-0-1-0-0-1	Thomas	
A. L. P. Larue	0-3-1-0-2-6	McCormick	0-8-1-0-2-8
Wm Littleton	0-1-2-0-1-4	Saml Morgan	0-0-1-0-0-0
Harrison Loyd	0-0-1-0-0-3	John McPhillin	0-4-2-0-3-8
John T. Lindsey	0-1-1-2-2-3	Jacob May	0-0-1-0-0-0
Rice W. Levi	0-0-1-0-0-2	Benjn F. Mayhew	0-0-1-0-0-0
David Loyd	0-0-1-0-0-0	Alexander	
James Larues heirs	0-0-0-0-0-0	Marshall	0-0-1-0-0-0
or Nelson Davis		Francis	
James Loyd Junr.	0-0-1-0-0-2	McCormick	0-17-1-0-1-29
Squire Lee	1-0-1-0-0-2	Mrs. Susan	
James Lanham	0-0-1-0-0-1	Marshall	0-4-0-0-0-6
Wm Levi	0-0-1-0-0-1	John Marshal	1-2-1-0-2-3
John K. Louthan	0-0-1-0-0-0	Wm B. Moore	0-0-1-0-0-0
John W. Littleton	0-0-1-0-0-2	John McConahay	0-0-1-0-0-0
John Longbeam	0-0-1-0-0-0	John Martz Senr.	0-0-1-0-0-1
Christopher Lee	0-0-1-0-0-0	Dr. & Saml	
Ben Longbeam	0-0-1-0-0-0	McCormick	1-24-2-0-0-31
John W. Luke	0-2-1-0-0-2	John McCoy	0-0-0-1-0-0

Clarke County, Virginia Personal Property Tax Lists 1836-1853
1853

C. C. McIntyre,		Revd. D. G.	
tax is on p. 25	0-0-0-0-0-0	Mallory	0-3-2-0-0-0
James Maddex	0-0-2-0-0-3	Henry Mason	0-0-1-0-0-0
Lorenzo Maddex	0-0-1-0-0-0	James W. Miller	0-0-1-0-0-0
Levi Marquis	0-0-1-0-0-1	P. McCormick	
Jesse Mercer	0-0-1-0-0-1	(Attorney)	0-6-1-0-1-8
N. Mercer	0-0-1-0-0-2	Milton H. Moore	0-7-1-0-1-8
Thomas Murphy	0-0-1-0-0-0	James McClaury	1-0-1-0-0-1
Col. Ben Morgan	on last page	Spencer Marquis	0-0-1-0-0-0
D° as Guardian for		Christian Moren [?]	1-0-1-0-0-4
Miss Alexanders		Wm G. Morris	0-0-1-0-0-0
John Morgan	1-7-1-0-3-10	Nathl B. Meade	0-8-1-0-0-8
James McCormick	0-1-1-0-0-10	John Mahoney	0-0-1-0-0-0
John N. Meade	0-5-1-0-1-6		
James Murphy	2-0-1-0-0-5	Dr. S. S. Neille	0-7-1-0-0-7
Revd. Wm Meade	0-0-1-0-0-0	Hugh M. Nelson	0-16-1-0-2-12
Stephen Marlow	0-0-0-0-0-0	Mrs. Sarah Nelson	on last page
Armishadie Moore	0-4-1-0-3-7	Thos F. Nelson	0-9-1-0-3-13
John G. McCauley	0-0-1-0-1-1	John Newcomb	0-0-1-0-0-4
David H. McGuire	0-8-1-0-0-7	James H. Neville	1-2-1-0-0-0
D° as trustee for		Jos Noble	0-0-1-0-0-0
children		Miss A. & R.	
Alfred P. Moore	0-0-1-0-0-0	Nelson	0-3-0-0-0-0
A. Ross Milton	0-5-1-0-1-5	John Nessmith	2-1-1-0-0-3
George Marple	0-0-1-0-0-2	Philip Nelson	0-0-0-0-0-0
Edward		John B. Norris	0-5-0-0-0-6
McCormick	0-0-0-0-0-0	Archie Nelson	0-0-1-0-0-3
Edwin W. Massey	1-5-1-0-1-9	John R. Nunn	0-3-1-0-1-6
John Marple	0-1-1-0-0-0	Wm M. Nelson	0-0-1-0-0-0
Province		Lucy Newman	0-0-0-0-0-0
McCormick Jr.	0-2-1-0-0-3		
Arabia		Elizabeth Orear	0-9-0-0-0-9
Seth Mason	0-5-1-0-3-10	George Orear	0-4-1-0-0-10
Harrison		David Osborn	0-0-1-0-0-3
McCormick	0-0-1-0-0-3	Mason Oliver Est.	2-1-0-0-0-1
Moses G. Miley	1-0-1-0-0-4	George Osborn	0-1-2-0-0-5
Richd K. Meade	0-4-1-0-1-10	Hugh ORorke	0-0-1-0-0-0
Wm McCormick	0-1-1-0-0-4	Elias Overall	0-2-1-0-1-2
Philip B. Martin	0-0-0-1-0-0	Benjn F. ORear	0-4-1-0-1-5

Clarke County, Virginia Personal Property Tax Lists 1836-1853
1853

Name	Values	Name	Values
Susan ORear	1-0-0-0-0-0	James M. Reed	0-0-1-0-0-0
Overseers of Poor	0-0-0-0-0-5	John Rowland	2-0-2-0-0-9
		Bennett Russell	0-9-2-0-3-12
Susan R. Page	0-31-0-0-3-30	John Reed	
John Pierce Jr.	1-4-2-0-0-15	(Col. Ware)	0-0-1-0-0-1
Mathew Pulliam	0-2-3-0-0-1	Elizabeth W.	
John E. Page	0-13-1-0-5-22	Royster	0-1-0-0-0-0
Eliza M. Page	0-5-0-0-1-0-2	Conrad Rinaman	0-0-0-0-0-0
John Page Junr.	0-9-1-0-2-12	Mathew Royston	0-1-1-0-1-10
Mann R. Page	0-9-1-0-3-15	Uriah B. Royston	1-0-1-0-0-4
Uriah Petitt	0-1-1-0-0-0	John Reed	0-0-1-0-0-0
Saml L. Pidgeon	0-0-1-0-0-6	Jos Ross	0-0-1-0-0-0
James M. Pine	0-0-1-0-0-0	Nancy Redman	0-0-0-0-0-0
Mary C. Page	0-2-0-0-0-0	George W. Rutter	0-0-1-0-0-0
Paul Pierce	1-6-1-0-3-6	Danl B. Richards	0-1-2-0-0-0
John Pierce Senr.	0-4-1-0-2-8	Saml B. Redman	0-0-1-0-0-1
James Puller	0-0-1-0-0-0	Addison Romine	0-2-1-0-0-4
Bushrod Puller	0-0-1-0-0-0	James W. Ryan	0-0-1-0-0-1
Peter McPierce	0-4-1-0-0-5	Jos F. Ryan	0-1-1-0-0-5
Pendleton &		John W. Russell	0-2-1-0-1-4
Richardson	0-14-2-0-3-30	Geo Reno	0-0-1-0-0-0
John Piggott	0-0-1-0-0-0	Mathew Rust	0-2-1-0-0-1
Washington F.		Thomson Ritt	0-0-1-0-0-0
Padgett	0-1-1-0-0-4	Beverly Randolph	0-16-1-0-7-22
Benjn F. Perry	0-0-1-0-0-0	Patrick Rodgers	0-0-1-0-0-0
Geo R. Page	0-3-1-0-1-3	Ross C. Randolph	0-20-1-0-4-28
Michael Pope	0-0-0-0-0-0	John Reynolds	0-0-1-0-0-0
Calvin Puller	0-0-1-0-0-0	Westley Russell	1-0-1-0-0-3
John Patterson	1-0-1-0-0-2	Thomas W.	
James S. Payne	0-0-1-0-0-2	Raynolds	0-0-1-0-0-0
Barnett Prichard	0-0-1-0-0-0	Richards &	
Simon & Wm		Wharton	0-0-2-0-0-1
Parker	0-0-0-2-0-0	Wm Riely	0-0-1-0-0-1
Wm Pyle	0-0-1-0-0-0	Michael Russell	0-1-1-0-0-1
A. C. Page	0-4-1-0-0-14	Jos Richardson	0-0-1-0-0-0
Michael P. Pierce	0-4-1-1-2-10	Wm A. Riely	0-3-1-0-0-6
Willis Prichard	0-0-1-0-0-0	John J. Riely	0-3-1-0-0-5
Alexander Parkin	0-3-1-0-0-4	Peter K. Royston	0-0-1-0-1-1
		Wm C. Ramey	0-0-1-0-0-5

Clarke County, Virginia Personal Property Tax Lists 1836-1853
1853

Thomas Roradan	0-0-1-0-0-1	Jackson Shaffer	0-0-1-1-0-0
Stephen Reed	0-0-1-0-0-0	Burr Smallwood	0-0-1-0-0-1
Thos W. Russell	0-0-1-0-2-1	Simon Stickles	0-0-1-0-0-1
Thos W. Ridings	0-1-1-0-0-0	Hugh T. Swarts	0-5-1-0-0-5
B. C. Raynolds	0-0-1-0-0-0	Danl H. Sowers	0-2-1-0-1-12
John Russell (Senr.)	0-0-1-0-0-1	Geo R. Smith	0-0-1-0-0-0
Theodoric Russell	0-0-1-0-0-0	Franklin Swarts	0-0-1-0-0-0
		Wm Strother	0-0-1-0-0-0
Wm D. & E. J. Smith	0-25-2-1-7-35	M. Shively Shivelys tax is included in	
Geo Smedley [?]	0-0-1-0-0-1	C. C. McIntyre's tax	
Smith & Lupton	0-0-1-0-0-0	John R. Shumate	0-0-1-0-0-0
Wm. B. Sowers (of Fielding)	0-0-1-0-0-0	Henry Shepherd	0-1-1-0-0-0
		Jos Sprint	0-0-1-0-0-0
Wm Sowers (Senr.)	1-7-1-0-2-13	John W. Sprint	0-0-1-0-1-0
Jos Shepherd	0-4-2-0-1-9	K. Shroud	0-0-1-0-0-0
John O. Snyder	0-1-1-0-1-1	Wm L. Smith	0-0-1-0-0-0
Champ Shepherd	0-3-1-0-0-6	Erasmus	
D° as guardian for son		Shackelford	1-0-1-0-0-0
Thos Shumate	0-3-1-0-0-9	B. H. Sinnott	0-0-1-0-0-0
John W. Sowers	1-8-1-0-3-18	Charles Showers	0-0-2-0-0-1
Danl W. Sowers	0-13-1-0-3-20	Susan T. Smith	0-2-0-0-0-0
R. H. Simpson	0-0-1-0-0-0	Emanuel Showers	
James A. Steel	0-2-1-0-0-0	(Junr.)	0-0-1-0-0-0
Thos Sprint	0-0-1-0-0-1	Alexander	
Saml Showers	1-1-2-0-0-0	Saunders	0-1-1-0-0-0
Barnett Smallwood	0-0-1-0-0-2	Paul Smith	1-4-1-0-1-10
Fielding L. Sowers	0-4-1-0-3-8	John Shell	0-0-1-0-0-0
P. D. Shepherd	2-5-1-0-0-13	Saunders & Ridings	1-0-0-0-0-1
Charles Swarts	0-0-1-0-0-0	Jonathan S. Smith	1-2-1-0-1-2
Philip Smith	0-22-2-0-4-20	Thomas J. Skinker	0-8-1-0-1-14
John W. Steele	0-0-1-0-0-0	John H. P. Stone	0-0-1-0-0-0
Threadwell Smith	0-16-2-0-4-18	Charles Slagle	0-0-1-0-0-0
Kerfoot Sowers Est.	1-7-0-0-0-15	Robt Stump	0-0-0-0-0-1
		Jos Stewart	0-0-1-0-0-0
James Sowers	0-2-1-0-1-7	Benjn Starkey	0-0-1-0-0-2
John Stewart	0-0-1-0-0-3	Stephen Shell	0-0-1-0-0-0
Elizabeth Strother	0-6-0-0-3-5		
John Shaffer	0-0-1-0-0-0	H. J. Chamblin	0-0-1-0-0-0

Clarke County, Virginia Personal Property Tax Lists 1836-1853
1853

Name	Values	Name	Values
Isaac Starkey	0-0-1-0-0-3	Wm Trenary	0-2-1-0-2-4
John Stonestreet	0-0-1-0-0-0	Adam F. Thomson	0-0-1-0-0-2
Bushrod Smallwood	0-0-1-0-0-0	Saml Tinsman Senr.	0-0-1-0-0-0
Gepton Smallwood	0-0-1-0-0-0	Robt Tapscott	0-0-1-0-0-0
Mary Stribling	tax is on p. 25	Wm Tomblin	0-0-1-0-0-0
John H. Spotts	0-1-1-0-0-0	Enoch Triplett	0-0-1-0-0-0
George W. Shultz	0-0-1-0-0-0	French Thompson	0-0-1-0-1-4
Joseph Shipe	0-0-1-0-0-0	Andrew J. Thompson	0-0-1-0-0-0
L. J. Schooler	0-0-1-0-0-0	Howard F. Thornton	0-6-1-0-1-6
Henry T. Shearer	0-0-1-0-0-0	Moses B. Trussell	0-1-1-0-0-3
Dennis Sheheen	0-0-3-0-0-2	Andrew J. Tinsman	0-0-1-0-0-0
Wm B. C. Sowers	0-2-1-1-1-6	Calvin Thacker	0-0-1-0-1-0
Reuben Sims	0-0-1-0-0-5	John B. Taylor	0-5-1-0-4-3
Wm M. Sowers	0-0-1-0-0-1	Wm D. Timerlake	0-2-1-0-1-6
Wm G. Steele	0-0-1-0-0-0	Ludwell Tinsman	0-0-1-0-0-1
Benjn Shipe	0-0-1-0-0-0	Baalis Thompson	0-0-1-0-0-5
		Geo F. Tomblin	0-0-1-0-0-0
Mrs. Sarah Timberlake	0-6-0-0-0-10		
Adison Timberlake	0-0-1-0-0-0	Jacob Vanclief	0-0-1-0-0-4
David Tristler	0-0-1-0-0-3	Jacob Vanmetre	1-3-0-0-0-5
John Turner	0-0-1-0-0-0		
Adam Towner	0-0-1-0-0-0	Geo B. West	0-0-1-0-1-1
Danl Turner		Wm Willingham	1-0-1-0-0-2
Greenberry Thompson	1-0-1-0-0-3	Allen Williams	1-10-1-0-1-14
James F. Thompson	0-0-1-0-0-2	Francis H. Whiting	0-3-1-0-1-6
Geo W. Thompson	0-0-1-0-0-1	J. W. Ware & Mrs. Stribling	1-17-1-0-6-20
Wm Taylor	0-17-2-0-0-17	Wm Webster	0-0-1-0-0-0
Saml Tinsman (Junr.)	0-0-1-0-0-0	Danl Wade & Brother	0-1-2-0-0-2
Saml Taylor	0-8-1-0-1-2	Horatio T. Wheat	1-5-4-0-2-5
Benjn Thomson	1-0-1-0-0-6	Hezekiah Wiley	0-0-1-0-0-0
Jos Tuley	0-30-1-0-4-22	Saml Wiley	0-0-1-0-0-1
Wm N. Thompson	1-4-1-0-0-0	John Willingham	1-0-1-0-0-1
John Trussell	1-4-1-0-3-6	Sydnor B. Wimdham	0-1-1-0-0-1
Charles H. Taylor	0-1-1-0-0-1		

Clarke County, Virginia Personal Property Tax Lists 1836-1853
1853

John Wilson	0-0-1-0-0-0		
Leroy P. Williams	0-9-1-0-0-9	Edwd Gormon	0-0-1-0-0-1
Jos A. Vasse	0-1-2-0-0-2	Edwd Smith	0-0-1-0-0-0
Francis B. Whiting	0-23-2-0-2-16	George W. Wiley	0-0-1-0-0-0
Wm W. Whiting	0-4-1-0-3-5	Wm Wolfe	1-0-1-0-0-1
N. B. Whiting	0-7-1-0-1-9	Jesse Wright	0-0-1-0-0-2
Louisa Washington	0-0-0-0-0-0	Robt Whittington	0-0-1-0-0-0
James V. Weir	0-4-1-0-0-5	Alexander Wood	0-0-1-0-0-0
Wm H. Whiting	0-7-1-0-1-11	James S. Welch	1-6-2-0-0-2
John F. Willingham	0-0-1-0-0-2	Jos Wood	0-1-1-0-0-5
James Wiley	0-0-1-0-0-1	James H. Willis	0-0-1-0-0-1
John Wiley	0-0-1-0-0-0	Benjn F. Wilson	0-0-1-0-0-1
Jacob Welch	1-0-1-0-0-4	Bennett Woods	0-0-1-0-0-1
David H. Wilcox	0-0-1-0-0-0	Walker B. Wilson	0-0-1-0-0-0
Obediah Willingham	0-0-1-0-0-0	G. W. Weaver	1-2-1-0-1-2
		Lucinda Washington	0-0-4-0-0-0
Col. B. Morgan	2-25-1-0-4-35	Col. James W. Walker	0-8-0-0-1-8
Mrs. Mary Stribling	0-4-0-0-2-1	Elias A. Smith	0-0-1-0-0-0
Edwd McCormick	0-12-1-0-2-17	E. L. Wager	0-1-1-0-0-1
		Francis M. Whittle	0-3-1-0-1-2
Mrs. Sarah Nelson	0-10-0-0-6-6	David Waddell	0-0-1-0-0-0
C. C. McIntyre	0-3-1-0-2-7	Wm Young	0-1-0-0-0-0
Philip Nelson	0-2-1-0-0-7	E. T. Hancock	1-3-1-0-0-6
John Ramey	0-0-1-0-0-0	John Walker	0-0-0-1-0-0

Clarke County, Virginia Personal Property Tax Lists 1836-1853
1853

Recapitulations from 1836-1850 tax lists

These are located at the end of each year in the tax booklets and on the microfilm.

1836 Recapitulation
15   merchants
1816   Slaves
2754   Horses
7   Studs
87   Coaches
3   Carriages
15   Gigs

1837 Recapitulation
1801   Slaves
2714   Horses
10   Studs
93   Coaches
2   Carryalls
18   Gigs
Deduct 1 slave & 1horse
Total of property $1190.14

1838 Recapitulation
1767   Slaves
2626   Horses
12   Studs
92   Coaches
1   Carryalls
17   Gigs
Total tax on property $1263.68

1839 Recapitulation
693 white tythes

1840 Recapitulation
778   Whites
23   Free Blacks
6   D° charged to whites
1605   Blacks over 16
1896   Slaves
2760   Horses

1841 Recapitulation
1873   Slaves
2878   Horses
3   Studs
113   Carriages
5   Carryalls
13   Gigs
35   Free Blacks

1841 continued: Total number of whites & free blacks 823, slaves 1579 = 2402
(13 slaves were addend on account of John B. Larue not turning in a correct list before the books were closed.)
Total tax on property $1516.92 ½

189

Clarke County, Virginia Personal Property Tax Lists 1836-1853
Recapitulations

1842 Recapitulation
1907	Slaves
2851	Horses
8	Carryalls
124	Carriages
12	Gigs
34	Pianos
69	Gold Watches
94	Silver D°
87	Clocks

Total tax on property $1715.49

1843 Recapitulation
745	White tithes above 16
28	Free Negroes
1869	Slaves
2924	Horses
80	Gold Watches
12	Levers D°
87	Common D°
91	Metal Clocks
147	Wood D°
27	Pianos value over $100
9	D° under $100 value

Total tax on property $2071.75 ½

1844 Recapitulation
1827	Slaves
2812	Horses
117	Carriages
3	Carryalls
12	Gigs
80	Gold Watches
21	Lever D°
60	Silver D°
108	Brass Clocks
168	Wood D°
32	Pianos
2	Attorneys
7	Physicians
114	Deeds etc.

Total tax on property $1932.82

1845 Recapitulation
1736	Slaves
2754	Horses
129	Carriages
5	Carryalls
5	Gigs
78	Gold Watches
18	Silver D°
59	Other D°
121	M Clock
174	Wooden Clocks
32	Pianos
1	Attorney
7	Physicians
1	Bridge

Clarke County, Virginia Personal Property Tax Lists 1836-1853
Recapitulations

1846	Recapitulation
1783	Slaves
2709	Horses
136	Carriages
77	Gold Watches
22	Lever D°
71	Silver D°
138	Brass Clocks
188	Wood D°
36	Pianos
1	Attorney
4	Physicians

Total tax on property $1513.64

"I have had more trouble with this Book than with any other I have examined, and still differ with the Commr 66 cents. It must be in some of his additions."

1847	Recapitulation
1808	Slaves
2641	Horses
146	Carriages
90	Gold Watches
22	Lever D°
73	Silver D°
146	Brass Clocks
204	Wood D°
30	Pianos
6	Attorney
10	Physicians
1	Press

Total tax on property $1557.00

1848	Recapitulation
2363	Levies [white tithables]
1817	Slaves
2650	Horses
160	Carriages
93	Gold Watches
25	Silver D°
68	Other D°
158	Mettalic Clocks
211	W Ditto
38	Pianos
4	Attorneys
11	Physicians

Total tax on property $1600.07

Clarke County, Virginia Personal Property Tax Lists 1836-1853
Recapitulations

1849	Recapitulation	1850	Recapitulation
1921	Slaves	1934	Slaves
2732	Horses	2685	Horses
172	Carriages	185	Carriages
106	Gold Watches	113	Gold Watches
39	Lever D°	40	Lever W
62	Silver D°	64	Silver W
205	Brass Clocks	237	Brass C
199	Wood D°	191	Wood C
41	Pianos	43	Pianos
1	Harp	1	Harp
5	Attorneys	6	Attorneys
11	Physicians	11	Physicians
Total tax on property $1747.27 ½		21	Free Negroes
		Total tax on property $2033.057	

Clarke County, Virginia Personal Property Tax Lists 1836-1853

Index

This index is only for those names that appear out of order in the regular text. You may find a space before and after the individual's name on the indicated page, but maybe not.

The index does not cover the free blacks (listed at the end of each year) or recapitulations. Those begin on page 189.

A

Akins
   Henry.......117
Alexander
   Miss..........170
Alexanders
   Miss..........184
Allen
   A. S. 183
   David H....175

B

Ballenger
   McCormick &
  5
Bel
   J. R. 153
Bell
   J. 70, 80
   J. R. 142
Bragg
   Thomas J. 175
Brown
   John............43

Burwel
   E. 172
Burwell
   L. G. 173
   N. 161
   P. 173
   R. P. 173

C

Carter
   [youngsters]
   ...129, 140
   J. B. & J. W.
   107
   Thomas... 161
Carters
   [children] 151
Castlemam
   James......... 86
Castleman
   Charles.... 108
   Henry...... 108
Clifton
   John......... 179
Clingon
   Mclain..... 175

Cook
   N. B. 172
Crampton
   B. 168
   Ben 181
Crawford
   A. 46
Crow
   & Snyder. 161

D

Davis
   Nelson 183
Dow
   J. 117
Drake
   J. 45
Duble
   Creager & 131

E

Eberhart
   Bowen &. 178
Edmunds
   Lewis....... 140

Clarke County, Virginia Personal Property Tax Lists 1836-1853
Index

Enders
   L   151
   L. 140, 164
   Leonidas 107, 118, 129, 177
Evans
   A. H. 76

F

Fitzsimons
   Jas 47
Flecher
   George 96
Fletcher
   John 47
Franks
   Henry 32
Funston
   Margaret... 76
Furgerson
   [young] ... 114

G

Gibbs
   James 32
Gibson
   Churchill C. 22
Gilkerson
   G. W. 79
Glass
   L. 113, 124
Gold
   Thos E. 48
Gore
   George G. 106

Gormon
   EDwd 188
Gourley
   Wm 43
Groves
   Groves 32
Grubs
   Wm 117

H

Haines
   Jacob 42
Hancock
   E. T. 188
   Eben T. 139
Harrison
   B. 114
Hay
   John . 76, 128, 139
Hays
   Doct. J. 121
Hefflybour
   Jacob 85
Hennis
   C. 96
Hicks
   Joseph 4
Huyett
   Saml 161

J

Jackson
   Thos 48
Johnson
   Butler & .. 108
   Spence 182

Joliffe
   Joseph M. 117

K

Kane
   Mrs. 46
Kelly
   John 153
Kerfoot,
   Franklin J. 117
Keyes
   Flore & 51
   Flore & Keyes 41
Killion
   Shederick .. 71
Kirby
   young 172
Knight
   Elizabeth . 161
   George 161
   Thomas 13, 22
   Wm F. 161
   Wm. F. 156
Kownslaw
   Dr. R. 106

L

Lanham
   James 34
   Samuel 34
Lewis
   Easther M. 161
   Lorenzo ... 106
Loving Est.
   161

Clarke County, Virginia Personal Property Tax Lists 1836-1853
Index

Littlejohn
  R. S. 161
Lock
  William 34
Lucius
  Charles 159
Lupton
  Smith & ...186

M

McCormick
  Edward ...117,
    128, 188
  Harriet.....117
  P. 174
McIntyre
  C. C. 188
McPierce
  Peter.......113,
    161, 172,
    185
Meade.............86
  F. B." 173
  Louisa 175
  Mary 161, 175
  P. N. 161
  R. S. 86
  Revd Wm.161
  Revd. Wm 175
  W. W. 86
Milton
  Charles H. ..96
Moore
  A. 117
Morgan
  Col. b 188

N

Neill
  West & ... 149
Nelson
  Mildred... 172
  Mrs. Sarah
    188
  P. 48
  Philip....... 188
  T. 172
Neuin
  H. M. 172
Nunn
  Doct. 76

P

Page
  Dr. Mat ... 103
  Mat 113
  Susan R. ... 161
Parker
  Elliott & . 167,
    180
  Richard ... 161
Pete ?
  Wm 113
Pickens
  Mary 35
Pine
  James M. 128
  Mary 37

R

Ramey
  John 188

Randolph
  Mary C. ... 161
  R. C. 172
Raynolas
  James W. .. 76
Reed
  A. 159
  Landon O. 113
  Sarah A. .. 148
Richardson
  Blackmore &
    29
  John 73
  Pendleton &
    . 136, 147,
    158, 172,
    185
Ridings
  Sanders &
    .. 159, 174
  Saunders &
    186
  Thomas W.
    161
Rowland
  John 161
Royston
  Mat 77
Russell
  James........ 66

S

Saratoga
  Farm 172
Saunders
  Wm H........ 96

Clarke County, Virginia Personal Property Tax Lists 1836-1853
Index

Seevers
  Blakemore & 49, 59
Shepherd
  Joseph 37, 106
  P. D. 40
Sherrick
  Philip 39
Shipe
  Joseph 123
Showers
  Emanuel 37
Smith
  E. L. 106
  Edwd 188
  Elias A. 188
  James W. 128
  Jas 43
  T. 48
Snyder
  John A. 161
Sowers
  Wm B. C. .. 161
  Wm K. 76
Stickles
  Simon 36
Stoll
  Brown & .. 164
Stolle
  Wm 161

Stribling
  Mrs 56, 75, 85, 95, 105, 115, 127, 138, 149, 160, 175, 187
  Mrs. Mary 188
  S. 47

T

Taylor
  Charles H. 161
  Hannah 76
  Wm 113
  Wm G. 117
Tidball
  A. S. 85
  Joseph 85
Timberlake
  R. M. S. 85
Trislar
  D. 43

U

Umbenhaur
  Peter 126

V

Vasse
  Jos A. 188

W

Ware
  Col. 185
Washington
  H. 66
Wharton
  Creager & .. 166, 179
  Richards & .. 173, 185
Whitescarver
  Mr. 46
Whiting
  Francis H. .. 37
Wigginton
  Wm P. 96, 106
Williams
  A. 167, 180
  Allen 109, 120
Willis
  Wm 128
Wood
  Bennet 161

Y

Yeakle
  S. S. 48

www.ingramcontent.com/pod-product-compliance
Lightning Source LLC
Chambersburg PA
CBHW072128160426
43197CB00012B/2034